The Silent Stones

Diana Cooper

The Silent Stones

A Spiritual Adventure

HODDER

MOBIUS

First published in Great Britain in 2002 by Hodder and Stoughton
A division of Hodder Headline
This paperback edition first published in 2004

A Mobius Book

3 5 7 9 10 8 6 4 2

A CIP catalogue record for this title
is available from the British Library

ISBN 0 340 82190 6

Typeset in Sabon by Palimpsest Book Production Limited,
Polmont, Stirlingshire

Printed and bound in Great Britain by
Mackays of Chatham plc, Chatham, Kent

Hodder and Stoughton
A division of Hodder Headline
338 Euston Road
London NW1 3BH

To my beloved daughter Dawn.
Thank you for the fun and happiness we have shared.

Author's note

This book has taken me on a quest. While writing it I have visited South America, California, and India twice. It started in 1996 when I woke one morning with a very vivid dream and knew instantly that it was the plot for the first half of a novel. I wrote it down and waited. The following year I visited India to meet my daughter, who was living and working in Hong Kong. We travelled together and parts of this novel are based on our experiences, for we found ourselves in the place shown me in the dream.

For some years I had worked with guides, those evolved spirits who help us from the spirit world. Later angels approached me, asking me to introduce them to the world and write about them. Angels are very high frequency light beings, who are messengers and intermediaries from Source. My guide told me that the information for the second part of the book would come through someone . . .

Some time later my son came to visit me after a year in South America. Nothing like this had ever happened to him before or since; he sat on my sofa and suddenly information started to pour through him. He told me to get a pen and write it down as he could not access any more until I had written what he was given. He channelled the information about Machu Picchu and told me he could feel the presence of the angels as he did so.

Two weeks later I was told that I was shortly to undergo a higher Initiation, which would increase my light levels, and that I must not write until after the Initiation. After it I wrote *A Little Light on the Spiritual Laws* as this was promised.

When I started *The Silent Stones*, Anne Vintner, a psychic artist, drew a beautiful Inuit woman called Saska for me, who was to be my writing guide for a spiritual teaching novel. 'Ah!' I thought. 'At last I can get on with it!' I finished the first draft and was then deluged with work and did not touch it for months. When I picked it up again I became totally involved once more. It was almost finished. At two o'clock one morning angels surrounded my bed and woke me, filling me with a great feeling of joy and delight. They wanted me to write another book about angels, called *Angel Inspiration*. It was to be written immediately. They stayed with me day and night until it was finished and it was published a year before *The Silent Stones*.

I finally completed my novel. I hope you enjoy reading it as much as I enjoyed writing it. Do use the symbols. They are very powerful.

With love,

Diana

TO ENABLE YOU TO CO-CREATE
WITH THE DIVINE

TO BRING HEAVEN TO EARTH

TO OPEN THE DEEPER MIND
AND EXPEL KARMIC DEBT

TO ACTIVATE THE HEART AND
CONNECT PEOPLE IN A WAY THAT
WILL OPEN THE LEYLINES ROUND
THE PLANET

TO COMBINE INTUITION
WITH LOVE

TO BRING FRIENDSHIP TO ALL
LONELY PEOPLE AND LIGHT UP THE
BEAUTY OF THE EARTH

TO TAKE THE MAGIC BURIED
WITHIN YOU AND BRING IT
OUT WITH WISDOM

Chapter 1

Those in the know say that you either have a love affair with India or you hate her. Certainly it takes the rose-tinted glasses of infatuation to be aware of the heat, the dirt and flies, the beggars, the smell, the babbling incompetence and mindless inertia of the place and yet feel overwhelming excitement and love whenever you visit her. These factors are the cause of intense aversion in those who despise India, of which there are inevitably a few.

But the moment Marcus stepped on to the dust of India, he loved the country – with its crazy drive from Delhi airport in a raucously honking taxi, round bullock carts, rusty buses, little men in whitish clothes slowly riding their stately bicycles and suicidal buzzing rickshaws. Being part of this frenetic world on the move, set against a surreal yellow orange sunrise, brought a lightness to his tired body as surely as would the sparkling eyes of a fascinating woman.

Marcus went everywhere and saw everything around Delhi. Tall and broad-shouldered, he dwarfed the Indians, and often bumped into them, as he strode through the crowded streets. But as he apologised, the laughter in his grey eyes was so appealing that they instantly smiled back and forgave him. It was easy to respond to the good-looking, open young man. He was a doer, a restless soul, unstoppable when fired with enthusiasm, and passionately interested in people. He read them, sensed their needs and moods, loved talking to and finding out about them. He sat in cafés, chatting to tourists, travellers and Indians alike and relished the East.

Seven days after he arrived in India, in a triumph of bravado over common sense, Marcus squeezed into a recycled tin can of a bus with a crush of curry-sweating humanity. His bag was balanced on his knee and the corner of someone's briefcase bruised his ribs as they jolted off to Rishikesh via Dehradun.

Dehradun! He savoured the name, rolling it deliciously over his tongue, while trying to close his ears to the constant honking of horns and to the loud and, to him, indescribably revolting, sound of spitting, which Indians feel is their passport to health. During the intermittent breaks he disembarked and stood with the men, a gesture of solidarity, communicating in pidgin English or sign language. Marcus thoroughly enjoyed the journey. The dust swirled as they passed through roadside villages of wooden shacks selling fruit and vegetables, and shops piled with colourful material, the tiny tailors hunched behind ancient sewing machines like the one his grandmother used.

They rattled past a young woman, her baby on her hip, a young child beside her, carrying a large laden basket on her head and leading a cow as she trudged through the dust. The rural Indian woman epitomised. He enjoyed the wafting aroma from the roadside chappati and curry makers. Crates of soft drinks were piled high outside shacks and everywhere shops were offering for sale more plastic buckets than he imagined an entire village could use in a year. Someone threw an orange peel out of the window but it was quickly gobbled up, for pigs, hens, cows, dogs, all wandered freely, walking dustbins. Single sex groups walked together and talked in clusters. Boys played together, girls helped mother. That was the way of it.

At Dehradun his new love affair with India suffered its first setback. He stepped from the bus into the fume-poisoned town, worse even than Bangkok. Gasping, he flinched, as if physically hit. The smell of traffic was so intensely concentrated that he could see the fumes rising like waves in the heat. With a handkerchief pressed over his nose, he had only one thought – to get a taxi out of the town to Rishikesh immediately.

Sitting back in the taxi, Marcus closed his eyes. Tired. Exhausted even. Defences down, he could no longer hold back the memories of the trauma he wanted to forget – the catalyst that led him to India. Pictures came back. His boss calling him into his office. The way he had innocently and eagerly responded, anticipating promotion to the Spanish desk because of his fluent Spanish. He had entered the office jubilantly. Then there was the humiliation and rage of being made redundant. It couldn't happen to him. He was good at his work. Believed he was indispensable. Marcus felt devastated, his ego shattered. He had charged out of the office, flushed with anger. He had not realised how much his self-esteem and reason for *being* were tied up in his work until that fateful moment.

Later on his girlfriend had snaked her arms round him and whispered, 'The eagle shot in full flight.' And that was how it felt. At work he was in his power, conquering the world. The arrow of rejection struck from nowhere. He fell heavily.

A week later he discovered that his girlfriend was sleeping with his boss, the man responsible for the redundancy decision. The double betrayal and disillusion were devastating. Thousands of miles away in the hot taxi, he groaned aloud as he remembered. His heart thumped and his chest hurt. 'Bastards,' he thought, clenching his fists. 'Bastards.'

The madness of his thoughts during the dark, unfocused weeks that followed the betrayal shook his core. Previously unknown feelings of hate, revenge and worthlessness thrust like a volcano from a place deep within and threatened to overwhelm him. Marcus, always friendly, and generous-hearted and understanding was presented with his shadow side and he did not like it. A sense of disorientation and plummeting confidence convinced him that he must change his life. Completely.

He was musing about it in the bar of his squash club when a girl he knew by sight struck up a conversation with him. She had just returned from holiday in India and painted a colourful and exciting picture of the country. As she rose to leave, swinging her squash bag over her shoulder, she laughed as she said, 'When I came back from India I had found parts of myself I didn't even know were missing. India does that to you.'

Marcus took an instant decision to travel there. From that moment everything fell into place as if unseen hands were fitting a jigsaw together with perfect synchronicity. He was beginning to learn that there is no chance or coincidence in life, that all is co-ordinated at another level. Until the betrayal and its consequences, he had always believed in chance, luck, an inhospitable universe and a punitive God who had to be placated. The latter was a legacy from his public school days, where daily affirmations that he was a miserable sinner had filtered into his subconscious mind. It might have done more harm were it not for his innate sense of self-worth.

A friend later postulated that for hundreds of years the Church had served the darkness by spreading a feeling of badness and guilt, which chained the human spirit. It was a revelation to Marcus, who saw the truth of this statement with blinding clarity and was determined to free himself from the grasping tentacles of other people's beliefs.

An old friend of his, Caroline, persuaded him to see a highly recommended clairvoyant with her. She managed to make an appointment for them both on the day before his flight and he agreed to go with her, feeling dubious but intrigued. The pleasant, ordinary looking, elderly woman gave Caroline a reading, which amazed and delighted her.

'How could you know all that about me?' she asked in wonder after the session. 'And will those things really happen?'

The clairvoyant laughed. 'I have the gift and as for your second question, your future isn't written in stone. I can only tell you your *possible* future, from which you can create your own life. What I have told you is a prediction based on the way you are heading now.'

Caroline glowed, determined to create the possibilities that had been presented to her.

It was Marcus' turn. As the clairvoyant tuned into him she went pale. 'You must go to India. Your destiny is calling.' She started to breathe heavily, then opened her eyes suddenly. She looked shocked. Marcus noticed that the little hairs on the woman's arms were standing up and he felt a shiver of apprehension run down his back.

'I'm sorry. I can't read for you.' She spoke abruptly, with a nervous laugh. She gave him his money back, ignored his questions and protests, and hurried them out of the door.

Marcus was bemused. He tried to shrug her words off with a smile and a few dismissive words. But he could not ignore the tight knot in his stomach.

Caroline was trying to distract him by babbling on about her reading. Everything the woman had said to her about her past had been astonishingly accurate and she was delighted about the predictions for her future. Although Marcus tried valiantly to listen and respond he could not get the clairvoyant's words out of his mind.

'Damn the woman,' he thought savagely, as he kicked a stone harder than he intended and heard it bouncing off a garden wall. 'What the hell was that all about!' The next day he set off for India and the wheel of fate started to turn.

Chapter 2

Rishikesh proved to be hot, dusty and swarming with so many people that the pigs could not keep up the waste disposal. Rotting fruit lay in the dirt, crawling with flies, and vendors shouted their wares. Small boys urinated against a dusty and ailing tree, dislodging the inevitable stream of climbing ants. The stench of the thick stew of humanity at close quarters, of rotting food, sweat and urine, of cooking spices and dung was overwhelming in the stifling heat.

Marcus was sticky and grimy. Sweat oozed from his pores, soaking his shirt to his back. Feeling suddenly dispirited, he slumped on to a rough cement step in a shady corner. Rickshaws, sounding like electric drills in competition, sped by. White-faced oxen stoically pulled heavy loads, as their emaciated owners sat on top. Brightly painted lorries belched fumes over him.

He watched people moving by: slender girls with long thick black braids, wearing colourful saris, laughing and chattering; ragged women, thin and grey; gaunt men, some busy, some idle; children, filthy or shining clean, all with big dark eyes. A one-legged cripple hopped with a crutch, a blind beggar whining as he was led along by his daughter. Hordes of people, all trying to eat and work and learn, to make friends and marriages, to have children and be happy, all specks of sand in a shifting desert – and he did not know one of them.

A sense of isolation gripped him. He was totally alone. He could die in an alien world and no one would know. He felt his tired mind leading him into an abyss and tried to pull his thoughts back.

'Hi!' broke in a cheerful English voice. 'Have you just arrived?'

Beside him stood a slender young woman in blue trousers, T-shirt and sandals, a black bum bag round her waist, swinging a thin polythene bag of oranges.

Marcus brightened at this apparition of Western civilisation. 'I've just come from Delhi on the bus.'

'No wonder you look tired. Got anywhere to stay yet?'

'Not yet. Got any recommendations?'

'There's a cheap smelly down there.' She pointed down an alley of material shops, jostling with hardware stalls, bookshops and travel agents. 'Or an expensive air con job on the hill.'

'Anything in the middle?' asked Marcus.

She screwed up her eyes in thought. 'Not much here. We're in Muni-ki-Reti, which is the next village. It's nicer and quieter than here – but it's mostly ashrams and they're full.' She paused. 'We're in a guest house run by a lovely Indian family. Proper beds, fans, own loo and Rima cooks local food if we want it.'

'Any rooms free?'

'Could be. A German guy left this morning.'

Marcus looked at her again. Shiny brown eyes, the colour of ripe chestnuts, short brown hair, curly at the ends, sharpish face with a straight nose and strong jaw. Interesting rather than beautiful, he decided.

'Not my type,' he thought. His type of women, or ex-type, he corrected himself quickly, was the blue-eyed baby doll – the flirtatious, dependent kind.

The girl introduced herself as Joanna in a natural, no-nonsense way, no hint of hidden messages. Just a direct, cheerful look. Marcus relaxed. She wasn't after him. She was simply one traveller talking to another. She read his mind and laughed. The laugh transformed her face, making it uncommonly beautiful.

She continued, 'I'm on holiday with my Mum at the moment.'

He was surprised. He had thought her highly independent. 'With your Mum!' he echoed.

'I've been working and travelling in Asia. Now I'm on my way back to England, so Mum and I decided to meet in India for a holiday.'

Marcus smiled. That seemed nearer the mark. Joanna darted off suddenly to pick up a stick dropped by a woman so emaciated and frail that she looked as if she could hardly walk, even with support. Joanna restored the stick with such a radiant smile that the old lady shuffled on with a straighter back.

The girl glanced across the road and said quickly, 'There's the rickshaw. Come on. If you want to see our place I'll show you the way.' She ducked round a coconut stall, avoided a mangy dog lying in the dust, waved away a hideously deformed beggar and jumped into a waiting rickshaw, without so much as a backward glance. Marcus followed, intrigued and energised by this self-assured, slightly abrasive, cheerful enigma of a young woman.

As he climbed into the rickshaw behind her, she explained, 'It's a rickshaw bus. Set price two rupees. It waits until it's full.' She pointed to faded pictures of Srdi Sai Baba, Krishna, Maharishi and Jesus Christ hanging on the windscreen amidst garlands of flowers and laughed lightly. 'Oh good, we're protected. All options covered.'

To the driver she said with a wide smile, 'Good rickshaw – very safe.'

He laughed uproariously, uneven teeth flashing white in his dark face and repeated, 'Sai Baba, Krishna, Maharishi and Jesus Christ,' touching each picture respectfully with a dirty finger.

Joanna grinned back. 'Very good journey.'

During this brief exchange at least eight Indians had squeezed into the space designed for six, so with the mandatory strident blare of horns, they headed for Muni-ki-Reti.

Chapter 3

Marcus' spirits soared when he saw the guest house, set high up on the hillside and approached by a steep track. Beyond iron gates the garden was carefully tended. Well-watered, fat-leafed shrubs burst with glossy vitality. Elegant trees and swathes of purple bougainvillaea graced the white marble steps to the raised veranda.

The house was pure white and decorated simply with tracery patterns, the veranda floors tiled in black and white marble. It reminded him of a Mediterranean villa.

Joanna laughed at his wide-eyed surprise. 'Unexpected, isn't it?' she acknowledged. 'Here's Rima. She's Raj's wife. He owns the guest house and she runs it. She's a wonderful cook.'

A small and slender Indian lady in a pale pink and blue sari appeared and welcomed them with the traditional hands-together position. 'Namaska,' she greeted.

Joanna responded easily in the same way and Marcus hastily followed suit. 'It means "I honour the Divine in you",' Joanna told him later. 'It's wonderful, isn't it? In some parts of India they say, "Namaste".'

Marcus could not help wondering how it would affect the City if its pin-striped materialists honoured the Divine in each other when they met. He grinned as he shared the delicious thought with Joanna and she laughed.

'Be the first to do it and see what happens,' she dared.

Rima had a room for Marcus and so, two hours later, showered, rested and once more feeling nurtured by a benign universe, he appeared for dinner and met Joanna's mother Helen for the first time.

She was smaller than he had expected, hair short with hints of grey, similar brown eyes to Joanna's, darker if anything, and set in a softer face. When they were introduced he had the most disconcerting impression that she looked through him for a fraction of a second before she smiled warmly and greeted him in a friendly tone. He immediately felt at ease, as if he had been checked and approved. It was odd but not unpleasant.

Their conversation was normal, even banal, as they discussed the weather, their travels and the usual superficial trivia passing as Western greeting ritual. Joanna had a keen eye for the ridiculous. 'You'll never guess what I saw this afternoon,' she giggled suddenly. 'A mangy puppy ran under a rickshaw and a huge German lady – and when I say huge I really mean it – stepped in front of it with her hand up like this.' She pantomimed an imperious hand gesture. 'She was pretty quick I must say. Then she crawled under the rickshaw, bottom in the air and emerged holding the poor little puppy at arms' length by the scruff of its neck. I saw her marching down the road, arm fully extended in front of her, with the puppy dangling like a snotty tissue. Goodness knows where she was taking it. I just saw her disappearing followed by a crowd of small boys.'

Everyone laughed and relaxed. Warm air scented with blossoms wafted through the open window. A dog barked somewhere in the distance.

Marcus' mind moved on. 'I must say it's nice to be away from the beggars.'

'Do they bother you?' Joanna asked.

'Well, yes,' he confessed. 'If I don't give them anything I feel terrible. If I do they either ask for more or grab the money without any thanks, so I feel annoyed.'

Joanna nodded. 'I know.'

'They're so persistent,' Marcus complained. 'Yesterday I was pursued by two totally relentless women with babies. I felt so awful.'

Helen and Joanna murmured sympathetically.

Joanna sighed, remembering some of the dreadful sights she had seen on the streets, and continued, 'It helps to understand it's their karma.'

Marcus took her up. 'What exactly is karma? I keep hearing the word bandied about and I know it's cause and effect but I don't really understand it.'

Helen answered, 'The theory is that every soul is on a journey. While you are on Earth you are accountable for your thoughts, words and actions, for they all have consequences. Consequences are karma. What Joanna means is that karma runs from lifetime to lifetime. So if you die with unresolved issues with people or you've done more bad things than good, your soul wants to come back and try to make amends.'

'Give me an example,' suggested Marcus.

'Well, it works in lots of ways. If you've been unkind to someone, you will inevitably meet them again in a later life and have an opportunity to be kind. Or at the other end of the scale, if you were a mercenary who butchered a lot of people, as your soul evolved it might want you to reincarnate as a surgeon to repay your debt to humanity.'

Marcus nodded. It made sense.

'Different religions have slightly different beliefs but basically all believe that there is a spiritual working-out for everything over lifetimes.'

'What about Christianity? Why don't they believe in karma then?' asked Marcus, intrigued.

'Oh, but they do. "As ye sow so shall ye reap!" Early Christians believed in reincarnation and therefore in karma. There is a body of evidence that Emperor Justinian wrote reincarnation out of the Bible at Constantinople in AD553. Later it was declared a heresy.'

Marcus was fascinated, 'Why should the Christian Church have wanted to do that?'

Helen's dark eyes were flashing. 'We're back to control by the Church. If you believe in reincarnation, you are in charge of your destiny. You want to connect with your own soul to understand the purpose of your journey in life. You then must listen to your own voice of conscience – in other words to the God within – to decide what is right for you. The Church wanted their priests to have the power to tell people what to believe and do.

'When they deleted reincarnation from the Bible they

stopped people from understanding that there is a spiritual working-out to everything, so they took away people's incentive to aim for the noble and good. The half-truths they preached did not resonate with people and caused unrest. That's when they started to preach hell fire and damnation to keep their flocks doing as they were told.'

Marcus observed that Helen spoke with indignation and a sense of frustration. 'It's interesting,' he said. 'I've never understood why one person seems to be good and yet they have terrible calamities in their lives and someone else gets away with everything. Life often seems pointless or unjust.'

'Of course it's confusing,' nodded Helen. 'But when you take the long-term view over lifetimes, it all falls into place.'

'There is another aspect to it,' Joanna put in. 'Toddlers need very safe boundaries. Unevolved souls who have only had a few experiences on Earth are toddler souls. Just like toddlers, they need to feel safe and so they try to restrict and control others. For instance, they congregate in fundamentalist religions, where they are told exactly what to do and can be totally fanatical in protecting the dogma.'

Marcus frowned with concentration as he grasped this concept.

'And teenagers tend to cause more hurt and damage than more mature people, don't they?' Marcus nodded, remembering a holiday project he'd done as a student, working with teenage tearaways.

Joanna continued, 'Teenage souls have had more

experiences on Earth but they still lack wisdom. They often incarnate into countries and situations where they can run riot. There are plenty of teenage souls right now in places like Africa, where there is unrest. Or they chase after the material life, become very rich and use the money to subjugate others. Like toddler souls, they tend to create a lot of karma for themselves.'

'I see,' said Marcus.

'So less-evolved souls tend to get into karmic debt. As they evolve over lifetimes into more mature souls their higher selves want to repay the debt.'

'No one gets away with anything spiritually,' reminded Helen.

'So very often people who are good and wise have difficult lives. They are mature souls repaying karma they earned before they evolved.'

'I see,' Marcus repeated.

'So bad luck is really bad karma and good luck is the return of karmic credit,' Helen added. Marcus thought for a moment. The concept made sense to him. 'But why would anyone want to reincarnate as a beggar?' he persisted.

'Millions of reasons,' replied Helen. 'As many reasons as souls who reincarnate as beggars. It isn't always possible to know why a soul would choose a particular experience. But for instance, if in one life someone was very rich and wouldn't help others who were less fortunate, the next time round their soul might want to experience poverty. Or say you refused to take responsibility for your life and always let others look after you, you might choose to experience having to fend for yourself.'

Marcus looked at Helen. 'It sounds as if you believe in reincarnation?'

She smiled. 'Absolutely. I believe our higher self makes many important choices before we are born.'

'What sort of choices?'

'Your family, place of birth, time and date of birth, as well as certain people and circumstances you encounter during life.'

Marcus thought about his family and pondered. Helen answered his thought. 'We often have karma to resolve with members of our family. That's one reason our soul chooses them. They represent the lessons we are trying to learn.'

'Even abusive parents?' Marcus was incredulous, remembering some of the abused teenagers he had worked with.

'Especially those!' Helen started to explain but Marcus, finding this inconceivable, had involuntarily crossed his arms. She recognised the shut-down signal and paused. Then she added gently. 'I believe our parents launch us on our life mission. They offer us the perfect opportunities we need to direct us towards what we came to Earth to accomplish. That's why one of our life tasks is to embrace the best qualities of both our parents and overcome their worst ones.'

Marcus fell silent as he considered this. He liked to evaluate all possibilities. Joanna leant forward, 'Remember it is the soul that chooses, not the personality.'

He nodded. 'Is there a way round karma?'

'Yes. By giving unconditional love. Basically we accrue karma by withholding love. Take the example of beggars again. If you give money to a beggar with real love – I'm not talking about sentimental or emotional stuff, cosmic love, I suppose – just accepting them as they are, that cancels out some of their karma and yours.'

'But how do you do that?'

'If you give anything, meet their eyes. That's looking into their soul. Try to see the divine in them and smile. When you do that you send a charge of love energy to them that dissolves some karma.'

Joanna could see this was hard for Marcus to digest. She reiterated, 'It's true, Marcus. Try it. It makes a whole lot of difference. But you may have to practise.'

Marcus shrugged, almost stunned into silence. 'Why do souls come to Earth in the first place?'

Helen replied, 'If you were a mountaineer, what would be your greatest goal?'

'To conquer Everest, I suppose.'

The older woman nodded. 'And a spiritual warrior wants to master Earth. You see, this planet is not just a haphazard lump of rock in space. It is a mystery school and one of the most difficult ones in the universe. Your spirit enters a physical body to learn lessons about emotions, relationships, sexuality, money and many other things. Your lessons are orchestrated by the universe and presented to you in the form of people and situations, which come into your life. Testing times are like exams. You have to get through them to progress.'

A million questions entered Marcus' mind but before he could formulate one into words, Helen said kindly,

'Your left shoulder and neck look very stiff and your lower back is really painful. Would you . . .'

Marcus was shocked. 'How do you know?'

Joanna laughed. 'Mum knows lots of things, Marcus, without your having to say.'

Helen continued smoothly, 'On a physical level you can blame carrying your bag. But there are always mental and emotional factors. Would you like me to give you some healing? It may help.'

'Yes please,' said Marcus, without a second's hesitation. 'I've heard of healing, of course, but I've never tried it. Are you a healer then?'

'Put it this way,' Helen told him. 'Joanna and I are both channels for healing energy.'

She rose and stood behind him, stilling her mind. Heat filled her hands and as she placed them on Marcus' shoulders, he felt a warm current flowing through him. A sense of calm and peace, such as he had never before experienced, filled him. He found himself relaxing, deeper and deeper.

When she had finished, the pain had melted away on every level.

'You'll sleep well,' Helen told him when he thanked her.

'One more question, please.' He frowned, remembering the clairvoyant's reaction. 'Have I got a destiny?'

'Of course,' she replied. 'A major one. That's why you're here. And you're about to find out what it is.'

Chapter 4

After sleeping the sleep of the innocent and waking early with a light spirit, Marcus was sitting on a boulder by the Ganges at sunrise. At last. The virgin sun, pure yellow white, was still soft, lighting the world gently. It was only at this brief, young time of day that India experienced this tenderness.

Near the town, the rocks lining Ma Ganga, the holy water of the life-giving mother, were used as a toilet. A strange way to treat a sacred river, he thought. But at this point he was above the pollution line. He sat with his feet in the waters, soothed by the drifting smell of incense and lulled by the sounds of chanting from ashrams and temples on both sides of the river. The music was overlaid by bird song and, as time passed, increasingly punctuated by the distant buzzing of rickshaws.

Here the sacred Mother Ganga was wide, deep and rushing in the middle, in a hurry to provide for her children in the plains. At the edges, the water frolicked round smooth boulders and caressed the shingle shore with careful fingers. The sunlight painted a million colours on the ripples, sparkled on the sand and rocks, and flirted through the leaves of trees. He sat contented.

Too soon the sun rose into maturity and power. The heat scorched. Persistent vendors selling their wares approached, even picking their way across the rocks, intruding into his quiet space with their eternal, shrill cries of, 'You buy' and 'Give you cheap price'.

Resigned to the inevitable, Marcus rose and bantered with them, until they laughed. As he walked along the shore, not even the hopeful greeting, 'School pens?' from at least twenty boys, one after the other, fazed him.

He smiled into the eyes of an emaciated beggar and was surprised to see, not the dullness he had expected, but clarity, brightness, a watchful alertness. The man obviously had an intelligent mind. It moved him to sudden compassion to think of a clever, thinking person being reduced to beggary – or choosing it.

He heard laughter ahead and saw a white woman sitting cross-legged in the dust under a tree, surrounded by children. He realised that it was Joanna, juggling.

'Hi!' she called cheerfully as soon as she spotted him.

Marcus squatted among the children. 'Hi,' he said easily.

'I've been teaching the kids to juggle. Do you want a go?' She handed him her juggling balls, deftly retrieving one from a small boy who had grabbed it.

'What do you do?' Marcus asked. Juggling had not been one of the skills required or acquired in the City. Joanna took them back and demonstrated. To her laughing chagrin he picked it up immediately.

'I've spent months practising,' she protested. 'And you've got it at once. It's not fair.'

For an instant he drew back, thinking of his sister. She was two years younger than he was and had always been jealous of him. In similar circumstances she would have pouted and huffed, until she was able to create a difficult scene about something seemingly unconnected. He had learned to pussyfoot around her. But Joanna was happily showing him a new routine, and when a Dutch traveller walked past she called out, 'Hello,' and he joined them for half an hour, practising passes and exchanging information.

'I must go,' Joanna said at last. 'I'm meeting Mum at the travel agent. We're hoping to go up to Kashmir for a few days, though we haven't really got suitable clothes.'

'I thought it was dangerous up there,' frowned Marcus in surprise.

'Yes, but Raj says his brother knows the area and will arrange something safe for us. We just want to see the Himalayas and there's a temple I want to visit.'

'Sounds interesting,' responded Marcus. 'I didn't think it was even possible to get there at the moment.'

Joanna laughed the laugh of adventure, pulled on a peaked cap that make her look younger than her twenty-five years, and sauntered off with a cheery wave.

A few minutes later Helen appeared, wearing a broad-brimmed sunhat of indeterminate shape. She was hurrying, and looked hot, sweaty and slightly flustered. She stopped when she saw Marcus. 'Hello. How are you today?'

He assured her with some awe that he felt wonderful. She smiled with genuine delight. Then she confided, 'I'm supposed to meet Joanna at the travel agent and I can't remember where it is.'

Marcus laughed sympathetically and gallantly offered to escort her. He had an excellent memory and sense of direction.

In that way, fate, with precise inevitability, pushed him forward, for it took only interest on his part, the sales expertise of Raj's travel-agent brother and the welcoming acceptance of Joanna and Helen to ensure that he joined them on their trip to Kashmir.

A couple of days later they set off in a convoy of two cars. Marcus and his new friends travelled in the first one with the driver, while the second car carried tents and cooking equipment, plus their guide, Krishna, and two boys to look after them.

They enjoyed the dramatic scenery with glimpses of the roaring Ganges below, although the road to Srinagar with its hairpin bends, sheer drops and much evidence of disaster, was as terrifying as it was spectacular. So when they reached their camping spot, which was perched in a niche in the mountainside looking over a tiny village set by a spectacular lake, they were relieved to be able to stretch their legs. They wandered in the clear cool air under the watchful eye of Krishna, while the boys set up camp and cooked for them.

Each morning they moved camp to somewhere more beautiful until, on the fourth day, their tents nestled in a slight bowl, surrounded by tiers of white peaks. Even at this height, huge rhododendron trees bloomed audaciously, their deep red startling against the shimmering patches of white snow. To complement the beauty, the tinkling of a stream provided music and the occasional glimpse of shy animals their entertainment.

That night they sat round a camp fire, expertly built by Krishna, eating a superb meal cooked by the boys. Entranced, the three Europeans watched the half-moon float above them in a nest of stars, touching the world in silver mystery.

Questions teemed through Marcus' brain. At last he asked, 'What's the New Age all about? Is it a philosophy, a cult or what?'

With a laugh, Joanna handed the question to her mother, who replied lightly, 'It's none of those things. It literally is a new age. The last one was the Piscean Age, when our planet entered the constellation of Pisces. It was heralded by the birth of Jesus Christ, who was bringing in the energy of Christ consciousness. He brought a message of unconditional love. Now earth is moving into the constellation of Aquarius, which is why it is called the Aquarian Age, and again new energy is coming in.'

Joanna added, 'This time offers the greatest opportunity for spiritual growth that there has ever been in the entire history of the planet.'

'Yes,' said her mother, the entire planet is moving to a higher frequency band, where everyone will live at a higher level of consciousness. The shift is starting now, which explains the turmoil everywhere. Even where change is positive, like moving to a bigger house, it causes chaos.'

'Do you think it will really happen?' Marcus saw the

world with the jaundiced eye of the average businessman and his voice expressed his doubt.

'Absolutely,' exclaimed Joanna.

'Why should now be so different?'

Helen took over. 'A number of reasons. Partly because of our shift into Aquarius, which influences everyone on earth, but also because right now massive bursts of light are being pulsed down to us from all the other universes. This used to happen occasionally. And now it is happening every two to three weeks. It's a bit like having high-frequency electricity passed through you. It shakes you up.

'This is the time that has been talked about throughout history as the end times. Not the finish of everything but the end of the old ways and the start of the new.'

'And,' added Joanna, 'lots of the babies and children being born now are wise old souls who are coming to lead the planet forward.'

'Yes, and many of those who incarnated to help with the shift and who have trained for aeons for this lifetime are waking up to who they truly are, ready to do their part.'

'Wow!' exclaimed Marcus, enthralled. He felt inspired and totally alive. He went to bed wondering what part he had to play in this incredible plan.

Chapter 5

The following day they were to climb through the snow to the ancient Buddhist temple, which Krishna assured them, in his thick Indian accent, would now be open for the summer. In the winter months it was covered in snow and the monks moved elsewhere. In the morning Helen woke with an uneasy feeling in her stomach. Her intuition told her not to go to the temple and she shared this thought over breakfast.

'Mum, you know you never like walking up hills,' Joanna responded with a laugh. 'It's an excuse to get out of it.'

'I don't think so,' Helen replied. A big black bird on a nearby tree shrieked a warning and goose pimples came up on her arms.

Marcus and Joanna, with the impetuosity of determined youth continued to tease her, to override her doubts. Her gut feeling was so strong that Helen decided to stay behind and wander in the locality of the camp while they tackled the snowy climb with Krishna, their guide.

Krishna was not happy. He had watched over Helen and Joanna like a mother hen and the thought of his chicks being separated clearly upset him. He gave Helen precise instructions about where she could go. She looked puzzled by his accent and Joanna, who was quicker of comprehension, had to translate his English for her.

'Do not go beyond that ridge, very dangerous,' Krishna admonished seriously.

All Helen could hear was a guttural slur. 'Pardon?' she said politely, striving to make out his words and feeling very inadequate, a feeling she hated.

'Do not go beyond that ridge, very dangerous,' Krishna repeated.

'Sorry?' tried Helen again, rolling her eyes towards Joanna for help.

The latter, stifling a giggle, said slowly and clearly, 'Don't go beyond that ridge. It's dangerous.'

'Oh.' Helen endeavoured to look as if she had really understood all along. She smiled, her face tomato red. 'No, of course not, Krishna.'

She dared not meet Joanna's eye.

Finally they were ready. Krishna was carrying a bed-roll on his head, which he solemnly explained was protection in case it started to snow. Joanna was inadequately and bizarrely dressed in trainers and just about every item of clothing she had with her, including a flowered sarong for extra warmth. She laughed at the odd look Krishna gave her. Marcus wore boots and an anorak.

Helen watched the odd trio disappearing round a bend in the track, little knowing that this would be the day that changed all of their lives.

For the first time since the betrayal Marcus lost the

niggling pain in his chest. He felt completely at ease, and he and Joanna played in the little patches of snow, throwing snowballs and laughing. This disconcerted Krishna, who was clearly not used to play. Life for him was a serious business.

Just below the snow line they passed through a deserted village. Only the piles of rubbish provided evidence of human existence. Krishna explained that the villagers moved away for the winter, but as soon as spring arrived they returned and repossessed their old houses. It was a frozen tableau waiting to be brought to life and they all felt the eeriness of the empty houses. Joanna shivered. 'It's spooky. There's a bad feeling here.'

Marcus was about to laugh it off but he stopped himself when he saw that Joanna's face was pale and pinched. He realised that she was sensitive to something he didn't comprehend and instinctively put an arm protectively round her shoulder. Though she said nothing, she did not pull away and he felt she appreciated it.

Krishna told them that bad things had happened in that village, 'Many die. Bad place.'

They hurried through the maze of derelict houses and were glad to get on to the bare mountainside where the snow was thick. Soon they were trekking through an enchanted fairy-tale world. There was no one to be seen and only old bear tracks suggested signs of life. Marcus had been watching Joanna's face and was glad to see her colour return as she regained her usual cheerfulness. She was a strange mixture of very sensitive and very independent, and he was only just beginning to get accustomed to it.

The snow was so deep that Krishna expressed doubts that the temple would be open. 'My boss tell me it is open but I do not think it,' he told them with a frown. 'It is too early. Too much snow.'

Joanna had really wanted to visit this temple and she felt irritated at what she regarded as inefficiency on the part of the organisers. Barbed words were on her lips but she did not utter them for Krishna was clearly a responsible young man who keenly felt the inappropriateness of bringing his protégés all this way to a closed temple. In fact, he looked so downhearted that she ended up by reassuring him that it did not matter. She decided to let it go and enjoy the day for what it was.

Before long, the snow was so deep that they had to walk in Krishna's footsteps as he led them on a zig-zag track up the mountain. When Joanna took an independent step, she found herself thigh deep in snow and unable to move. Marcus and Krishna had to pull her out, which she found hysterically funny, especially when the ever serious Krishna cautioned her earnestly to walk only where he had prepared the way.

An hour later they caught a glimpse of the temple. It was obviously closed, still submerged in snow almost up to its roof. Suddenly Joanna had a tense feeling inside her. Her stomach clenched and she felt sick. Was she picking up the same thing that her mother had tuned into that morning? It was completely different from the sense she had in the village. This was a feeling of danger.

All looked peaceful and she persuaded herself she must be imagining it. But the feeling persisted and she found herself telling Marcus to be careful. She knew something was wrong and he did not doubt her. But when he looked around he could see nothing. Nevertheless he walked warily.

It was not until they reached the temple that they came across footprints and signs of a scuffle in what had been virgin snow. With a sickening wrench they saw the blood, still red and glistening in the snow, and bloody drag marks as if an injured person had pulled himself to the other side of the temple. Two sets of footprints came and went, disappearing round a rock in the distance. Joanna's stomach lurched. Marcus felt a rush of adrenaline.

'Stay here, please,' faltered Krishna. His dark face looked white around the eyes and lips.

Marcus pushed past him and charged, like a bull, through the snow around the temple. Joanna, feeling nauseous, her heart thumping, legs like jelly, was close behind. In the lea of the building lay the huddled figure of a monk, blood seeping from several gaping wounds. He looked Tibetan and had evidently been stabbed, repeatedly.

With a screaming feeling inside her, Joanna knelt beside him and took his wrist to feel his pulse. He stirred, barely alive. She held his frozen hand and desperately willed him to live. She'd never seen anyone die. She didn't want to, not here. Not now.

Marcus pulled off his anorak and laid it over the injured man, who half-opened his eyes.

'It's all right,' Joanna tried to say soothingly through trembling lips, but her words fell on deaf ears.

The dying man desperately sought Marcus' eyes. 'Scroll!' he whispered urgently, holding his eyes. 'I hide . . . They not find. Scroll . . . there.' He tried to raise his arm to point but the effort was too much. Marcus followed his eyes to the eaves. He nodded reassuringly to the dying man. Then he clambered precariously through the thick snow on to the temple roof. The monk was watching him, compelling him to find whatever precious item he had hidden.

Marcus reached under the eaves and felt beneath them, hands moving cautiously.

'Yes . . . yes,' the monk whispered, excitement giving him energy. At last Marcus felt something. With a struggle he pulled out a sealed packet, wrapped in polythene. Holding it carefully he jumped down into the snow and held it out to the monk.

'No, no! Take to Mahathat Temple at Joshipur,' he gasped. 'I bring from Tibet . . . important . . .' Every breath was a rasping struggle. 'They chase. I hide . . . hurry. They watching. Important hurry. Go, go! Mahathat Temple.'

'What about you? We must get you to hospital,' Marcus protested, though he knew no hospital could save the old man.

In a final effort the monk clutched Marcus' hand as if to impress on to him the urgency and importance of the Scroll. 'Me not important. Go, go!' he implored. 'You sent by God. Scroll save world. You blessed.' He smiled gently, almost lovingly, and Marcus never forgot the look in his eyes as the old Tibetan monk died.

He had never seen a dead body before, so pale and

peaceful. Nor had Joanna but, white-faced and practical as ever, she leant over and closed the old monk's eyes. They felt warm and jelly-like under her fingers and the sick feeling inside her intensified. She shut his jaw firmly. It was harder to move than she had expected, but she had seen it done on television and was glad she had the courage to do it. He looked incredibly peaceful and she kept her eyes firmly on his face. She must not look anywhere else. She wondered if his spirit had left his body and, if so, where it was. The sun reflecting off the white snow was too bright. She was beginning to feel strangely detached and spaced. Marcus caught her arm firmly as she swayed.

At that moment they heard a shout and two men appeared over the next crest, slithering, sliding and wading towards them as fast as the deep snow would allow. One was Oriental and one Indian.

The sound of a whip cracked behind them and reverberated round the mountain. In horror they realised it was a shot.

'Run,' shouted Marcus.

'What about him?' Joanna, instantly back in her body, indicated the dead monk.

Marcus grabbed her hand and pulled her to her feet. 'He's dead. There's nothing we can do for him.' He sounded harsh even to himself.

In one movement he grabbed his blood-stained anorak off the monk and zipped the packet containing the Scroll under it.

The three of them struggled and floundered through the snow, frantic to get away from the men. Dreading another shot, they cowered low as they pushed through the drifts, desperately stepping in the footsteps they made on the way up. Terror speeded them but they sensed the men getting nearer.

'The bedroll,' Joanna gasped suddenly. 'It'll make a sledge.' She grabbed it from Krishna, who was unresisting with terror, and laid it on the snow. It took precious seconds.

'Sit on it,' she commanded. Immediately grasping her intention, Marcus threw himself down at the front and she clung closely round his middle. Krishna, at the back, held on to her and they found themselves hurtling down the slope.

It was terrifying. Out of control on the steep slope, they narrowly missed rocks and tree branches poking out of the snow. Marcus, in taut command of himself, did his best to steer with his boots. Joanna, holding on tightly, put her head on Marcus' back and shut her eyes in free-fall anxiety. Krishna screamed and screamed, the sound lost in the snowy wasteland.

Finally they careered into the leafy edge of a rhododendron bush and were thrown off, bruised but unhurt. They regrouped, their clothing soaked.

Now that they were on lower slopes there was a veritable minefield of rocks and bushes thrusting through the snow. When another shot rang out, they resolutely decided to brave the bedroll sledge again. It was the fastest way. They could hear their pursuers crashing and slithering, as they gave chase.

As the snow became thinner, the rocks and bushes were too hazardous. They abandoned the sledge and slid on their bottoms, unaware that they were cut and bruised beneath their soaking, frozen clothing. They knew only that they carried information that could change the world. And men with guns wanted it and would not hesitate to kill them for it. When the snow thinned, they ran for their lives.

Chapter 6

Helen felt increasingly tense and restless. She sensed that something was wrong, but had no idea what it could be. She kept looking at the sky, thinking bad weather was going to set in, but the sky was a clear, innocent blue.

As the day progressed, her anxiety grew. But it was not until midday, when she was sitting quietly on a rock, gazing at the icy stream that trickled from the snow-covered mountains through its tiny gorge, that she had a sudden doom-filled flash of death. It was so strong that she could not deny it. But whose death? Was it here or at home? She sensed it was here and prayed that Joanna was all right. She asked the powers-that-be to protect her, and then did the same for Marcus and Krishna with a greater sense of detachment. But she still felt sick with apprehension.

She had to get out of the camp and found herself pacing up and down the track that led to the mountain. 'We've got to get out of here,' she muttered to herself, and was embarrassed to find she had spoken aloud, though there was no one to hear. Her scalp was taut and a headache, like a tourniquet round her brow, was inexorably tightening. She must do something active to dispel the awful tension, she decided. On impulse she went to the tent she shared with Joanna and packed both their rucksacks.

'They'll think I'm mad when they come back,' she thought. But still the sense of danger persisted. 'We've got to get out of here,' she repeated aloud and, swallowing a sense of guilt, she peered into Marcus' tent. Helen almost smiled as she remembered he was a public school boy. Everything was already neatly stowed in his bag.

The driver and the boys were sitting cross-legged playing cards under the flap of the cooking tent among the pots, pans and cartons of food. Chattering and laughing, they appeared to be completely unaware of trouble in the air and for a moment Helen wondered if she was imagining it all.

Soon she could stand it no longer. Striding over to them, she communicated in pidgin English and mime to indicate to the driver that she wanted him to take the car up the track in the direction the three had headed earlier in the day. He could feel the tension crackling round her and it made him nervous and obdurate. Reluctant to put down his cards, he pretended not to understand and ignored her as he engaged the boys in a torrent of Urdu. But, her voice rising a decibel, she persisted.

Eventually he stood up with an exaggerated shrug that said, 'Who can understand an English memsahib's mind?' He riffled through his cards and put them down carefully, as if to make her feel guilty. Then, changing mood to the normal happy disposition of an Indian, he grinned engagingly and together they walked to the car, which started noisily. At last they jolted up the track.

After a mile they stopped and waited uncertainly

where the path branched off to the temple. Helen asked him to turn the car round. Then she got out and stood in silence, straining all her senses, like a hound on the scent. She heard them before she saw them as they crashed through undergrowth, slipping and clattering over muddy stones, wild with fear and panting, near exhaustion.

As she saw them, Helen experienced an instant of relief that all three were safely together, but that feeling was quickly followed by dread as she felt their terror. She threw herself into the back seat of the car as the three heaving, sweating bodies crashed around her.

The driver needed no telling. He smelled of fear as he frantically tried to start the car again. But the engine turned over and over without firing. For several ghastly moments they screeched at him to move.

'Bloody hell! Get the thing going, can't you?' yelled Marcus, sweat pouring down his scarlet face.

'Hurry! Hurry! Oh God, move!' screamed Joanna, white round the eyes and lips with exhaustion and fear.

Krishna had started to shake and shout urgently in guttural Urdu, while Helen kept repeating inanely, 'What's happened? Are you all right?'

At last the car shuddered away and they craned behind them to see how close their pursuers were. Seconds later one of the men reached the road and started to run after them. Then, to their horror, the Oriental appeared in front of them. He had evidently taken a short cut. Krishna pushed Helen and Joanna down as a wild shot rang out.

Suddenly the Chinese man launched himself at the car and his thin, lithe body sprawled across the bonnet, his face contorted and grotesque at the windscreen, as he clawed at the wiper blades to gain a hold. The driver blindly, instinctively accelerated and the man bounced off into the road. They were all too shocked to scream, but as Joanna looked back, she saw him pick himself up and watch them for a moment. Then he darted off on to another track, which led down the mountain.

Common sense demanded they should drive without stopping until they escaped, but as they neared the camp, Krishna, whose brother was one of the cooking boys, started shouting frantically, 'Stop! Stop for brother. Bad men shoot him.' His accent became thicker and more incomprehensible as he grew more agitated.

Then everyone was shouting at once. Incongruous with shock, Joanna wanted to stop for her diary. 'It's got all my notes in it,' she bleated.

'What's going on? Who are those men?' Helen shouted.

'Don't know,' replied Marcus grimly. And then they were jolting too severely to speak, as the car roared over craggy potholes.

At last Marcus declared very decisively, 'We ought to warn the boys.' They agreed to stop for a moment. It would take their pursuers fifteen minutes to reach the camp on foot. They had not, however, bargained on the driver, who did not want to stop. He did not mind sacrificing his friends. He made no effort to slow as they passed the tents, so Marcus hurled himself between the seats, grabbing the steering wheel and the handbrake, forcing the car to halt.

The cook boys were in the trees at the far end of the camp fetching wood for the fire. Krishna jumped out of the car and screamed and gesticulated loudly to them. They abandoned the branches they were carrying and started running towards him.

Helen's stomach felt even worse, her head tighter. She hadn't used up any adrenaline in running. No one had explained anything and she was desperate to know what was going on. Joanna tried to scramble out of the car but her legs were shaking and she almost collapsed.

'Stay here,' commanded her mother. 'I'll get your bag.'

She jumped out and Marcus followed her.

'Forget the bags, Helen,' he called. For a moment he was going to stop her, but seeing the determined look on her face and realising that it would only take an instant, he went to help her. Already she had shouldered her bag and, dragging Joanna's, was pulling them back to the car with the superhuman strength derived from sheer terror. Marcus grabbed them from her at which, to his amazement, she ran to his tent and lugged out his rucksack. She must be mad, he thought.

He was halfway back to the car when he heard its engine roar. The driver had taken off without them. But he had underestimated Joanna, who instantly regained her strength and, from the back seat, started to hit him and strangle him like a tigress. The man had never experienced anything like this in his life and, half-conscious, he swerved to a stop.

Marcus reached the car in an instant, dragging the driver out unceremoniously and dumping him on the grass. 'Bastard!' he hissed. He pushed Helen and the bags inside and jumped into the driving seat.

As they raced away, Marcus saw Krishna and the other Indians scrambling into the second car. They were right behind him.

Joanna began to unwind, 'Good old Mum,' she murmured 'I wish we'd paid attention to your intuition this morning.'

They started to tell Helen what had happened. She was ashen and now that the immediate danger was past, beginning to look for a higher meaning to the tragedy. 'You were meant to be there, Marcus, to take the Scroll,' she announced.

Marcus touched the Scroll under his anorak and remembered what the old monk had said before he died, 'God sent you.' Perhaps everything had worked out as it should. He set his jaw in a line of steely determination and made a vow on the life of that innocent monk to do his best to deliver it as promised.

Minutes later he noticed that another car had appeared in the mirror. He tensed all over, and his palms grew sweaty. It was the men! Who the hell were they? Joanna noticed Marcus' reaction and immediately turned to look behind.

'Oh no! It's them. Where did they get a car from?' she screamed in fear.

'Hijacked it, I expect,' Marcus responded tersely.

Face set in intense concentration, Marcus drove as he'd never driven before, racing round corners and swerving round potholes, children, dogs and other obstacles in the track. He prayed that nothing would get in their way.

Joanna became intensely practical, her way of staying in control. 'How much petrol do we have?' she yelled.

'Quarter of a tank,' Marcus shouted back, daring to take his eyes off the road to look at the gauge as they swept round a bend with a sheer drop on one side. 'Is there a map in the car?'

'Yes,' replied Joanna, 'but it's scruffy and practically illegible. Can this car go faster than theirs?'

'God knows.' His foot flat on the floor, he was racing at suicidal speed.

Helen and Joanna held on with white knuckles and invoked the angels to help and protect them. As if in response, the car behind them containing Krishna and the boys immediately juddered to a halt in the middle of the track. They guessed it had run out of petrol and felt a rush of relief. It would gain them time. But to their shock the hijackers jumped out and, putting their shoulders to the back of Krishna's car, shoved it off the road with the petrified Indians still inside.

Before they turned the next corner, they could see it hanging with one wheel over the cliff edge. Had it gone over? Were they all right? What sort of men would do that? They all knew the answer – desperate men. Already the Scroll had proved important enough to kill for. Marcus gritted his teeth more tightly, gripped the wheel so that his knuckles were white and tried to ignore his pounding heart. 'Keep cool,' he repeated to himself. 'Keep cool.'

'We'll reach the main road in a minute, I think,'

Joanna screamed. 'Go left.' She was trying to follow the map while being jolted around in the car.

The glimpsed their pursuers occasionally in the distance as they flung themselves round hairpin bends, praying they wouldn't meet anything coming towards them.

After what seemed like hours their car ran out of petrol in the middle of a small town. Marcus directed it into the side of the road and it died. They leapt out with their bags and, even though they had not discussed it, ran with one accord towards the bus station.

One very crowded bus was ready to leave. Push as they might into the mass of humanity already on board, it was clear that only one of them would be able to get on. Helen tried to compose herself.

'I'll take the Scroll. They won't recognise me,' she yelled above the hubbub. She could not hide the fact that she was shaking.

Marcus paused. She was right. It wouldn't enter their minds that a middle-aged woman they had never seen would have it. He handed her the packet containing the Scroll. His grey eyes locked for a moment into her brown ones, willing her to be strong. Behind them a fat man spat loudly.

'Take it! Get off when you can and head back to the guest house at Muni-ki-Reti and we'll see you there,' he whispered into her ear. 'Good luck!' She nodded and he pushed her with all his force into the bus. She could hardly breathe, standing wedged in a sea of bodies. She had no idea where the bus was going or when she would see the others again but she did have the Scroll.

Through the window she caught a glimpse of Joanna and Marcus going in different directions. Oh no, they're separating, she thought in sudden terror, her stomach clenching. No! no!

Her head ached intolerably. She could hardly move and waves of heat flushed through her. Suddenly she felt very lost and alone.

Chapter 7

Heart exploding with fear Joanna forced her cotton-wool legs to carry her. She hurried down the squalid streets, her terror a palpable force field around her. She wanted to be invisible. Giddy with panic, she knew she must lose herself in the crowds.

Suddenly she remembered a mystery story she had once read. The thieves had been unable to find a letter they were looking for because it was in the letter rack – inconspicuous among the other letters.

If I want to disappear I must fit in, she thought. Of course, she must buy a sari! The thought took over her mind. Oblivious to anything else, and frantic as a beetle in distress, she scuttled into a corrugated shack calling itself a sari shop and pretended to look at fabric in the dark interior.

The overweight man and his wife eyed her with the insolent impassivity of the Easterner who has ceased to be astonished at the antics of Westerners. That is, until she fainted. All changed instantly to infinite compassion and concern.

As she was revived with strips of cloth soaked in cool water, her wild glances at the doorway and evident terror persuaded them she was being hounded by a man. Then they noticed with horror that she had blood on her clothes. It must be bad. There is a silent conspiracy among women worldwide to shelter their sisters from persecution. From nowhere appeared tiny thin women, sisters, cousins, mothers, aunts, black hair scraped back, replicas of the wife behind the counter.

Instantly the man of the shop left his accustomed post and stood on the pavement staring into space. Some things men question – others they do not. The sorority nurtured Joanna with infinite tenderness. They sat her on the single chair and brought her chai. When she relaxed and rewarded them with a faint smile they beamed with delight. She noticed that there were always two or three women between her and the doorway and felt peculiarly safe. She heaved a sigh. They eyed her expectantly. She smiled wanly and they smiled back at her, with caring, delighted smiles.

Only for an instant.

Then she thought of her mother and Marcus. She remembered the danger. Sick fear swept through her again. She swayed giddily in her seat, blackness engulfing her, and closed her eyes. What was it her mother always said? 'Fear attracts danger. The invisible powers can't help you through fear, so relax. Put white light round yourself and call for protection.' Joanna could hear her mother's voice in her head.

Conscious that the women were all watching her with concern, she tried to relax by controlling her breathing and gradually felt the tension seeping away. She stopped shivering and her colour returned. She visualised white light around her and called for all the spiritual help she could.

When Joanna opened her eyes, she was able to thank her saviours, if not with serenity, at least with composure. She explained that she wanted to buy a sari and was touched by their evident astonishment and delight. They produced an underskirt and a *choli*, a top worn as a bra under a sari, and they held up a piece of material so that she could take off her T-shirt and trousers in respectful modesty.

The little women patiently taught Joanna how to put on a sari. Their tiny, deft hands, soft as butterfly wings, stroked the fabric into place, and Joanna felt inexplicably soothed. As she relaxed, they giggled behind their hands at her ineptitude. Grinning wide, toothy grins, they produced huge safety pins to clip where she could not manage the intricate drapes. Joanna forgot her fear and laughed, too, as she looked in a chipped and grimy mirror. The deep blue colour that she had chosen to render her invisible in the night enhanced her beauty. But she cared only that no one would realise that she was a Westerner. She felt safe, as though she was among friends.

Moments later a shadow passed the doorway and Joanna froze instantly, staring at the entrance. It was only the shop owner wishing to reclaim his territory. He glanced within and withdrew.

Her new friends, observing Joanna's reaction, exchanged concerned glances. It was time to speak.

'Problem?' voiced the wife after a questioning silence.

Joanna nodded. She tried to explain slowly, with

eloquent gestures, what had happened and how she had been separated from her mother and her friend. Even though they did not fully understand, their shock reverberated through the darkening shop. Such happenings were beyond their comprehension. After a whispered consultation in their own language, the women went to fetch the man. Looking impenetrably solemn, he indicated that Joanna was to repeat her story. The women stood and stared at her.

She repeated her story, adding that one of the murderers was Indian and the other Oriental. They all frowned.

'I don't know where my friend is,' she faltered as she finished.

'Name?' the man asked. It sounded abrupt, but she knew it wasn't meant to be. It just reflected his fear.

'Joanna.'

'Friend name?'

She hesitated. Then said, 'Marcus.'

'What look like?'

She described him.

He did not doubt her sincerity. His eyes rolled. 'What to do?' he said and stared at her. Then he appeared to take a decision.

'Wait!' he barked and disappeared into the outside world. Now all of the women were apprehensive. They too felt in danger.

Joanna tried to apologise, but they touched her lightly to indicate solidarity. They sat together in what seemed to be an interminable frightened silence until it grew so dark that they ought to light a lamp – but did not.

Suddenly a car drew up outside and men's voices

called out. Amid an urgent babble of Urdu, she heard, 'Quick! Quick!' Hands pushed and pulled her out of the shack. 'Go! Go!' She resisted in terror. The sari restricted her.

'Okay! Okay! man found,' reassured the wife looking at her with huge liquid eyes.

The wizened grandmother added toothlessly, with innuendo totally inappropriate for the moment, 'Pretty girl, nice man.' She cackled and several of the women uttered a high-pitched, tension-releasing giggle.

Joanna scarcely had time to call 'Thank you' before she was being bundled into the back of an ancient car. Marcus was there already, looking tired, strained and overwhelmingly relieved to see her.

She almost fell on to him and he grabbed her, holding her tightly in mutual reassurance.

'Are you all right? Thank God. I searched everywhere for you.'

'I'm okay. I hid in a sari shop. What about you?'

'I'll tell you later. Your Indian family mafia soon found me. They found the other guys, too. They're still searching for us. One's still at the bus station.'

'Oh no. What are we going to do?' The pit of Joanna's stomach dropped.

'It's all right. Everything's arranged,' Marcus reassured her. 'Our friends are putting us on a bus at the stop after the bus station. The driver is your friend's cousin. I gave them the money and they got our tickets to Rishikesh.'

'Thank goodness.' Joanna breathed a huge sigh. 'They were good people.'

'They were brilliant. They got everything sussed and sorted in no time. Amazing for India.'

'We were being looked after by someone upstairs, I guess.'

'Let's hope they're looking after your mother, too, and that she and the Scroll are safely on the way back to the guest house.'

'Oh, please. I do hope she's all right.'

Chapter 8

Gasping for breath in the crowded bus Helen wished she had not impulsively offered to take the Scroll. She should have stayed with Joanna. Then she reminded herself firmly that Joanna was a very capable young woman. She's probably far better at looking after herself than I am, she thought ruefully. Besides she was with Marcus. Helen had to admit that she wished she was with them, too.

She must keep her mind focused on the positive. She made a mental picture of the Scroll being safely handed over to the temple, and saw herself being reunited with Joanna and Marcus. She kept visualising this and asking the powers-that-be to energise her vision. She must not let any other thought enter her mind. She must not.

The bus kept putting people down in the middle of nowhere and at last she got a seat. One exhausting hour later it stopped at a filthy, smelly hotchpotch of wooden huts with corrugated iron roofs, one of which bore the sign 'Travel Agent'. That was enough for Helen. She dragged herself wearily off the bus and made her way into the shop, past the two mangy dogs lying in the dirt in front of it.

The two men in the shack were asleep, heads lolling awkwardly. They opened their eyes when she entered.

Surprise at the sight of a middle-aged white woman in a battered hat registered on their faces. She was red and sweaty, with a dirty smudge across her cheek, and she clutched a tattered parcel as if her life depended on it.

'Taxi to Muni-ki-Reti,' Helen said firmly and clearly. 'How much?'

'Yes, yes.' They smiled at her with the usual bobbing of the head. They talked among themselves and then one ventured, 'Taxi . . . you go where?'

'Muni-ki-Reti.'

They talked again. She realised they had no idea where it was. 'Near Rishikesh,' she added more loudly.

That was better. 'Rishikesh!' one repeated. Then the other said it. 'Rishikesh!' They laughed.

'Rishikesh,' they said again and they all laughed together, including Helen, who had no idea what she was laughing at.

Helen was getting impatient, a fatal sin in India. She also realised she was filthy, tired, scared and clutching the dirty, scruffy package in an incongruous way.

'How much?' she repeated, her voice rising another octave.

The two men consulted again. One went to fetch the boss, returning with him almost a quarter of an hour later.

'Tomorrow,' he said.

'Tomorrow!' echoed Helen in dismay. 'Now!' she said firmly.

'No! No!' They all laughed in conspiracy. 'Dangerous in dark,' smiled the boss man. The others nodded, smiling, as if they were incredulous that she could have thought of such a thing.

Half an hour later the conversation had gone full circle and they had reached an impasse. The price they had agreed, but the Indians were still smilingly adamant that the journey could not take place until the following day.

'Hotel?' she asked defeated.

They were delighted. 'Very good hotel!' they all exclaimed in unison pointing to a derelict looking flea-pit on the other side of the road. 'Owned by my brother,' said the travel agent proudly. 'First class! Five star!' his white teeth flashed in an impudent grin.

'Five star!' Despite her stressed and weary state Helen chuckled. More like a fifth of a star, if that.

'Okay,' she said, 'taxi at five in the morning!'

They promised on their lives that the taxi would be there at 5 a.m., and all three of them jubilantly conducted her across the road to what was undoubtedly the filthiest, dingiest hotel room she had ever seen. Paint peeled off the uniformly grubby cream walls. Dirt and dust tickled her nostrils and made her sneeze. The building smelt of urine and decay.

She looked round her room and for a moment her will failed her. She couldn't stay here. But what else could she do? She gathered her strength and went out to buy bottled water, fruit she could peel and a packet of biscuits. Then she returned, locked the door of her room and sat on the dusty bed in despair.

Helen endured one of the worst nights she had ever experienced. For hours her mind churned in a loop.

Were Joanna and Marcus safe? What was the Scroll? What secrets did it hold? Why was it so important? Who were the men? Why did they want it? And another thought intruded. Was there an organisation behind these men?

She dreamt that something big and anonymous with dark tentacles was spreading out to find the Scroll and catch her. She woke exhausted and was outside waiting for the taxi in the dark at 4.30 a.m. Thankfully it arrived by five.

She would have felt less safe if she had known that a Chinese man and an Indian would be knocking at the hotel door two hours later.

Helen sat in the back of the car as red streaks filtered across the sky. She saw every inch of the sun rise in all its glory and become hotter and more fiery as the day passed. She watched the early-morning workers trudge to the fields and become listless and slower as the drowsy inertia of the day overcame them. All the while she listened to the two men in front droning, like foreign bees. India is a companionable land. If someone drives, a friend or child comes along for the ride.

She felt separate, apart, a watcher and listener, a being in two worlds, one a tourist and the other a fugitive on a mission, separated from her companions.

Late in the crumpled afternoon the golden finger of fate caused her to look up at a temple perched on a peak overlooking the Ganges. It looked Buddhist, she thought vaguely. Then her eye caught a faded sign. Temple Mahathat.

I don't believe it! she thought and shouted, 'Stop!' so abruptly that the driver swerved and pulled in. 'Stop now!' she repeated. 'Is this Joshipur?' she demanded, harsh with sudden anticipation. The two men looked blankly at each other. Either they did not understand her English or they did not know.

Inevitably there was a little chai stall down the road. Helen indicated to the driver to move forward to it. She got out and bought them each a cup of chai. The girl serving the drinks spoke a few words of tourist English.

Helen pointed to the mountain-top where the temple roof was visible. She said, with a question mark in her voice, 'Temple Mahathat at Joshipur?' and made a praying gesture. The girl nodded.

'I want to go there,' Helen declared. It took some time before the girl got her meaning. Then she giggled behind her hand and said something to the various people standing around, all of whom guffawed. Apparently Helen's suggestion was very funny.

'Men only. Women no!' she gurgled at last.

Helen was still clutching the Scroll. She screwed up her eyes and gazed up at the ornate roof of the temple visible above the trees. Filled with impulsive determination, she said to the driver, 'Wait here.'

She picked up her bag from the car and strode off in the late-afternoon sun towards the temple. She could hear the laughter and comments from those hanging around the chai shop. It served to increase her resolve.

The climb was steep and Helen had never been good at hills. Legs aching, chest and lungs tightly hurting, she persevered up a well-worn stony track. In places, where it was very steep, there were rough steps hewn into the hill and sometimes a welcome handrail. Hot, panting, but utterly determined, she blanked out worry about Joanna and Marcus or their pursuers and simply held on to the vision of handing the Scroll to the Chief Lama.

As she approached the temple, the stronghold of masculine spiritual energy, underlying doubts began to attack her. Dusk was beginning to fall and what seemed obvious in the bright light of day appeared obscure in the time of shadows. Her worst worries and fears started to haunt her. Would they let her in? What if it wasn't a temple but some strange dark place only disguised as one? Would their pursuers catch Joanna and Marcus? Who were they? What would they do to them? The path was dark as she passed under trees. A predatory night bird screeched. A leaf brushed her arm and made her jump.

She stopped and forced herself to breathe calmly. She must not let her imagination lead her into fear. She could use images to change her feelings. She pictured a warm welcome at the temple and Marcus and Joanna safe at the guest house. At once she felt more relaxed. Before long, deep, melodious chanting floated from the temple. They were evidently holding a service. She sat on a rock to listen and take time to compose herself completely.

Held in the sound of the sacred chanting, she became quiet, still and attuned to the great Oneness. She felt soothed, peaceful. All was well. Her fears dissolved. When the chanting ended she rose, softly approached the huge ornate gold inlaid door and pulled a bell. The sound clanged into the night.

After what seemed an eternity, she heard shuffling footsteps. A small thin monk with glasses opened the door and looked totally shocked to see her. She rose and pressed her hands together in a Namaste gesture. Then she held out the package, saying, 'Important. Do you speak English?' in as calm a voice as she could manage.

The monk pushed the door shut without closing it and disappeared. Helen prepared for a long wait and sat quietly on the step, holding the Scroll carefully, watching darkness fall like a cloak over the countryside.

Sooner than she had expected the monk returned with a brother and Helen asked to speak to the Head Lama. She stayed very calm and centred. She pointed to the package containing the Scroll and said, 'Very important.'

The two monks scrutinised her dishevelled appearance, but her calm manner seemed to reassure them and they disappeared again. She noticed many faces appearing at windows, and soon monks gathered round her in little groups, staring and nudging each other like children. She ignored them, closed her eyes and sat, trying to radiate peace and the importance of her mission. The monks soon fell silent, confounded and curious.

She heard quiet footsteps approaching and opened her eyes. A different monk stood in front of her. He was older, more dignified and quiet; his hands in the Namaste posture. Slowly she returned the gesture. He motioned her to follow him. She rose with as much dignity as possible, stiff from sitting on the stone step, and followed him in silence, through ornate corridors and winding stone stairways, possibly the first woman ever to grace the building. The monk paused in front of a door hung with a beautiful tapestry, embroidered with a fish. He shuffled his feet slightly and a tinkling bell from inside summoned them in.

Sitting motionless and cross-legged were several inscrutably dignified monks. She wondered if any of them spoke English. How would she explain? How would they respond?

The man sitting in lotus position on a mat on a slightly raised dais was small, elderly and wizened. This was clearly the Head Lama. Helen observed that he had a look of infinite calm and wisdom about him and felt pleased, recognising him as an old soul.

He honoured her by rising and greeting her, hands together, Namaste. She responded quietly in like manner. No one had spoken. She did not know the etiquette. She knew that only her silence and her stillness had brought her into this man's presence.

She held out the package to him as if it was a precious diamond. Puzzled, he took it and placed it on the floor in front of him. They both sat on mats with the parcel between them. Commensurate with the gravity of the situation, he welcomed her seriously in measured English and invited her to speak.

The room was impregnated with the atmosphere of meditation and prayer and as she told her story Helen felt supported by the deep sense of peace. She faltered only once, lips quivering, when she said she did not know where her daughter and Marcus were. For an instant, as she looked into the Lama's eyes and blinked back tears, she saw the infinite compassion with which he observed her.

'I hope your daughter and friend are safe,' he said quietly. Shocking as the story had been, and full of curiosity as they all must be, he had taken the trouble to reach out to her pain first. She realised he was a man of heart as well as mind. She nodded, grateful for his concern.

'Excuse us,' he said with impeccable politeness, as they consulted among themselves in their own language.

He turned to her a few moments later, exuding oceans of patience and calm. 'First we must offer prayers for our brother monk from Tibet who died, and for the safety of your daughter and friend. Then the seal must be broken very carefully, in a special atmosphere. The contents are undoubtedly fragile. Our temple specialises in such knowledge. The monks here study old manuscripts. We believe that is why the Scroll was being brought here.'

Helen felt exhausted. It had been a very long two days. All she wanted to do was sleep. She felt all their eyes on her, kindly, wise and devoted to doing what was the greatest good.

'Yes,' she nodded, grateful and relieved.

Two monks were assigned to look after her and the senior monks left for meditation. She heard the bell clang again and sensed excitement in the building, but it all felt far away.

Her two carers fetched some hot rice and vegetable curry. She ate a little and felt better. Then they led her through corridors to a small room, placed a pillow on a mat on the floor and invited her to lie down. She was too tired to do anything other than obey gratefully. She was unaware that the thoughtful monks had sent a message down to the taxi driver and his friend to wait overnight.

She slept through the ceremony of the breaking of the seal, which took place in front of the Chief Lama. She did not know that the Scroll was a fragile, ancient parchment covered in hieroglyphics, understood only by a few people in the world. Three of these scholars, who had devoted their lives to this study, were brothers at the Mahathat Monastery, attached to the temple, which was exactly why the Tibetan monk had been so determined to bring the Scroll here.

She was oblivious to the fact that they had sat up all night in mounting excitement, filming, copying and beginning to decipher the Scroll, whose information could change the world. It was the most significant moment in the history of the temple.

Helen slept through it all.

Chapter 9

Helen woke feeling stiff, sticky and disorientated, with the lingering memory of dreadful dreams – dreams of Joanna as a little girl, lost. She'd been searching everywhere, frantically searching, and she could not find her. She was falling over precipices, dropping. Then she was alone, totally alone, in a boiling cauldron. She woke with her head thumping and a horrid feeling in her solar plexus, all her worst fears coming back to hit her.

When she opened her eyes, she realised that someone had placed a light blanket over her, welcome in the relatively cool early morning. She appeared to be in a dark green cocoon, as the solicitous monks had placed dark green silk screens around her, offering her privacy where there was no door.

They were evidently aware of her waking movements for when she sat up and gently moved the screen, several smiling faces waited to greet her.

Helen felt that they treated her with as much politeness but with more deference this morning.

'The Scroll?' she asked and they all nodded, Indian style, eternally smiling. She suspected they spoke no English.

'Wash,' she said, miming. Even a cold shower would be welcome. But she was pleasantly surprised. She was led to a communal washroom and a youthful monk brought her a bucket of hot water. He put it down in the shower space, turned the tap on to show her she could also have a cold shower, then carefully turned it off again.

'Namaste,' he bowed. 'Honourable guest!'

She smiled. He beamed as he withdrew. She wondered if he knew what 'honourable guest' meant or whether he had been told to say it.

She could hear the monks chattering outside the washroom door so she knew no one would walk in. Showering in cold water, then decadently sluicing herself in hot, Helen emerged feeling like an English memsahib again. The young monks conducted her directly to the Chief Lama. As before, several older monks flanked him. He greeted her most graciously in the traditional manner, asked how she had slept and enquired after her health. There was no hint of the total irregularity of having a white, middle-aged English woman sleeping in his temple.

Have you opened the Scroll? What's it like? What have you found out? The questions burned on her lips but, ever controlled, she waited politely for him to speak first.

Instead of giving her information, he asked if she would tell them again how it had been acquired. Biting back her irritation and reminding herself that it was a lesson in patience, she once more recounted the story, giving more detail than before. This time they broke in occasionally to ask questions, which she answered as fully as she could.

She was in mid-flow when, shockingly, the loud, continuous clanging of the main bell interrupted her story. She was aware of the monks' surprise and discomfort, as the noise shattered their concentration. The bell demanded to be answered.

Soon a monk silently appeared to give the Lama a message. Behind him were sounds of a scuffle and voices raised, as Marcus rushed in, a tall, impetuous European fending off tiny Tibetans who were trying to prevent his entry.

Helen leapt to her feet, laughing with relief, 'Marcus! How did you get here? Where's Joanna?'

He grabbed her and gave her a bear hug of delight. 'Helen! Are you all right? Have you given them the Scroll?'

She nodded. 'Where's Joanna?' she asked again.

'On a bus back to Muni-ki-Reti to find you. She's okay, I hope.'

'Thank heavens,' she sighed, and her headache dissolved as if by magic.

'How did you find the temple?' they asked together and laughed again.

The monks had fallen back in disconcerted silence as they watched this public Western display. The Chief Lama, however, had laughter in his eyes. He was known to say, in his light way, 'Laughter is good. Good is God.'

He rose and shook hands with Marcus, for all the world like an English gentleman. Surreal, thought Helen. The monks stared.

Without beating about the bush, Marcus demanded, 'Where's the Scroll?'

The Chief Monk replied calmly, 'It is safe.' Then he motioned his visitors to sit.

He seated himself deliberately and waited for silence. Then he addressed Marcus, 'You should know that this temple is renowned for research into old documents. We specialise in this work. We have already explained this to your revered friend,' he nodded towards Helen. 'We believe this is why our brother monk was bringing the Scroll to us. Here there are experts in such matters and also special conditions in which to examine ancient documents.'

He paused and spoke to both of them, 'We believe the Scroll is an authentic document. We do not yet know how old it is, for it was sealed in special fabric we have never before experienced. There is nothing like this in the world today and we believe that for hundreds of years the Scroll was in the custody of the temple in Tibet.'

'What's it about?' Marcus wanted to know. 'The monk who died said it could save the world.'

The Chief Lama looked at him for a silent instant. Then nodded. 'Yes. The Scroll appears to contain sacred and secret information, which is needed now. I will tell you.' He looked at Marcus. 'You are the chosen one.'

Marcus felt a shiver go through him. He remembered the words of the dying Tibetan, 'You sent by God. You save the world. Blessed.' He remembered Helen's words, and the reaction of the clairvoyant. He dropped his eyes, confused.

The venerable Lama turned his glance to Helen and bowed. For a moment she thought he was going to ask her to leave the room but he honoured her, too.

'You are a Wise One.' She smiled and blushed, feeling unaccountably pleased. It was the same feeling she had experienced when she was chosen to be a prefect at school.

He told them that the Scroll appeared to be written in an ancient Tibetan dialect, in which one of the brothers at the temple was an expert. This brother believed that Buddha had prepared him all his life for the sacred task of translating the Scroll.

Helen and Marcus nodded. With the synchronicities they had already observed regarding the Scroll, it did indeed seem likely.

'The Scroll reminds us that our beautiful earth is a sacred planet and holds a special position in the universe. It is also unique because here God gave His Creation free will. You know humans have free will?' he checked. They nodded and he continued, 'The Scroll says our Creator observes but never interferes.'

They nodded again, and Helen said dryly, 'So we blame God for tragedy and disasters instead of taking responsibility for our behaviour and actions that cause them.'

'Exactly,' agreed the Lama. 'According to the Scroll, when God put humans on Earth, He created four portals through which He and His messengers could be contacted more easily. And through these special places, God could pour a higher vibration, which would help humans to live in cooperation and harmony.'

'Just a minute,' interrupted Marcus. 'That sounds a bit like parents letting children camp on an island, where they can do what they want. But at the same time they make sure there are bridges to the island, so they can pop over and check that everything's okay or the kids can get help if they need it.'

'Exactly,' nodded the Lama. He continued. 'These four portals were connected to other places on Earth by a grid of communicating lines. Divine information and messages of hope and inspiration were transmitted down the lines. People were able to link through the network to other special high-energy places and to God.'

'Sorry to interrupt again. Are you saying that the four portals were kind of like electricity generators, sending high-voltage currents through a network of cables?' questioned Marcus, who needed to translate everything into a concept he could understand.

'And at these portals the vibration was higher, so it was easier to communicate with God?' checked Helen.

'Just so,' the Lama nodded to both of them. 'Very good. The Scroll says there were many points on the network, like substations, which stepped down the power where it was too much for people to cope with. Special people, Holy Ones, looked after the portals and subportals, using ritual and ceremony, and kept them pure. They devoted their whole lives to this purpose.'

Helen and Marcus looked at each other. 'What happened to change it?' asked Marcus.

'Two things. First people started to get more materialistic. Think of the energy lines as telephone cables. Once people became denser, they couldn't get a clear line. There was interference or crackle on the line, which meant they could no longer communicate easily with

God. Many stopped trying and let intermediaries, like priests, do it for them.

'Secondly, and this is really important. Whoever controls the portals and the energy grid has power on the planet. With the development of industry and technology, money and power became more of an issue.

'The dogmatic religions started to be taken over by men of dubious spiritual credentials. Some, for instance, started to tell their followers that they must not communicate directly with God or his messengers. They claimed that their priests were the only intermediaries to God and they must pay them for this service and obey them. People believed this because there was now interference on the line.'

'And,' interrupted Helen fiercely, 'they had witch hunts to eradicate all the natural mediums and healers.'

The Lama continued patiently, 'As soon as the Churches controlled the lines, they set about making the people powerless by distorting the Divine Truth.'

'Not deliberately, surely?'

'In some cases, I think so.' The Lama's voice was almost apologetic. 'Take Christianity, for instance. After the death of Jesus, his followers started telling people that to follow Jesus was the only way. They must give up their wealth and do as the priests told them. Otherwise they would go to hell.'

Helen, eyes flashing, commented, 'They even sealed the third eyes of babies at baptism.'

'What's the third eye exactly?' queried Marcus.

'You know, the spiritual point in the centre of the forehead. The all-seeing eye. It's a divine point of connection and priests seal it with a cross of holy water! Then they have closed the baby's connection to God and they can take power.'

'Oh!' Marcus exclaimed, disturbed. He considered what she had said. 'Surely that wasn't the original intention.'

'Possibly not.' Helen shook her head. 'They certainly wanted the flock to follow a few leaders, which they would automatically do if their third eye was closed. But you also had to believe in it. Now I think a lot of people don't believe, so it has less power to control.'

'Mmm,' Marcus glanced at the Lama as if for confirmation.

The old man continued carefully, 'The Scroll talks about the preaching of false beliefs. It calls them illusions. But it also says that it is not just the Churches who have control over the energy lines.

'Originally kings and queens, earls, lords and those of position worked for the light. They were evolved souls who, before they were incarnated, dedicated their lives to ruling honourably. Over the centuries inbreeding diluted the pure lines. Self-interest prevailed rather than the will of God and many did deals to preserve their position. Greed and corruption often won.

'Then other groups of people banded together to battle for the material wealth and power. Governments, banks and big business took over from the High Born. Now they have taken control of the energy grids.'

'Is this deliberate? Do they know they have done this?' Marcus demanded.

'Very rarely. In the beginning, of course, the Royal

Ones knew all about the power points and grids and used them carefully. Even then black magicians could use a line and block or distort it, but there were relatively few of them. Now there are many businesses who have built on the lines with a view only to profit.'

'How would they know they were building, say, a garage or a warehouse on a ley line?' Marcus persisted.

'Easy,' Helen responded. 'All the villages and towns, churches, meeting places and ceremonial sites were built on ley lines. We use those same sites now because unconsciously we recognise they are energy points. However, when the motive is wrong, the energy becomes dark.

'Now most parliament buildings, town halls and even schools have dark energy lines radiating from them carrying vibrations of fear, greed, control and other illusions.'

The Lama pursed his lips and sighed in agreement. 'So ruthless, materially minded people have waged a war for the subtle communication network on the planet and they have succeeded almost entirely to take it over. The planet is now ruled with fear.

'The network must be reclaimed for the Light *and the scroll tells how this can be done,*' he emphasised. 'Of course this is a danger to those who want money and control. They will fight and kill to retain power, as we already know. Furthermore, whoever holds the information contained in the Scroll will hold the secret of immense power, greater than anyone has ever had access to. This power can be used for evil or to spread truth and bring equality of health and wealth to all on the planet.'

He looked directly at Marcus. 'You have an awesome task.'

Part of Marcus felt sick, inadequate and numb. He wanted to shout, 'Why me?' The other half felt inspired, excited and ready.

To his eternal shame and regret, 'Why me?' popped out of his mouth. He could have bitten his tongue off.

Compassion tempered the words of the Lama. 'Because you were chosen and prepared for this task before you were born. You will be helped. That is why you met this good lady.' He indicated Helen.

'I know,' Marcus sighed. 'Tell us more.'

The Chief Lama smiled politely. 'Regretfully I have other duties that call me away. One more piece of information I can give you. All that has happened on earth was a possibility that was forecast all those years ago. The Scroll has appeared now because it is imperative that the downward trend of inhumanity be stopped.

'It may take weeks, months, even years for my scribes to decode it all. But, because we know it is so urgent and important, we are looking at the first section immediately. If you could be so good as to return here at three o'clock I will update you.'

'Of course.'

'We'll be here.'

The Chief Lama paused as he was about to leave, then he turned suddenly and spoke softly, 'Incidentally, the Scroll describes the understanding of the portals and the grid network as the first Great Mystery of earth.'

Chapter 10

Their faces alive with excitement, Helen and Marcus walked through the cool temple discussing the first Great Mystery.

'I hadn't realised how controlled we all are,' Marcus frowned. 'Then I realised that it's happening all the time. Like banks, for instance, holding us in thrall by lending imaginary money and charging interest on it.'

'Especially the extortionate rates they charge under-developed countries, keeping them eternally burdened,' agreed Helen. 'Then there's the pharmaceutical industry, which blocks and devalues natural healing methods and promotes expensive drugs, which do terrible damage and cost people a fortune.'

'And the tobacco and drugs lobby.'

'And guns in America!'

'England's not much better. The average person may not hold a handgun, but our wealth is based on arms exports.'

'We could go on for ever,' sighed Helen, 'but we're energising the darkness. And it looks as if the Scroll holds the secrets to re-empower the people. No wonder the controllers everywhere, whoever they are, want it destroyed. Who do you think they are, Marcus?'

'I don't know. I've gone over it and over it in my mind.'

'Those two must work for someone – or an organisation.'

'Of course. It could be the drug barons, the Triads, the Mafia or the CIA, even.' Helen shivered. An even more awful thought had struck her. 'It could be the Elite.'

'The Elite?'

Marcus noticed she had gone pale. A frisson ran down his back.

'Those who control the world by manipulating the people who seem to be in charge. They're a group of powerful black magicians, headed by a guy called Sturov. Many of them work behind the scenes as advisers to decision-makers but they can be doctors, businesspeople or shop assistants.'

'And are they consciously aware of what they are doing?'

'Some are. Certainly those at the top. But many are not. People who are afraid or angry can be working for the dark forces without realising it. Their negative emotions leave them vulnerable to control by Sturov's lot, who push them into positions where they can do damage. They're in the media and government and in religions – even the New Age movement. They often work by spreading confusion and undermining the efforts of those who want the highest good for all.'

'Can you give me an example?'

'Well, if Sturov's men can control the mind of a newspaper editor, they can influence him to distort the truth and ridicule light-workers who are standing up for peace or bringing in higher perspectives.'

'I see.' Marcus looked grave.

Helen said, 'They *seem* very ordinary but their real power is in the inner planes.'

'You've lost me.'

Helen paused. 'I don't know how to explain.' He waited, knowing this could be important.

She took a deep breath. 'We live in a material world – the physical plane. But this is interspersed with other planes. For instance, ghosts, the stuck spirits of people who have died are in another plane. Angels are in a higher plane.'

He nodded.

'Light-workers focus on spreading light, love and healing to others. They can use divine energy to do this and they access it by developing purity, mind control and higher consciousness. Dark beings with selfish or even evil intent can manipulate energy, too. However they draw their power from other people's fear, sexuality and focus on evil, and by stealing energy from others, especially the pure and innocent.'

'Okay, I get that,' nodded Marcus.

'For everything light there is a balance working for the dark. So there are Dark Ones who wish to control the minds of everyone on the planet and cause destruction and chaos. An ordinary seeming person or even someone who appears to be good may be in thrall to the Dark Side. These are led by Sturov.'

'And he or his henchmen would provoke discontent, disruption and even killing?'

'Yes.'

'But you said that we all have angels who constantly whisper our highest potential to us?'

'We do. All the time. But there are also dark angels and energies. That's why we have to use discernment. And constantly focus on the Light. Dark can't harm light or put it out. Dark beings get at us through our fears and insecurities and try to undermine or frighten us through those.'

'What would they gain from this?'

'In the inner planes, chaos, destruction, the obliteration of the light of humanity. Then they can take over the minds of everyone on the planet and use them to do their will. They want power and control, pure and simple. To be top dog.'

'And in the material world?'

'Same thing. If they can foment enough wars and spread drug dependence, they get the arms and drug money. They use the chaos to legislate to take away freedoms. When they control the food, medicine, water, banking systems, police forces and everything else, people become dependent. The Elite then take over the communication networks and they control the world. They hold the money and the power. It feeds their ego.'

'Is this the Battle of Armageddon? The battle between dark and light?'

'I suppose so. We light-workers everywhere have to mobilise ourselves and the Scroll will show us how to do this more effectively. That's why Sturov is determined to stop us.'

* * *

When Helen and Marcus emerged from the cool of the temple, the heat hit them like air from a roasting oven. They could barely breathe, let alone speak.

Nevertheless they felt they had to go down the hill to the chai shop to speak to Helen's taxi driver. They decided they would ask him to wait until after their next talk with the Chief Lama. Then they would return to Muni-ki-Reti and find Joanna.

They scuttled from one patch of shade to another.

'What happened after I caught the bus?' Helen panted when they paused under a tree. 'I saw you and Joanna separating. That really worried me.'

Marcus responded tersely, 'We had no idea the men were so close behind us. As you got on to the bus we saw them and just ran in opposite directions. I thought they would go to the train station so I found a shady corner behind a wall and hid for ages. My heart was thumping so damn loudly I was sure they would find me. It was the worst time. I didn't know where Joanna was or if they had caught her or where we would meet again.'

He glanced at Helen's face and decided to lighten the story up for he didn't want to worry her any more than she was already.

'Typical woman,' he grinned. 'It turned out she found a clothes shop and very cleverly bought herself a sari. The women showed her how to put it on. That took about an hour and a half, apparently, because they were all giggling so much at her ineptitude. With her dark hair, it really suited her.' Marcus sounded surprised.

'I bet she looked great.' Helen tried fleetingly to picture her daughter in a sari and failed.

'How did you find each other again?' she wanted to know.

Marcus' eyes were teasing. 'I suppose the powers-that-be looked after us. The Light Angels! After a time I got up and started to search for Joanna. I must have lurked behind every wall and tree in the place. I didn't see the men but I couldn't find Joanna either. I was getting pretty desperate, I can tell you.' He heaved a sigh.

Helen nodded.

He continued, 'The men from the sari shop found me. They took me to her by car! Boy, was I glad to see her. And how about this, while I had been searching for her, she had managed to ask the sari ladies about the Mahathat Temple! They had never heard of it but they asked a cousin, who knew someone and on down the chain until someone said it was on the road to Rishikesh. They were able to tell her fairly precisely where it was and she had a good feeling it was the one we were looking for. Incredible luck in the whole of India. I thought it would be like looking for a needle in a haystack.'

'No!' Helen reminded him. 'Don't forget there is no such thing as chance or coincidence on this planet. You weren't there to take the Scroll from the monk as he died, just by chance.'

'I'm beginning to understand that,' admitted Marcus.

'And if the powers-that-be wanted us to deliver the Scroll now, they would provide the synchronicities and opportunities to make that happen. I guess that for us to find the Temple so quickly and easily means that the universe is giving us the message it is really urgent.'

'Oh!' said Marcus, lost for a moment in silent thought. 'Going back to what we were talking about. They put Joanna and me on a bus to Rishikesh. I got off at the Temple and she went back to the guest house because we thought you might be there with the Scroll. We didn't think you would find the Temple.'

'There you go,' said Helen lightly. 'I was guided.'

'So,' said Marcus, 'does our task end now that we have handed the Scroll over?'

Helen merely raised her eyebrows in disbelief.

'I thought not.'

They woke the taxi driver, who was quite sensibly asleep under a tree. He was astonished to see them, for no Indian can possibly understand Europeans who walk in the full heat of the day. The inner forces that drive the latter are incomprehensible to the former.

Using the universal currency of persuasion, they made a deal with him to wait another few hours. Then after a rest and cold drinks, to his concerned incredulity, they clambered, hot, red and breathless, up the hill again to the temple.

They would not have felt so contented if they had been there as dusk fell, when a car containing one Indian and one Chinese man rattled past towards Muni-ki-Reti and a second car filled with armed men stopped at the chai stall.

But Helen and Marcus were oblivious. By then they had returned to the sanctuary of the temple to meet the Chief Lama and were unaware of the drama about to unfold.

Chapter 11

Helen and Marcus sat on their mats in the Chief Lama's chamber, where he was flanked by his retinue of elderly monks. After the obligatory salutations he informed them that his scribes and scholars had been working all day on the Scroll. The information contained in it was very, very important, even more than they had realised earlier. He glowed with excitement and enthusiasm, and the elderly monks were smiling too, their eyes sparkling with light.

The Chief Lama spoke in his soft voice, 'The Scroll informs us that, if the portals and energy grids become polluted, our planet will not be able to evolve and eventually this will hold back the evolution of the entire universe. Therefore, destiny decrees that it will be released at a certain time in history if the knowledge contained in it is needed. That time is when Earth is ready to move into a new phase, which is to be the Golden Age. It is now.'

He looked at them over his half-glasses. 'As you can see, our planet is far from ready, mainly because of the corruption of the energy network. The power-seekers have also apparently taken control of the main portals. This must be stopped and the gateways reclaimed for the Light ... The Scroll tells us this is urgent.

People have been shackled and disempowered for too long.'

'How can we clear and reclaim the grids?' demanded Marcus.

'Let me continue,' the Chief Lama gently rebuked him. 'The Scroll tells us that Earth was designed to be a Mystery School. It says there are seven Great Mysteries, which are the Laws governing the Earth plane. We enrol for this experience when we are born and then we have amnesia about these Laws and our true selves. It's known as the veil of forgetfulness. Our lessons are presented to us in the great school of life. Every person, every situation we come across is a lesson.'

Helen was nodding in agreement and the Chief Lama smiled at her. 'You may be surprised that I, as a Buddhist, can say all these things. But the messages of the Scroll are spiritual and apply to all religions. I would say they are the foundations for all religions. Written through the Scroll everywhere is the reminder to love each other.'

'That's what religions say but don't practise,' Helen agreed. 'And me too a lot of the time, I guess.'

The Lama raised one eyebrow at her with understanding and continued, 'The Scroll tells us about the seven Great Mysteries. I explained this morning that the first seems to be that there are four direct portals from Earth to God and a network of energy lines intended to carry divine communication.

'It tells us that, when you discover the Scroll, the illusions of life will be drawn to your attention. This will happen seemingly by chance but in fact will be coordinated by your spiritual guides and helpers.'

'Amazing!'

'What are these illusions?'

'I think they are things that everyone has accepted as truths but which are not. They are distorting our perception of life.'

Marcus decided to think about that later. He repeated his earlier question, 'How can the grid be cleared, purified and reclaimed? And what will happen on Earth when it is?'

The Chief Lama nodded. 'To answer your first question, the clearance can take place by use of the power of the mind and of certain symbols. With it must be used the vibration of certain sounds. Just as the right notes brought down the walls of Jericho and certain high notes shatter glass, some sounds can clear darkness. We believe the Scroll contains esoteric information. We think it gives us the symbols and the keys to the sounds.'

There was an excitement-filled silence.

Marcus broke it. 'I don't understand. What can sound and the mind together do?'

The Chief Lama spoke again. 'When you think a thought, it starts to send an energy impulse into the universe. Enough thoughts make things manifest. Such is the power of thought. When you open your mouth and speak words, the sound energises the thought and manifestation takes place more quickly. Sound waves are most powerful.'

'You mean that when people send the appropriate sounds and thoughts along the grid, they can cleanse it?' Marcus asked.

'Most people's thoughts are too scattered to be of any

use. However, groups of people with specially trained minds have the power to focus appropriate thought and intention. We believe that if this is used in conjunction with the right sounds we will soon have the keys to raise the vibration on the planet.'

Marcus looked dubious and disappointed. He had expected practical instructions.

Helen spoke up. 'They say that in Atlantean times tumours were dissolved by the use of sound and that vehicles were propelled by sound vibrations stored in crystals.'

The Chief Lama looked at her with an unfathomable expression. 'We have reason to believe the Scroll was written by those survivors of Atlantis who came to Tibet.'

Marcus, Helen and several of the monks felt a shiver run through them. Marcus felt the hair at the back of his neck prickle. Helen's arms were covered in goose pimples.

'The sacred and most powerful portal in Tibet has been overrun by negative forces.' The Lama referred to the Chinese. 'But some of our monks are trained in the discipline of the mind. They will be able to practise the sounds we have been given and use them to focus on reversing the illusions as we are presented with them.'

He looked at Marcus and Helen. 'I have consulted with my fellow Lamas and we believe that you must take the Scroll to England to try to retrieve the two-way inter-dimensional portal there at Stonehenge. It has been allowed to fall into disrepair. The ancient keepers of the

Henge are kept away from it and it is under threat from the forces of darkness.'

They were startled. Neither had appreciated the full significance of Stonehenge. 'Is it one of the four main portals?' asked Helen.

'According to the Scroll, yes. It is urgently in need of restitution for the healing of the planet.'

'Why must we take the Scroll? Surely you will need a long time to work on it?'

'Indeed, I do not mean the original,' the Chief Lama smiled and shook his head in gentle self-deprecation. 'I mean take the copy we have made, so that it can be examined by your experts.'

'However did you make a copy of ancient parchment?' exclaimed Marcus.

'This is no ordinary parchment. It is of a material we do not recognise. They had technology in Atlantean times we have no concept of yet. The material is flexible and durable and hasn't crumbled.'

'Oh!' Marcus was dumbfounded. 'Surely that is very generous of you to let a rival institution see it?' he queried, slipping into Old Age attitude.

'We believe it is for the highest good. All must cooperate to raise the vibrations of the planet before it is too late.'

Marcus flushed, feeling rebuked. 'Who must we take the Scroll to?' he asked.

'You will be guided to the right people,' replied the Lama enigmatically.

Helen nodded. For some reason she had started to feel very anxious. The recently familiar sick feeling had punched her in the solar plexus. Marcus noticed suddenly how white she was. He reached over and touched her arm reassuringly with his big warm hand. 'Are you all right?' he whispered, concerned.

'I've got that feeling again, as if there is something wrong,' she responded apologetically. A week ago, Marcus would have brushed this off. Now he was worried. He looked around.

'Excuse me!' he said to the Chief Monk. Getting up, he strolled to the window and peered out. There was nothing to be seen, for impenetrable darkness had fallen.

Marcus realised that he too was starting to feel uneasy, unless he was catching it from Helen.

'Where is the Scroll?' he said to the Lama.

The Lama and his retinue of monks had been watching him with disquiet. 'In the manuscript room, where it's being examined,' he replied.

'I'd like to check that it is all right,' Marcus demanded. Suddenly it seemed urgent. The monks had become alert and watchful. At a nod from the Chief Lama, a couple of them rose and moved towards the door.

Marcus followed them and, with an apologetic 'excuse me' to the Chief Lama, so did Helen. The monks walked unhurriedly along the corridor and down the stairs, impatiently followed by the Westerners.

In the manuscript room, bespectacled scribes were poring over the Scroll. The room was kept at a constant temperature to allow the examination of invaluable documents brought here by scholars from all over the world. The walls were lined with brown-covered books and papers and the room felt like an ancient library, silent, dusty and poorly lit, apart from incongruous high wattage beams focused on to the Scroll lying on a table in the centre of the room.

Their entry disrupted the atmosphere of total concentration. The Scroll was not what they expected. 'I suppose,' Helen said, 'I expected it to be like the Dead Sea Scrolls, bits of flaky brown parchment, ready to collapse to dust.'

One of the scribe monks, obviously highly erudite and speaking educated English, responded that this was much older than the Dead Sea Scrolls and they did not know what it was made from or how it was inscribed. It was of material not recognised by them.

Another said, with reverence and wonder in his voice, that he had never seen anything like this before. The others all nodded in agreement.

Indeed, the parchment was brown and cracked, but it had not collapsed nor did it look as if it was about to reduce to dust. The Chief Lama joined them unexpectedly. He, too, looked with awe and reverence at the Scroll that had arrived at his temple. Then he asked the monks for something. One fetched a small brown paper bag and handed it to him.

Helen felt another kick in her solar plexus. What was it? She tried to open up her senses and could only feel a sense of urgency. She felt an overwhelming need to leave the monastery.

She whispered this to Marcus.

'Okay,' he nodded. He felt torn because he wanted to

ask a million questions about the Scroll but he too was feeling strangely anxious.

'I think we must leave now,' he said quietly to the Chief Lama.

That was when they heard the first scream. Seconds later they smelt smoke.

More screams and shouts followed and the scribes, totally frozen in their cerebral state, sat unmoving.

The Chief Lama thrust the brown paper bag into Marcus' hands. 'The microfilm of the Scroll,' he said. 'Take it to England. Keep it safe.'

Everything went into automatic. One of the monks turned the heavy key of the lock in the door just as fists started pounding on it.

The Chief Lama spoke calmly into the feeling of doom that had enveloped the room. 'Better destroyed than in the wrong hands.'

Marcus tried to open the window. Then picked up a chair and smashed the glass.

The monks started to break up the Scroll. 'No,' screamed Helen in horrified disbelief, and grabbed pieces of it, shoving them into her bag.

The door started to splinter as the invaders used some form of battering ram to gain entry. She saw the old Lama, white-faced, standing outstretched in front of it, calling out to Buddha.

Marcus took her hand with violent force and pushed her roughly through the window. She had forgotten that young men had such strength. She fell gasping, cutting her leg on the glass and scraping her knee on the ledge. She landed on baked earth.

Marcus had vaulted over her and was dragging her with mighty strength into the shadows. Behind them they could hear shouts, screams and the crackle of fire.

Adrenaline, determination and the vice-like grip of Marcus' hand on her arm got Helen down the steep, dark path. She thought she would have a heart attack but all she said between gasps for breath was, 'Go on without me.'

Marcus, through gritted teeth, replied, 'No!'

As they reached the bottom of the hill, they could see that the trees and buildings at the top were on fire. Bright orange flames turned shadows into gargoyles and bright sparks shot up from the roof of the temple like fireworks into the night. The smell of smoke drifted to them on the air. In the tinder-dry conditions there was a danger of the fire spreading down the hill. Suddenly everywhere was heaving with excited people, who appeared like a swarm of mosquitos to see what was going on. Marcus pushed a way through them to the waiting car.

Thankfully the driver was close by. He and his friend saw them and hurried over. They obviously wanted to stay for the drama but Marcus' expression soon persuaded them otherwise.

Within seconds they were in the car and inching their way through the curious crowds on their way to Muni-ki-Reti to find Joanna. They prayed she was safe.

Chapter 12

When Marcus got off the bus at Joshipur to go to the temple, Joanna felt unexpectedly bereft. She had always been light-hearted, capable, even streetwise, but nothing had prepared her for the shocking events of the last few days.

Nor had she realised how much Marcus' masculine presence had supported her. Alone, she felt fear. She worried about her mother. Was she all right? Where did the bus she had got on to take her? Did she still have the Scroll? Had she been caught? Concerns that had been whirling clouds on the horizon when Marcus had been there became dark, crashing thunderclouds overhead. Like forked lightning, her imaginings illuminated more anxieties.

It had seemed such a good idea earlier to travel in the sari. Now it felt ludicrous, restricting and out of place on the bus. The folds of material round her legs made her so hot that her legs felt sweaty, jumpy and twitchy. Her fear of capture by the men caused her to cover her head, so no free air could circulate.

Mercifully she dozed.

Dusk was falling by the time she eventually climbed the steep hill to the guest house in Muni-ki-Reti. Her mother was not there. The hope that had sustained her crashed. Feeling insecure and tearful, she showered and dressed in clean clothes. She felt better, but her neck and head were in a vice of tension and nothing stilled the screaming fear in her stomach. What had happened? She sensed something was badly wrong.

It did not suit Joanna to wait. She did not even like sitting, except in meditation, and then only when her life was flowing smoothly. This was not such a time. Her mind was hopping like a deranged flea.

Not daring to contemplate what had happened to her mother, or Marcus for that matter, she focused her mind on a simple mantra. *All is well*. This she repeated constantly. *All is well*. She pictured Helen smiling with the Scroll, and Marcus smiling and safe. *All is well*, she reminded herself. Over and over again.

She could not even get into a sacred mantra like *Om Sai Ram*, which she often used, calling on Sai Baba, or *Kodoish Kodoish Kodoish Adonai 'Tsbeyoth*, said to be the most powerful mantra of all. They seemed too nebulous. She needed an affirmation. *All is well*.

When she was younger she used to swim lengths, affirming, 'I am confident and capable.' She knew it worked. *All is well*.

She could not face dinner with Raj and Rima and their family. They were already looking at her with big questioning eyes, asking why her Mother and Marcus had not come back with her. Picking up her fear they were probing tactfully. She had to get out. With an apologetic excuse she picked up her torch and strode down the path to find somewhere clean to eat.

She took a rickshaw to Rishikesh and wandered round until she met up with a couple of travellers, two girls. One of them had her hair in dreadlocks, spoke in a cockney accent, and was wearing a torn T-shirt. The other sported a neat, shiny bob and was dressed in an elegant blouse and trousers.

Unlikely travelling companions, thought Joanna, smiling at their disparity despite herself. With easy friendliness she joined them for a curry, little realising that they would soon give her an awareness of her first illusion. Even though she knew nothing consciously of the contents of the Scroll, the work was already beginning.

The conversation travelled round India, through finances and then on to boyfriends. They all shared stories of their worst experiences with men and laughed together.

Joanna said, 'Being in love is great. It's when reality sets in that the problems arise.'

Daph, the tattered Eastender, frowned slightly and said, 'I think that's an illusion actually.'

Joanna was surprised. 'Why?'

The girl flushed and said awkwardly, 'I know that's what everyone says – that when you are in love you are living in fantasyland, just seeing the best in the other person. And that reality is when people see the worst parts of each other. But I believe it's the other way round. Being in love is reality. That's when you see the wonderful essence of the person if you like.

Illusion sets in when your ego starts clashing with their ego.'

Joanna was amazed. 'You're right,' she breathed. 'Go on.'

'Well,' continued Daph. 'We've been taught to believe that people are bad. So we keep looking for the bad bits in others, instead of looking for the real beautiful, kind, nice parts of them.'

'So,' summarised Joanna, 'when you're in love you see your partner's best qualities. That is the real person, who they truly are. What we call reality is the illusion of their personality traits, which disguise their true essence. Yes, it makes good sense.'

Daph added, 'So we find the truth of another when we look for the best in them.'

Fragments of old relationships flashed through Joanna's mind and she realised, with a shock, how many had been ruined by ego clashes. She had not had a serious boy friend for over a year now – just friends. I'll have to look at my ego, she decided. Surely I'm not a control freak?

She looked at her watch. They had chatted for longer than she had intended. She knew she must go to the travel agent to see if Krishna and the boys had got back. It was something she did not relish doing. What if they were not all right? She shook off the thought and pushed her chair back.

'Nice meeting you,' she said, meaning it. 'I've got to go. Maybe see you guys around again.'

Back in Muni-ki-Reti she was about to cross the road

to the travel agent when her heart stopped. Inside, talking to Raj's brother, were two men, one Indian and one Chinese. They were standing over him, clearly threatening.

Krishna must have led them here. She hoped that meant he was safe.

White-faced and heart thumping, she pressed herself into the shadows, where a stray dog eyed her without curiosity and a small boy with lively interest. There are eyes everywhere in India. What if the eyes told the men where she was? She shivered. What if her mother or Marcus had arrived at the guest house while she was out? Could she warn them in time? What if . . . ?

There was a commotion at the door of the shop as the men left and jumped into their car. Raj's brother ran out after them shouting and holding his telephone line in his hand. They had pulled out his phone and she knew they were on their way to the guest house. Every part of her body was screaming, 'No! no! no!' How could she stop them? She glanced desperately around for help.

A small boy was still standing near Joanna. She had seen him hanging around the travel agent shop, so he was probably related to the family. With slippery, sweating hands, she rummaged in her bag for a pen and scrawled on a page of her diary: 'Mum and Marcus. Danger. Get out. J.'

She tore the page out and held it in front of the child. Then pointed up the hill to the guest house and shoved the note into his hand with a few rupees. 'Quick, quick. Hurry, hurry,' she whispered loudly.

She knew that the car would have to go the long way

round. Her only hope was that the boy could scramble up the hill more quickly and deliver the note.

Then she walked as invisibly as she could to the start of the track which led to the guest house and hid behind a bush, waiting for she knew not what.

Suddenly her stomach clenched. What if they caught the boy and hurt him? Surely they wouldn't do that? Burdened as she was with guilt at her thoughtlessness, it was fortunate she did not know what had happened at the temple.

Fifteen minutes later, to her inexpressible relief, the small boy joined her, grinning as if to say, 'You thought you could hide?'

'No,' he said shaking his head and giving her back the note. She knew he could speak no more English and hoped he meant that her mother and Marcus were not there. Her anxiety increased. What if one of them arrived with the Scroll while the men were there?

She sat behind the bush, eaten by mosquitoes, haunted by fears and poked by twigs. She waited. The boy had long since slipped away, bored, she presumed, and the night had become silent as the rickshaws stopped plying their trade. The lights in the house had all gone out, except one. Either the men were inside or they were watching the place. She hoped they had not harmed Rima and Raj and their family.

'If I had more courage,' she thought, 'I'd go and peer through a window.' But fear and common sense kept her immobile.

What seemed like hours later she heard a car turning into the track. She could not see who was driving it but something made her leap from the bush in front of it. Her legs were so full of pins and needles, she stumbled and fell in the dust. The car only just stopped in time and her mother and Marcus leapt out.

'Thank God it's you,' Joanna whispered. 'They're here.'

Immediately they pulled her back into the car and ordered the driver to reverse. He grumbled automatically but let the car run backwards down the drive. They knew that the headlights and the sound of the car would have alerted the men waiting at the guest house. They had to escape quickly. They drove all night, never knowing if lights behind them were those of the enemy or of some innocent traveller.

Morning found them at Delhi airport. All of the headlines shouted of the massacre at the Temple, where eleven of the monks, including the Chief Lama, had been killed. The building was burnt to the ground and the newspapers suggested no motive, no possible reason for the attack.

The exhausted travellers felt devastated. Grim-faced, they tried to change their tickets to an earlier flight. When three people did not show up for the fully booked early-morning flight to Heathrow, they thanked every spiritual being they could think of. It was not until the plane took off that they felt safe.

Chapter 13

It is universally accepted that if you buy a sky-blue car, you suddenly see them everywhere. If you talk about a rare breed of dogs, one will turn up in the next street. What's more, it may have lived near you for years but you'd never noticed it before.

So it was hardly a surprise for Marcus to find himself seated on the plane next to a young couple who were talking about the use of sound for healing.

They introduced themselves as Bill and Jill, which Marcus privately thought was unfortunate. They thought it lovely.

When he asked them about sound healing, they told him how they used singing bowls, cymbals and gongs to heal imbalances in a person's energy field and bring them into alignment.

'What does that mean exactly? How do you do it?' he asked cautiously, for the new terminology was still very strange to him.

Smiling, the young man told him that they felt the person's energy field with their hands and if it felt depleted they would create appropriate sounds to fill it up.

'Start at the beginning,' suggested Marcus. 'I'm not even sure what an energy field is.'

'Okay. Every living organism radiates its own energy.

With humans it's made up of our thoughts, beliefs, fears and emotions as well as the energy we take in through what we read or watch on TV or even talk about. That's known as our aura. It is our own personal electromagnetic field.' Bill paused, trying to find the right words to enable Marcus to grasp the concept. 'If someone has good vibes, that's their aura you're sensing. Are you with me?'

'So far so good,' agreed Marcus.

'If someone is very materialistic or under stress there will be lots of red in the aura, which has the longest wave-length and slowest vibrational rate. And if someone is very spiritual, the colours will be higher up the spectrum, the blues and violets. Violet has the shortest wave-length and the fastest vibrational rate.'

'How do you know?'

'Clairvoyants, who can see things that normal people can't, have always told us of the colours round people. Saints were depicted with golden halos, because that's the colour that clairvoyants could see round their heads. Gold is the colour of wisdom by the way. But now we have aura cameras, which can photograph the energy round you.'

'Really?' Marcus nodded. 'How do they do that?'

'I'm not sure how it works. I think the camera picks up heat radiations. All I know is, it works.'

'Fair enough. Tell me about auras.' Marcus knew he would not get a scientific explanation. Part of him realised it really was not necessary.

The young man relaxed, 'If someone is confident and strong, they will have a strong aura. It acts as a kind of buffer round them, to protect them from other people's energy and it keeps them healthy. But if someone is weak, or had a shock, or is very negative or even been ill, their aura will become thin and wispy or even totally broken. And it feels cold. Then they are easy to influence. They catch things because they have no immunity. And if someone is full of suppressed anger their aura feels hot or clogged and it needs to be cleared out. Our job is to check people's energy fields and we help to strengthen them with sounds.'

'How do you know it works?' asked the still-dubious Marcus.

Jill, who had been leaning forward, listening intently and nodding enthusiastically, chipped in, 'First because the person feels better. Also we can feel the difference in the aura with our hands. And we have lots of before-and-after photos taken with the aura camera, which are really interesting.'

Marcus felt a spurt of interest. 'What's an aura camera?'

'I'll show you some pictures taken with one.' The young man got up and unzipped a bag that was in the overhead locker. He took out a packet and handed Marcus some photos. 'Look,' he said.

He held a photo of a person surrounded by a murky cloud of whitish, grey and red colour. 'That's before healing. Here's after.' He produced a photo of the same man surrounded by light blue. The cloud had lifted from around him and gold and green streamed into the area around his head.

'That's quite impressive,' said Marcus nodding in

surprise as he handed it back. They showed him several more, including one of a woman with a very dark blob over her heart. After the sound healing the dark blob had gone and was replaced by a deep green light. 'She'd been very ill. She recovered after the treatment,' said the girl laughing with a refreshingly innocent delight.

'And take this one.' The youth showed Marcus a picture of a woman almost enveloped in a brownish-red aura. 'What do you think of that?'

'She doesn't look too healthy,' Marcus grimaced.

'Too right. She was exhausted and anxious. Her husband had moved out and was living with someone else and she couldn't stop thinking about it. She was totally obsessed about it. Look. Here's after the sound work.' Now her aura, though still dingy, was showing patches of colour.

'The fascinating thing is that when her energy field became stronger, she let go of her husband and got a life for herself.'

'You obviously do really good work,' commented Marcus.

'We don't just work with people. We dowse houses and clear ley lines, too,' Bill chipped in.

Hello, thought Marcus, here we go.

'What's a ley line?' he checked.

'It's a line of energy connecting two places. Originally pilgrims would walk from holy site to holy site and the path they created formed a ley line, and high-vibration energy would flow down it. Wherever people gathered, such as a market place, lines from different directions would meet.'

'And where lines cross an energy vortex forms.'

'Yes, and anything done there, especially with ritual or ceremony, is charged with energy. It is very powerful.'

'Unfortunately,' sighed Jill, 'many of the lines have been blocked or distorted.'

'Or taken over by the darkness,' put in Bill.

'What do you mean?'

'Well at first the lines were pegged with symbols and crystals, programmed to work for the light. Often it didn't matter what held the line. The intention with which it was done was more important and it meant the lines were kept clear for good energy to flow.'

'Why would anyone want to block a line?' Marcus demanded, though he felt he already knew the answer.

'It's part of the battle between dark and light. Whoever runs the ley line has control. For instance, we have found several ley lines where black covens have met.'

'You mean witches?' asked Marcus, startled. 'I've always thought talk of witches and covens was hocus pocus.'

'No way! Though most witches are white. They are the healers and others who work for the light. But there are plenty of black ones out there and active, on their own and in covens. More than you have any idea of. It's not a good idea even to talk about them for it allows their evil intentions to be drawn to us.'

Marcus, though he found it difficult to believe a word of it, felt a shiver running down his spine. Instinctively he pulled up his thin aeroplane blanket.

Bill continued. 'If people of evil or avaricious intent

block or tap into an energy line they can use the current for their own purposes.'

'Deliberately, you mean?'

'Some have tuned into the dark power and they use it deliberately. That would mostly be the covens. But there are lots of black magicians who don't even realise they are magicians. They just know they can make things happen. Mostly people just sense the energy and use it without really knowing what they are doing.'

'What can they use it for?'

'Like they get the planning permission they need or the licence to do something detrimental to people. On the inner planes the dark workers band together to help each other. It is dangerous work trying to free those lines but there are groups of us working to do this.'

'Hang on. What are the inner planes?'

Bill laughed. 'The physical world that you can feel, see, hear and touch is the outer world. But we all have an inner world, made up of thoughts and emotions and images. That is the inner plane. If someone sends out dark angry thoughts, they create a cloud of energy in the inner planes. On its own it may not be able to hinder or harm someone. But if several people create a cloud of energy and it joins together, it can cause a lot of harm.'

'What can it do?' Marcus was curiously sceptical.

'I'll give you an example. If someone is confused a dark cloud of anger could enter the vacant spaces in his mind and cause him to go out and commit an atrocity.'

'Or,' added Jill, 'if someone was terrified and their

friends sent thoughts of courage and positivity to enfold that person, they would find the strength to go ahead. If lots of people were worried for him, the dark worry thoughts could form a negative energy round him and cause him to fail.'

'Let's get this straight,' said Marcus. 'If some people are fighting to clean up the environment for everyone's good while others are polluting it for profit, there is a clash of wills. That's the physical world. And at the same time, the thoughts and emotions of those same people create energies, and dark workers can manipulate that energy for their own ends?'

'Yes, but it happens unconsciously. We are not always aware of the shadow we haven't dealt with.'

'Oh!' Marcus exclaimed.

Jill went back to her old tack. 'A friend of ours dowsed round our county council offices and found that all the lines running from it were black.'

'What does that mean exactly?' asked Marcus.

'Corruption. Those in control trying to cheat or hood-wink the people in the county. For instance, they may give permission to dump nuclear waste into the earth or allow ugly buildings to be built because it's lucrative. And much worse things.'

'Take supermarkets,' put in Bill. 'They buy in bulk offering the producer a measly profit, pay miserable wages, sell cheaply and force all local shops to close. Then they have a monopoly and can put up the prices.'

'Another thing,' Jill interrupted, impatient to say more. 'Along black ley lines there is much greater incidence of illness, especially cancer. Dark forces have an investment in keeping people sick because that way they buy medicines, which are chemical drugs. No one listens to their own bodies any more. They give doctors power over their health. Then drug companies subtly influence the doctors. The medical profession try to make herbal treatments illegal.'

Marcus found his mind spinning. The intensity of the girl's anger disturbed him. He wanted to move the conversation on.

'Do you use sound to clear energy lines?' he asked. They nodded.

It turned out they lived near Avebury in the West Country. 'It's a really spiritual part of the country,' said Jill.

His thoughts wandered while she talked about the power and wonder of Avebury but snapped back to attention when she mentioned that it was connected to Stonehenge and Glastonbury.

'Have you been to Stonehenge?' he wanted to know.

Predictably they both nodded. 'Of course. It's a power point. Very sacred energy there.'

'It's an ancient sundial, isn't it?' he asked.

'We think it's an entry point for beings from other planets,' Jill told him.

'Our friend Tim, who knows about these things, says Stonehenge links us to other galaxies,' added Bill.

Once more Marcus was amazed. It was all so similar to what the Scroll was saying.

'How do you think it was built?' he wanted to know.

'Certainly not by men pulling the Stones up,' laughed

Jill. That would be impossible. 'We think it was tele-kinesis and sound.'

'What's telekinesis?'

'The use of mind control to change matter,' Jill replied promptly. Information revealed in the Scroll was being trotted out at him by some New Age hippies. He was beginning to wonder if everyone knew except him. He said that it was very strange but he'd recently heard something very similar.

'Well, you're obviously meant to hear it then,' smiled Bill. 'People everywhere are opening up like flowers, ready to receive the higher truths. But there's still a long way to go yet.'

'It was really lucky I sat next to you,' Marcus told them.

'That's an illusion,' responded Jill quickly, giving him quite a shock.

'What is?'

'Luck, man,' took up Bill. 'There's no such thing as luck or chance. The truth is that everything is a response to our energy and our need to know or experience.'

'I think of it like this,' added Jill, with those big, innocent blue eyes, all seeing, all knowing. 'We humans are like actors on the stage of life. The spiritual world, our angels and guides, who are invisible, set the stage and hand out the props so we have them at the per-fect moment. We call it synchronicity or coincidence or luck.'

Angels and guides! thought Marcus, bemused. Where do they come into it? He must ask Helen. In fact he couldn't understand why he had not already done so. He felt a strange reluctance to do so, as if he was entering a mysterious world that felt strangely out of control.

'Do you do healing?' Bill broke into his thoughts, suddenly veering him off tack.

Jill added, 'If not, why not?' and they both laughed.

Marcus said, 'No. What's so funny?' He remembered that Helen had told him that he could be a healing channel.

'It's just that clearly you're a healer with special work to do, but I guess you don't really understand yet.'

The same message again. Marcus was stunned into silence. They were landing in Abu Dhabi to change planes. He had not even noticed the plane coming down.

'Hey, write down your names and phone number,' he implored, as Bill jumped up to retrieve their hand luggage.

Jill obliged on a scruffy piece of paper, in strangely childlike handwriting.

'Bye,' she said. 'See you again, I expect.'

What did that mean? Marcus frowned.

If this is the way the universe works, he thought, I wonder who Helen and Joanna sat next to.

Chapter 14

On the second leg of the flight, from Abu Dhabi to London Heathrow, there were only two seats together. Helen wanted to sleep and give her leg, which had been badly cut by the glass when they escaped through the window of the temple, a chance to rest and heal. She was happy to be alone.

So Marcus sat next to Joanna, who nearly had a panic attack when an Oriental walked up the aisle of the plane. Sharply she dropped her face to hide it. For a moment she was like a tiny, frightened, shaking bird. Marcus realised instantly what had happened and wanted to protect her. He took her hand and held it firmly. Her vulnerability made him feel stronger.

'It's okay,' he whispered. 'It's not them. You're safe.'

She relaxed, feeling foolish, and disengaged her hand with a nervous laugh. 'Phew, that gave me a terrible shock.' She breathed deeply for a few moments. 'I'm still shaking,' she said, holding out her trembling hands. 'Thanks for your help.'

When she took control of herself again, she became the light, laughing, cool young woman he had originally met in Rishikesh. He felt frustrated by her invisible defensive wall and suddenly he wanted to breach it again and get to know the real Joanna underneath. He had always felt that he understood people, but he suspected Joanna was more fragile and complex than he had ever realised.

He told her about his conversation with Jill and Bill, and she laughed at his description of them. She was surprised that two long-haired hippies in matching tie-dyed T-shirts could have made such an impression on him and said so.

'I thought you only gave credence to logical, scientific knowledge,' she teased, her brown eyes glinting mischievously.

He protested, 'Come on! I'm not that bad, and the aura photos were impressive.'

Joanna laughingly retorted, 'You're improving. Anyone who can juggle as well as you has to be okay.'

His eyes glowed with pleasure as he accepted the compliment. She had an uncanny knack of making him feel good.

'I think it was the synchronicity with the information in the Scroll. It is stunning that the validation should have come so quickly.'

'I expect the universe knew you needed that,' smiled Joanna. 'So they arranged for you to sit next to them. It wouldn't have had such an impact on Mum or me because we knew some of it already.

'Oh! And they gave us another illusion!'

'What is it?' Joanna was immediately alert and interested.

'Bill said what I've heard you and your Mum say. There's no such thing as luck or chance. The truth is that everything is a response to our energy and our need to know or experience.'

'Absolutely,' agreed Joanna. 'We ought to write them down.' She got out her diary and said them aloud as she recorded the two they had received so far.

'Being in love and seeing the best in others is truth. When reality sets in and two egos clash, it's illusion.'

'That really got me thinking,' she admitted. 'I realise that most of my relationships have ended with power struggles.'

'Have they?' He gave her an opening to share more of herself but she ignored it and carried on writing.

She said, 'Knowing that luck and coincidence is the hand of spirit at work is truth. Thinking that luck, coincidence and synchronicity are chance is illusion.'

'That's not quite what he said. He said that luck, coincidence and synchronicity are a response to our energy and need to know.'

'Same thing.' She tossed her head and grinned cheekily in a way he was beginning to recognise. It said, 'Don't bother to argue. I'm right and that's that.' He decided to let it slide. Besides he rather liked it.

Joanna changed tack suddenly. 'We should have a plan for when we get to England. What are we going to do?'

Marcus was pleased that she said 'we'. Somehow he wanted her to be part of whatever was going to happen. He only had the haziest idea of what that was, but he knew that there was work and probably danger ahead too. At that moment he had no idea of just how much work, adventure and danger they were all to face.

'Where are you going to stay?' she demanded. 'You've let your flat, haven't you?'

'Yes. I didn't expect to be back for six months. The Scroll had other ideas.' He automatically patted the microfilm in his money belt to check it was safe.

She said lightly, 'I expect it'll knock you about a bit more before you've done what you contracted to do.'

'What do you mean?'

'You know. Your contract for this life. It included something about the Scroll. Quite likely you were one of the Atlanteans in that past life who escaped to Tibet. Now you're back to continue the work.'

Marcus was cottoning on. 'So I suppose that as you're with me in this, you were one of them, too.'

She grinned at him. 'I was probably your wicked stepmother or your cruel uncle then.'

'No, we feel too comfortable together,' he countered.

But Joanna lightly veered tack, saying, 'I'm going to stay at Mum's in Surrey. If you can't get into your flat, you can stay with us for a while, I'm sure.'

'Won't your mother mind?'

'No, of course not. There are always people staying. Not that there's much room. It's a bit cramped. But it's always open house.'

There was a slight pause, then Marcus expressed their worst fears. 'Do you think they would trace us there?'

Joanna stared at him and he stared back, grey eyes looking into brown ones, seeking soul-level information and sustenance. She sighed, 'I hoped you wouldn't say that.'

He took her hand and she let him. Mutual comfort.

What would they say to Helen? 'Helen, we don't think it's safe for you to go home?'

As ever, they had underestimated Helen. While Joanna and Marcus arrived at Heathrow looking untidy and haggard, and in his case unshaven, she had slept and emerged from the plane looking somewhat crumpled but alert.

'I've been thinking,' she announced as they walked the never-ending corridors of civilisation with only the clothes they stood up in as a reminder of India. 'It may not be safe to live in my house. I've a friend with a holiday house in the New Forest. I'm sure she'll let us use it. We'll just go home to fetch some things.'

'What about your work, Mum?' Joanna asked.

Helen looked amazed. 'Let's get our priorities straight. The Scroll's more important than my work. It could change the world.'

'You know it's dangerous,' warned Marcus. 'You could even die doing this.'

'Death is an illusion,' replied Helen and then stopped with the words barely uttered.

'There's another one,' gurgled Joanna.

'What do you mean, death is an illusion?' questioned Marcus.

'Oh, just that our spirits go on for ever. Death is only the release of our physical body, which is a sheath for the spirit. Just like the caterpillar shedding its cocoon and becoming a butterfly.'

'Some people think death is final,' added Joanna.

'They don't realise it is just like moving from one room into another.'

'I see,' said Marcus. 'But you were both pretty frightened there in India – so was I for that matter, especially when we were being chased.'

'That was our little self being scared of the unknown,' Helen reminded him. 'Our higher spiritual self knew that all was well whatever happened, whether we lived or died.'

'Okay, I'll buy that,' said Marcus, while Joanna got out her diary as they queued for customs and added to the list: 'Death is an illusion. The truth is our spirit is eternal.'

As their belongings were still in the guest house in India, they had no baggage to wait for. They took a taxi to Helen's house and before they even put the kettle on, she phoned her friend, who was happy for them to move into her holiday home for a few weeks. They could go there the next day.

She phoned various friends and told them briefly about the Scroll and its contents. She thought one of them might know of a group to which they could entrust the further decoding of the Scroll. She drew a blank.

It was, typically, a mind-blowing coincidence that found them someone who could decipher the code. A forgetful old aunt of Helen's, very old, in fact, who had not remembered they were supposed to be away on holiday, happened to phone.

The slow and shouted conversation, for she was nearly deaf, took strange turns from the welfare of the children, to India to Tibet. Auntie Peggy was inclined to ramble. 'I had a great friend once, who was Chinese. He became a professor and studied ancient Tibetan. What a strange way to earn a living. He was a suitor of mine but of course was totally unsuitable.' Auntie Peggy cackled in delight at her own pun and Helen hoped she would be as sharp at nearly ninety.

Her mind flew in circles. Why was the universe presenting her with this information now?

'Is he still alive?' she asked.

'No. Of course not. He died years ago.' Helen had expected as much.

'But his widow is. Tough old bird, despite being a refugee from Tibet. I expect she'll go on to a hundred.'

A Chinese man married to a Tibetan woman? It sounded intriguing but Helen did not want to deflect the old lady towards a wild goose chase, so she teased lightly, 'I expect she will and so will you. You'll get your telegram from the Queen yet! Do you have any contact with his widow now?'

'Only Christmas cards. She moved to Hampshire with her son when he retired. He followed in his father's footsteps. Dry as dust he was.'

'Oh, no!' Helen had an uncharitable picture of ancient mother and nearly as ancient son, living together. 'Do you have their phone number or address, Auntie?' she asked.

'Yes, but I can't read it without my magnifying glass and I don't know where it is.'

Helen tried to be patient. 'Please can you find it and their number and I'll phone you back?'

'No use phoning them, dear. Both as deaf as posts.'

Helen gritted her teeth. 'Okay. It would help if you could find their address and phone number anyway. I'll phone in ten minutes.'

'Can't think why you should want to know that. She was never good enough for him anyway.'

'I'll speak to you in a minute, Auntie,' Helen said, and firmly put down the receiver.

Joanna and Marcus had been listening to the conversation with a mixture of amusement and impatient anticipation. Now as Helen put down the phone they collapsed with laughter. It was the only way of dealing with their tension.

Ten minutes later they had the address and phone number of someone who could hold the key to the secrets of the Scroll.

Chapter 15

Helen had always loved her little detached cottage in its pretty garden. She spent as much time as she could tending the plants and never allowed chemicals to be used on them. If anyone asked why, she would say, with a twinkle in her eyes, 'It kills the fairies.' No one quite knew if she was serious or not.

She loved the log fire in her sitting room in winter and the way the sun flooded into her room in the mornings where she saw clients for healing and counselling. She had bought the house at the end of a cul-de-sac seven years ago after her husband left her and it had been a happy house. Whenever she approached it, she felt that it smiled a welcome at her.

As far as she could remember, that night when they returned from India was the only sleepless night she had ever spent there. None of them slept well, and because of the time difference they were all awake at 4 a.m. They were all tetchy and irritable. They bickered.

Helen snapped at Joanna for slurping her tea right next to her. Joanna told her mother she was slovenly because she had not cleaned the bath properly. Marcus felt as if he was sitting close to a time bomb and was irritated with both of them. When he pointed out quite reasonably that they were all tired, they both turned on him.

He had two options, snap back or soothe troubled waters. Typically, he took a deep breath and chose the latter. Opening his big arms wide he enveloped them in a huge caring hug and, with a hint of laughter in his voice, told them they were two wonderful women.

Helen relaxed despite herself. 'Are you sure you're not Irish?'

Joanna shrieked, 'The witches must have turned the ley line under this house black.' Suddenly they were all laughing. Friends again.

They were showered, in Marcus' case shaved, packed and ready to leave for the New Forest before six. It was sheeting with grey vertical rain, cold and miserable as only English rain can be, pouring like dirty bath water from a leaden sky.

'Come back, India. All is forgiven,' moaned Joanna. 'I'm sorry I ever complained about the heat.'

The holiday home turned out to be a small house set alone amongst trees, isolated at the end of a rutted track, rather dilapidated and depressing. Inside it felt damp and chilly. They did their best to make themselves at home, though the tap in the kitchen was jammed, half the lights did not work and they could not switch on the gas fire.

Joanna moved into manic mode, rushing round looking for a spanner and spare light bulbs. She found a couple of bulbs in a cobweb-filled cupboard and teetered on a stool stretching to reach the socket. Marcus lifted her off it and effortlessly replaced the bulbs.

Then she hunted for some tools to mend the tap in the kitchen, so they could have a cup of tea. In normal circumstances, she was extremely capable, but as she attacked the tap, water flooded out of the sink and on to the floor.

Marcus managed to stem the flow and swiftly mended the tap. Joanna was forced to admit with good humour, 'Okay, I hand it to you, you're handy despite your public school education!'

'Oh, so I get two points then. One, I can juggle. Two, I can mend a tap,' he bantered.

She tossed her hair and grinned broadly, 'I expect I'll think of something else if you give me time.'

Helen had been putting a bucket under the leak in the bathroom and she returned to find them jesting like children. She looked round the dingy, unwelcoming kitchen. 'At least it's safe and no one will find us here,' she breathed thankfully.

'I'm going to phone the professor's old wife or son,' Helen announced a few minutes later. They all gathered round the phone and hoped against hope someone would hear and answer. It rang and rang. Just as she was about to give up, a man's sleepy voice answered. Helen realised to her horror that she had got him out of bed.

It turned out to be the old professor's son, who called himself Tony and spoke with an impeccable English accent. He sounded much younger than she had expected and was totally charming despite the early hour and disruption of his sleep.

Helen gave him an abridgement of the Scroll saga,

trying to focus on the message rather than the drama. Tony sounded interested and invited them all to lunch. They were only half an hour's drive away. What luck, she wanted to say!

There was time to stop to buy some warm English clothing for Marcus, who had been walking round in Indian cotton trousers and a sweater borrowed from Helen's friend, Miranda, and to do some other essential shopping.

Of course, nothing turned out as expected. Old Auntie Peggy's memory proved to be as defective as her hearing. Tony was a good-looking businessman in his late fifties. Perhaps his hazel eyes had a slight Tibetan slant, but his silver grey hair was typically English. He was kindly, avuncular even. Probably as hard as nails in business, thought Marcus cynically.

Tony welcomed them graciously into his large elegant Tudor house, which was surrounded by carefully tended lawns. A middle-aged woman who was clearly a house-keeper brought them coffee. There were several photos of a girl growing up, evidently his daughter, while a single oil portrait of a rather beautiful woman who must have been his wife hung over the fireplace.

Helen related a sanitised version of the story her aunt had given them about Tony's background.

He chuckled. 'Sorry, it's not nearly as romantic as that. My grandmother was Tibetan but my grandfather was English and both my parents were boringly English.'

'So your father wasn't a professor of ancient Tibetan?' asked Joanna, disappointed.

'Yes, he was. He died some years ago but I'm afraid I didn't follow in his footsteps. However, I still have close links with the academic world and think I can find someone to help you.'

They beamed at him, half-disappointed that it was not to be instant gratification but more than delighted that he could find someone to translate the Scroll. They trusted him immediately and over lunch told him the whole story. He appeared to have a grasp of esoteric matters, albeit from an intellectual standpoint. Most important of all, he pledged to help.

After lunch he went into his study to make some phone calls and returned with the news that a friend of his, Professor Smith, would see them that afternoon in London. He had the facilities to look at the micro-film and the tattered portion of Scroll that Helen had grabbed before she was pushed out of the window of the Temple.

It was agreed that Tony and Marcus would leave immediately, for Marcus refused to part with the micro-film. He clearly felt that he was the sacred guardian. They left together in Tony's BMW. Marcus slept most of the way.

Professor Smith was the archetypal, desiccated, bespec-tacled, gnome-like and taciturn academic that they had expected to find in Tony. He made it clear that it was only Tony's impeccable credentials as his father's son that had granted them entry.

However within an hour of looking at the bits of Scroll and the microfilm, he became animated and voluble. 'If this is genuine, it is unique. The find of the century. Unbelievable.' His grey cheeks flushed pink.

He arranged for a colleague to examine the Scroll, part of which was protected by a brown roll of cardboard. The remaining fragments were still in an Indian brown paper bag, slipped into the pages of a book. Several more of his colleagues filtered in to look at the incredible find.

To Marcus they seemed more interested in the material the Scroll was made from than anything else and he felt a knot of frustration in his stomach. He murmured to Tony out of the side of his mouth that they had missed the point. Then he said more loudly than he intended, 'We just want to know what the Scroll says, in English.'

There was an affronted pause. No one could commit to an actual translation. It all had to be carefully studied. It would take experts weeks if not months and years to understand the Scroll.

Professor Smith had been sitting examining part of the Scroll very intent. He appeared to be completely lost in concentration. Just as Marcus was feeling very despondent, he said in a slow and measured voice that, as far as he could understand, the Script mentioned an esoteric society, whose members had the mind training and knowledge of sound to affect matter. With the appearance of the Scroll, these people would simultaneously be ready and prepared to work with the information revealed.

Marcus felt incredulous, totally awed by the secret interweaving of universal energy.

'Is there any name given for the society?' he asked Professor Smith.

'Strange hieroglyphics spell out something like *Kumeka*. It says it is a new energy, which is coming into the planet now.'

'Wow!' Marcus felt mind blown. He sat in silence for the next hour turning this over in his mind. How would they find the society? Where was it? Would the universe, with its now familiar synchronicity, push them in the right direction? He had to trust this.

Professor Smith was speaking again. 'Apparently the Scroll contains symbols and details of an interplay of musical notes, which can be used to change the vibratory rate of matter.' He frowned, his eyes boring into the script. 'There are warnings that this information must not fall into the wrong hands.'

Everyone nodded sombrely.

Tony asked, 'How soon will it be before you can let us have this information in usable form?'

The professor was unwilling to be drawn. He said severely, 'This is only a very preliminary and rough translation. I give it only because you press me. We do not know yet if the Scroll is genuine. The information will be presented when it is ready.' Then he added, 'There appear to be several sections to this document. One contains mathematical formulas.' He screwed up his eyes in concentration. 'A second appears to be headed. "The Great Mysteries" or something like that. Then there is "The Codes of Power". I don't know about the others. I'll look at the Great Mysteries tomorrow.'

*   *   *

It was after midnight when they left the building. Adrenaline had kept Marcus going. As they walked into the cool night air the effect of jetlag and sleepless nights hit him suddenly. His head was throbbing and his eyelids drooped over burning eyes. Everything felt woolly and he swayed slightly.

'Steady there,' said Tony in concern, grabbing his arm to hold him.

Marcus had intended to stay with a friend but it was too late to phone. Tony had a small pied à terre in London and offered Marcus the sofa for the night. Gratefully he accepted. Exhausted as he felt and despite the late hour he wanted to phone Joanna and Helen to tell them what had been discovered. The phone rang and rang. There was no answer.

Chapter 16

It was only when Marcus phoned Helen and Joanna at eight, nine and ten o'clock the following morning without success that he really began to worry. Until then he had rationalised that they were deeply tired and fast asleep. Now he had a tight knot of anxiety in his stomach.

Tony had arranged to meet a former business colleague while he was in London, intending to drive Marcus and himself back to Hampshire in the afternoon. Tony was a successful businessman, and he believed that two factors were the reason for his achievement. One was his ability to follow his intuition, and the other his willingness to be flexible. Sensing Marcus' increasing anxiety – hardly difficult as he was restlessly pacing the floor and jumping every time the phone rang – Tony cancelled the meeting.

He was a kind person and he liked the open-faced young man, who was of an age to be the son he never had. Until his wife died three years ago and his daughter married and virtually disappeared from his life, he had never regretted not having more children. After Mary's death, he lost all incentive to accumulate wealth, so he retired early and started to write a book, something he had wanted to do for years.

He was outwardly composed and charming, generous with his hospitality but rarely let anyone become close, and few knew how lonely he had felt these last years. He suggested they drive back to Hampshire immediately and was gratified with the look of relief on Marcus' face. 'It'll be all right. I'm sure there's a good explanation,' he said reassuringly.

Marcus played the game. 'Yes, of course. I'm sure there is.'

As they raced back to the holiday house, Marcus' imagination started to work overtime. He convinced himself that the men had discovered their whereabouts.

'I'll kill them if they hurt Joanna or Helen,' he burst out. 'They'll never get away with it.' His fists were clenched like lumps of gnarled hardwood and Tony tried to distract his train of thought.

'My sense is that it's an illusion to think anyone gets away with anything.'

Marcus stopped short. 'What did you say?'

'I don't really think people get away with things. There's a kind of spiritual working-out for everything eventually.'

'Is that one of the illusions?' wondered Marcus aloud.

'Oh, I see what you mean,' Tony replied. 'Well, I suppose it is or I wouldn't have said it.'

Marcus was pulled away from his rage, and beginning to concentrate again. 'You really think that everything is evened out spiritually? Do you believe in reincarnation then?'

Tony pursed up his lips. 'Put it this way. I keep an open mind about it. I certainly don't disbelieve it. But even if someone doesn't reincarnate to right a wrong, the spiritual working-out could happen in other planes of existence. I certainly don't believe that the spirit dies on death. In fact, one thing I'm absolutely sure of is that the whole of creation is so much vaster and more ineffable that we have any concept of. Our planet is such a tiny insignificant part of the whole.' He shrugged in disbelief. 'And we have the illusion we are so important!'

'What do you think of the Scroll?'

Tony slowed down and said deliberately, 'I think it could be the most monumentally important thing that has ever been discovered.'

Marcus was stunned. 'Do you believe it's genuine?' he persisted.

'There's no doubt in my mind at all,' said the older man, rather to Marcus' surprise and relief. 'That's why I'm prepared to do anything I can to help you.'

Marcus sighed, pleased. 'So it's illusion to think we can get away with anything. The truth is that everything is resolved spiritually in the end,' he mused.

'It doesn't mean we don't do our utmost to sort things out in the physical world, though,' warned Tony.

'No, I didn't think it did, but it is good to know that there is a higher force overseeing things,' Marcus responded.

'By the way, did you notice when I was talking about the role of humans on the planet?'

'What about it?'

'It just slipped out. It's an illusion to think we're so important!' The older man shook his head with a surprised smile. 'It's amazing how it happens. I just heard myself say it.'

'So you did. It's coming back to me. What was it? It's an illusion that humans are so important in the grand scheme of things. The truth is . . . ? What?' He looked at Tony.

'I suppose the truth is that everything is divine and our role as humans is to be caretakers while we are on earth.'

'So God doesn't consider us to be better than animals, just different?'

Tony nodded in agreement. 'We're more evolved, but that doesn't mean we're more important or more loved. You don't love a child less because it's younger than its siblings, or think it's less important. So I'm pretty sure God doesn't consider us humans as more important in his scheme.'

'I like that analogy,' agreed Marcus. 'So animals are our younger brethren and it's up to us to look after them.'

'I think so.'

'Helen says dolphins are more evolved than humans,' Marcus put in tentatively.

'I'm sure she's right,' commented Tony automatically. He was concentrating on passing a slow lorry before a bend.

When they arrived at the house there was no sign of life. Everything was locked up and the beds had clearly not been slept in. The men searched the house with a sense of mounting dread.

Within minutes the phone rang. Marcus snatched it up and heard Joanna's chirpy voice.

'Hello, it's me!'

'How are you? We were worried to death about you? Are you all right? Where are you?' Marcus was incoherent with anxiety.

'We're fine. I just had a freak-out at the thought of Mum and me sleeping in that place alone. It felt all wrong and so we found a hotel for the night. I've been phoning every half an hour because we didn't have your number.'

Now that he knew they were safe Marcus felt enraged. How dare they put him through nightmares! How dare Joanna sound so cheery!

'Yeah. We raced all the way back from London because we were so worried about you,' he said frostily.

'Sorry. It's a pain, I know, but we agreed to follow our intuition. What did you find out?'

'I'll tell you later when you get here.'

'No. You don't understand. We don't want to be there. We've got a bad feeling about it. Please can you bring our bags and meet us here?'

'You must be joking!' Forgetting how their intuition had saved them before, Marcus felt less than charitable about this latest whim.

Joanna was unfazed by his grumpiness. 'Hey, your anger is your stuff. Don't dump it on me. We've been true to our feelings.'

Marcus felt his usual reluctant admiration for her honesty and apologised.

'Meet us at the hotel,' she suggested, and gave him directions.

Tony was watching him with a curious expression on his face. 'This place is really very spooky,' he commented. 'If I'd been through what you've all been through, I don't think I'd want to sleep here.'

'Wouldn't you?' Marcus asked, surprised. Then he laughed. 'You're right. It's got bad vibes. I'll grab the cases. Then let's get out.'

It was while they were loading up the car that the phone rang again. Marcus picked it up, expecting it to be Joanna and said, 'Hi.'

The receiver at the other end clicked and Marcus felt the hairs on his neck prickle.

'No one there,' he said to Tony. 'They put the receiver down.'

'Dial 1471,' urged Tony. But that only revealed that the call was not traceable.

'Quick, into the car. They've found us.' They threw in the cases and raced down the track, expecting to be ambushed at every turn.

Joanna and Helen were already waiting in the hotel lounge. They were desperate to know what had transpired with Professor Smith and the Scroll. Marcus brought them up to date. When he talked about the Kumeka energy, the women looked at each other in amazement.

'That's too much of a coincidence,' interrupted Helen excitedly.

'That's unbelievable,' shouted Joanna, her mouth open.

'What?'

'We've been invited to a place called Kumeka House tonight!' Joanna's voice had risen an octave.

Everyone talked at once for a moment and a few threads emerged from the bedlam. 'When we left you we drove back to the holiday house and took a detour via Stonehenge. We decided to park and buy tickets to go in,' said Helen.

'And while we were there we chatted to some people who were talking about ley lines and energy points and how the henge was really built. They were really nice people – and very interesting. Knowledgeable, too.'

'Yes,' agreed Joanna. 'One was a doctor who had moved away from allopathic into natural medicine. He's particularly interested in biofeedback techniques to slow down the brain waves and allow self-healing to take place. His wife teaches meditation and yoga and the third, a thin Irishwoman, I can't remember her name, writes books about the mind–body connection.'

'Something unusual . . . Mairaed, I think,' said her mother.

Joanna went on, 'I think you are right. Anyway they talked about this place called Kumeka House, which is apparently where a community of men live, who are dedicated to raising light on the planet. They have a very strict regime and meditate daily. They also practise mind control, sacred ceremonies and live a simple life devoted to God.

'Apparently they have always been a closed community, having little to do with the outside world. However, they recently received channelling.' She looked at Tony and Marcus. 'You know, messages channelled from a higher spiritual source.' They nodded for her to continue. 'These messages said that they must open up Kumeka House in preparation for people to bring them important work to do. They believe that all their work so far has made them ready to do a special task that will be revealed to them soon.'

Tony and Marcus said simultaneously, 'The Scroll!'

'Of course, the Scroll,' triumphed Joanna.

Chapter 17

That evening they were all buzzing with excited anticipation as Tony drove them down the long, tree-lined gravel
approach to Kumeka House. The sweet summer-evening
fragrance of newly mown grass and lilac, with occasional
wafts of lavender, drifted through the open car windows
and they felt the next few hours could be vitally important.

Helen and Joanna had no doubt whatsoever that these
were the people who would work with the information
contained in the Scroll.

The drive curved and Kumeka House stood in front of
them, a large, square building with the solid air of eternal
safety. The orange rays of the evening sun reflected from
the windows, illuminating it in a welcoming glow. There
was something most pleasing about the house. Later
they were told that it had been designed according to
sacred geometry to affect the consciousness of anyone
who visited it.

A young man with a shaved head and fathomless black
eyes opened the door. He greeted them with a warmly
welcoming smile and showed them into a large sunny
room, empty but for a few chairs around the walls and
a beautiful arrangement of flowers and candles on a low
table. The smell of incense and soothing music created a
serene and peaceful atmosphere.

Each of the residents who entered greeted them in a way that made them feel welcome. Marcus noticed that everyone spoke quietly. Yet each of the men seemed to have an air of dignity and authority. He felt comfortable and at ease in their presence.

Helen, Marcus and Tony opted for chairs. Joanna sat cross-legged and straight-backed on a cushion on the floor, as did the fifteen or so residents, all men. Their ages varied from about twenty to a man in his seventies. All had that still, centred, serene air of those dedicated to a contemplative life. There was a sense that they were happy to speak in order to help their visitors relax but that they felt comfortable with silence themselves.

The only other visitors arrived a few minutes later and they were the three people who had talked to Helen and Joanna at Stonehenge: the doctor, his wife and their friend, the writer.

The man who appeared to be in charge of the community was in his forties, a bulky-looking man with a strong face and clear blue eyes. His shaved head made him look like a monk. He introduced himself as Zoranda and welcomed them in a quiet voice. Then he talked for a little while of the visions and intentions of the community. Its members clearly dedicated their whole lives to service and to mind training.

Marcus was deeply impressed when he realised that these men had devoted themselves to a monk-like life without the financial and structural safety and backing of a religious order. They seemed to work in total trust that God would provide their needs and tell them what He wanted them to do. He also had a sense that they practised intense self-discipline individually and collectively. Their greatest delight was evidently in serving others and God. They radiated a genuine sense of peace and joy.

Marcus felt inspired and strangely humbled in their presence.

After his introductory talk, Zoranda suggested a ten-minute silent meditation to focus on the purpose of everyone being together. Marcus found it a very peaceful few minutes. He had the strange feeling that he was being held and supported.

A somewhat reflective and drawn-out discussion then took place, with the doctor doing most of the talking. Marcus began to feel impatient. He could see that Tony had withdrawn and was watching the proceedings as an observer, while Helen appeared to be in dreamland. He could not see Joanna's face behind her hair.

He burst out suddenly, 'I think we're here about the Scroll.' Zoranda gestured to him to continue.

He started at the beginning and told them everything frankly – the whole story. Either they would embrace it or be so terrified of the danger they would kick him out. Then he would know where he was.

When he finished the silence was crystal clear. Zoranda said simply, 'This is what we have been preparing for.'

Marcus felt a tremendous rush of relief and then everyone started to talk and ask questions.

Helen and Joanna shared their experiences. It emphasised for everyone the dangers involved in bringing forward the message of the Scroll.

Tony confirmed that he also felt they were in danger, not just from the armed men, whose task it was to retrieve the Scroll for the Chinese, but also from those who had an investment in holding on to power and control in the world.

He was impressed when Zoranda looked him in the eye with a total lack of fear. He said in his quietly commanding voice, 'We believe that we chose to come to Earth on a special mission, for which we have trained for many lifetimes. We know that we are a soul group who have incarnated together many times to do certain work and now we are together again.' The other community members nodded. He continued. 'We are not afraid of danger. Why should we be? If we are to die then nothing can save us and it would be an honour to give our lives in such service to the planet. However, I believe that if we are to work for the release of the portals and the cleansing of the energy network round the planet, then we will be protected.

'Our aim is to stay centred and serene for then we are able to connect to God and be guided by His divine will. We practise radiating harmlessness and love to all creatures so that nothing feels threatened by us or wants to harm us.'

'I think you might need more than that to stop these people,' commented Tony sceptically.

A younger community member shook his head slightly with a smile. 'We believe that serenity and loving intention confer great protection. With the power of our minds we have surrounded Kumeka House with white light. As long as we hold this light steady people of dark intention cannot penetrate it.'

Another resident confirmed, 'We are surrounded by an impenetrable force field.'

Joanna broke in. 'The theory is all very well. I know it in my head, but does it work in practice?'

'I feel we may soon find out,' responded Zoranda calmly. A deep silence followed his words.

Marcus broke it. 'How do you feel you can clear the energy lines? Do you use sound?'

'There are certain sounds, which are the basis of manifestation. One of these is the sound *ah*. When you focus on your vision and chant *ah*, it manifests more quickly. The Bible says, "In the beginning was the word." In fact, that is a mistranslation or, rather, wrong choice of words to convey the true meaning of the original Sanskrit, which was "In the beginning was sound". In other words the basis of creation is the vibration of sound. Other translations say the manifest universe started with *aum*. You have probably heard people chanting *aum* and even chanted it yourselves?'

They all nodded.

'*Aum* is made up of *ah-oo-mm*, so every time you chant it, you are increasing your power of manifestation. Of course, if your mind is blank or scattered, you create confusion. However, if you focus your mind on something that you wish to manifest, you increase the power to make this come about.'

'Wow!' exclaimed Joanna and looked at her mother, who nodded thoughtfully.

Zoranda continued. 'From what you have said the Scroll contains information about certain specific notes, which can be used to materialise and de-materialise matter as well as to clear the portals and ley lines. It also contains symbols which, when used with the sounds, enhance the power.

'I believe that when we have that information we may be able to restore Stonehenge to its former state and purify that particular gateway to heaven.'

'Are you talking about telekinesis? Do you practise it?' asked Joanna curiously.

Zoranda paused for a moment and glanced at her. 'It is one of our powers but we only use it when Divinely guided.'

Joanna looked nonplussed for a moment. She guessed he knew she had intended to ask for a demonstration. Then she smiled and acknowledged the rightness of what he said. He was pleased when he saw her response.

'When will you have the information from the Scroll to start work?' the doctor asked.

'Soon, I hope,' interjected Marcus impatiently

'In God's time,' replied Zoranda. 'It's an illusion to think you can push the river, for all things happen in Divine right timing.'

He was surprised when four of his visitors laughed and Joanna got out her diary and solemnly wrote: 'Illusion: We are in control of time. (We can push the river). Truth: All things happen in God's time.'

Helen changed the subject to the benefits the information in the Scroll could bring to everyone.

'When we know the right notes, I imagine sound frequency will heal people instead of drugs,' she ventured.

'There are sound machines that do that already,' said the doctor. He told them of a man called Reif who invented just such a machine many years ago. He discovered which frequencies were needed to break up the disease in the body. 'A few doctors started using it with startling success to heal everything from cancer to sinusitis, but their machines were broken and some of the doctors were murdered, presumably by representatives of the controllers of power. Now it is slowly coming back but drugs are big business.'

'Could it be used to levitate people who had burns, for instance, so that they could heal?' asked Joanna.

'That would be interesting!' agreed the doctor.

He looked at Zoranda who nodded. 'I'm sure this will all come about soon.'

'And cars that are powered by alternative energy? It could speed up construction work.'

'Could sound purify polluted water?' asked the doctor's wife.

'I imagine it could,' answered Zoranda.

When the discussion died down, the doctor announced that they were part of a group who had permission to go into Stonehenge during the evening, when it was closed to the public. 'We go in once a month and meditate for peace on earth,' he told them. 'This month we have a pass on Wednesday, which is the day before the full moon.'

'Can you go right into the Stones?' Helen wanted to know.

'Yes. Sometimes one of the wardens stands on the perimeter, but they know us and usually leave us in peace.'

'What does it feel like in there?' asked Joanna.

'If you'd like to join us, you can find out for yourself.

Unfortunately it's quite expensive because we have to pay for the pass. It's limited to thirty and usually about twenty of us go in.'

'I'd like to come if you have room,' said Helen.

'So would I,' echoed the others and it was agreed that they would meet at the entrance to Stonehenge at six o'clock the following Wednesday evening to feel the energy of the Stones for themselves.

The expectation of going into the sacred Stones at full moon charged them up still further and everyone was talking again.

Suddenly a bell sounded and Zoranda explained that it was the 10 p.m. meditation bell. Marcus had been talking to one of the younger men. Half-expecting to be turned down, he asked if he could stay at Kumeka House as a visitor for a few days. The young man replied graciously that they would be honoured. It was agreed that he would stay and participate in their life for a week, unless work for the Scroll dictated otherwise.

Tony had been deeply affected by the honesty, love and togetherness at Kumeka House. Even though he had sat slightly apart and participated very little in the discussion, he had felt cocooned. It was a heart-warming feeling and he wanted to hold on to it longer.

He realised, too, that he would miss Marcus' company – strange when he had known him for such a short time. Marcus had been so genuinely interested in his writings that he had opened up in an unaccustomed way. He sighed quietly. Helen noticed and put a gentle hand on his arm, which he acknowledged with a half-smile.

He was to drive Helen and Joanna back to the hotel. Almost to his own surprise, he said shyly, 'Would you two like to stay at my house tonight?' Then he added hastily, as if fearing his suggestion might be misinterpreted, 'There's plenty of room and it might be safer.'

They accepted with alacrity.

'I'll take you to collect your things from the hotel tomorrow,' said Tony.

'Oh!' exclaimed Helen. 'That's very kind of you. Would you mind?'

'Of course not.'

'We'll surround your house with white light,' said Helen. 'We'll be safe then.'

Chapter 18

When they got back to Tony's house there was a message from Professor Smith.

Tony and Helen thought that eleven o'clock was much too late to phone him back. Joanna teased them that they belonged to a generation that did not make calls after nine-thirty in the evening.

'Now the truth is,' she declared, 'that academics don't go to bed early because brains don't need much sleep. It's physical and emotional energy that makes you tired.' They allowed her impeccable logic to win the day.

'I hope you're right,' said Tony, laughing despite himself as he dialled the number. His hazel eyes twinkled and the creases deepened in his cheeks when he laughed, giving him a youthful air.

She was right. Professor Smith's dry voice answered. He had expected it to be Tony and was not in the least put out by the lateness of the hour.

He told them carefully that as far as he could tell the Scroll was unique. Several of his colleagues, eminent experts in the field, had examined the parchment and were cautiously optimistic. Not only did they feel, on first impressions, that it was genuine, but they had never come across anything made of material like it. Even the little of the content they had explored was extraordinary.

His monologue was rather full of such words and phrases as 'cautiously', 'first impressions only', 'with reservations', 'subject to more testing' and 'as a hypothesis'. However, he did tell them that one of the symbols seemed to be a six-pointed star, though the others were more complex.

'What are the symbols for exactly?' questioned Tony.

'It seems that they are to be used in conjunction with certain notes to clear a grid of energy round the planet – but this is just my initial observation.'

'That's wonderful,' said Tony. 'Is there anything else?'

'Mmm. Indeed there is.' The usually dourly cerebral professor paused, almost dramatically. To his surprise Tony thought he could detect a hint of excitement in his voice and it lit a corresponding spark in him. He gave a thumbs-up to Helen and Joanna who were both trying to listen on an extension.

The professor continued, 'You mentioned the Great Mysteries. There seems to be some very specific reference to these. It states that all is energy. A human is a dense vibration, a tree even denser, a thought is a slight vibration unless it carries a big emotional connection. All is floating in a sea of energy. All interacting. In this cosmic soup of interconnecting energy everything is evolving in its own way.' He coughed. 'Any physicist could tell you that, of course.

'Then it says, "Humans have free choice, so they have special opportunities to evolve or devolve as the case may be. Free choice offers responsibility about the use of thoughts and emotions." According to the Scroll, humans differ in this from the rest of creation and this gives them great opportunity for evolution.

'Every vibration that a human sends out causes a reaction in the cosmic soup and affects everything else. Ultimately, every vibration a human chooses to transmit comes back to him or her. Thus a human can measure his progress by what is happening in his life.

'The Scroll states that if a human is very negative, he will sink into the thick dregs of the cosmic soup. When he does evil actions, bad vibrations emit into the soup and it may take many, many returns to come back to him through the heavy frequency of his personal world.'

The Professor paused fractionally as if to say something in explanation. Then he appeared to change his mind and continued, 'The evil man will experience the dark until he listens to the prompting of his soul and wants to rise again. When a human makes Godly choices, the pure vibrations he emits ensure he rises into the lighter part of the cosmic soup and good fortune will be his return.'

'That sounds like the Laws of Karma,' commented Helen.

'Yes,' breathed Joanna.

'Shh!' Tony mouthed at them, irritated by the interruption and putting his hand up to quieten them.

'Sorry,' Helen mouthed back, embarrassed. She hated being told off.

Joanna shrugged. She was a different generation from Helen and laughed at her mother's hang-ups.

The Professor was continuing as if he had not heard the interruption. 'It seems that at the time the Scroll was written it was forecast that the energy, or cosmic soup, if you like, on the planet would become very thick and murky as humanity moved into greed and materialism. If that indeed happened, then the Scroll would be released to give humanity the opportunity to change.'

Professor Smith paused and cleared his throat. 'Presumably that is where we are now.'

'I agree,' said Tony nodding.

The Professor continued, 'It is written that the Scroll will come into air when it is time to herald the Golden Age, which cannot come about until the impenetrable soup of fear, greed and desire is lightened with the pure water of spirit.'

As he paused, Tony remarked encouragingly, 'Clearly the whole energy of the planet has to change.'

Helen and Joanna nodded silently.

'Yes, yes. I'm coming to that. This is quite extraordinary.' His voice changed as he evidently looked down at his notes again. 'If the forecast of heavy vibrations on Earth indeed becomes reality, many highly evolved souls, who vibrate on a higher frequency, will volunteer to incarnate at the beginning of the Golden Era. They offer this service in order to lighten the energy on the planet.

'The likelihood is that most of these . . .' he paused and they could sense him peering over his glasses down the phone as he explained. 'The Scroll refers to these high-frequency beings as star children. I resume. The likelihood is that most of these star children will be asleep to their true spiritual nature. They need to remember who they truly are and the pulses of higher energy coming through the energy grid will wake them up, so that they can start their service contracts.'

Tony, Helen and Joanna were completely silent now, listening in fascination to every word.

'When a human is in the thick soup – in other words, when a human being is very materially minded or nega-tive – the vibrations which emanate from him come back to him in equal measure. But when he becomes more spiritual and sends out a higher frequency, they return to him threefold. When he becomes totally spiritual they return tenfold.

'Those who are awake will become vortices of light, which spin faster than the average human, so that the radiations penetrate matter more quickly and return more quickly.'

He paused again. 'I really can't tell you any more. I have read this from my rough preliminary notes. Normally I wouldn't release anything like this at such an early stage. There may be nuances I have missed.' Then he paused again and said with a half-cough, as if embarrassed:

'It is a peculiar observation I have made that working on the Scroll has been unlike working on any other document in my experience. I hardly know how to describe it. It is as if the words and shape of the translation have dropped into my mind as I study it.' He sighed faintly. 'And another thing: it was as if I had been prepared in advance for this study. I had to do very little research or investigation, as most of the words and phrases have appeared in my recent works, in different context, of course. But it seemed an extraordinary coincidence and I felt compelled to let you have this information, however preliminary.'

He coughed apologetically and added formally, 'I'll fax it to you in the morning. I'll let you know more when I can.'

'Very many thanks,' said Tony. 'I can't tell you how grateful we are. You must have been working very hard on it.'

'I haven't stopped. It is intriguing, fascinating. The opportunity of a lifetime to be presented with such an artefact.'

'Well, thank you again,'

'There's just one thing more – a warning! If the Scroll is destroyed or the work is not done, there will be darkness beyond anything earth has experienced and all will be trapped within it for aeons of pain.' He paused, but the only response was thick silence from Tony.

'I'll speak to you tomorrow. Goodbye.'

'Goodnight.' Tony clicked off the phone and they all looked at each other.

'We've just got to make it work,' said Joanna.

'We will,' added Helen resolutely. 'Let's start by visualising white light round the house and the Scroll. We'll ask the powers-that-be to protect it, too.'

Chapter 19

Helen, Joanna and Tony arrived very early the following morning at Kumeka House, fax in hand and buzzing with suppressed excitement. Though they were bursting to tell everyone what they had learned, they agreed to say nothing until they could all be together.

One of the residents opened the door and smiled at the sight of their beaming faces. Marcus was right behind him.

'What's it like being in a monastery?' Joanna teased, grinning broadly.

'Bit quiet, but really interesting,' Marcus spoke seriously, but with a hint of laughter in his eyes. 'I'm learning loads.'

'I'm jealous,' responded Joanna. 'I'd love to live in these beautiful surroundings.'

Tony raised an eyebrow. He could not imagine the energetic Joanna living the quiet life. He imagined she would be bored in no time. He refrained from saying so, but when he caught Helen's eye, her lips twitched and he knew she was thinking the same. In fact he was surprised at the restless Marcus opting to stay here, but maybe it would do him good.

'We're in the middle of *sava*,' the resident told them.

'That's selfless service. We each do two or three hours a day to keep the place running smoothly.'

'We'll help,' burst out Joanna eagerly. 'What do you want us to do? We've got a fax about the Scroll. The sooner the work's finished the sooner we can discuss it.'

'You've got a fax about the Scroll?' echoed the resident.

'Let's see it, then!' Marcus' voice rose in excitement. 'What does it say? When did it come? Is there . . . ?'

'Hang on,' calmed Tony. 'We agreed not to say anything until we could all be together.'

'Sorry,' apologised Joanna, mortified. 'It just came out. It's so exciting. I want to tell everyone.'

'Excuse me a minute,' murmured the resident and slipped away.

Marcus smiled reassuringly at Joanna. He did not want her to feel bad. And Tony caught an expression he recognised in Marcus' eyes as he did so. Joanna, cross with herself, bit her lip and walked away to smell a yellow rose. Helen followed her.

Tony murmured to Marcus, glancing at Joanna, 'The door's not open yet.'

Marcus sighed. 'What would open it?'

Tony was about to shrug and say he was no expert on relationships. That would have been his pattern in the past and the conversation would have died with both sides feeling uncomfortable.

But he heard himself say, 'Consistent kindness and steadiness, I imagine. Underneath the confident and streetwise girl I often see a wild fawn, watchful and ready to run.' He startled himself. The Scroll must be working on him already.

'Thanks!' replied Marcus.

Moments later the resident returned to tell them that Zoranda had agreed that *sava* could be interrupted for half an hour. Before they had a chance to respond, he hit the gong three times and the sound rippled round the house. Even the gong was melodious at Kumeka House!

Instantly the residents, silent and dignified, appeared from all directions and congregated in the meeting room, where a huge bowl of white narcissus with orange centres filled the room with a beautiful fragrance. There was a distinct current of excitement in the air.

As Tony read the fax aloud, he was the focus of intense concentration from everyone in the room.

When he finished, there was silence until Marcus spoke, 'It's amazing – a bit much to take in. So it's saying everyone has a vibration that affects other people and their future because everything we give out comes back to us.'

'And the lighter we are, the more quickly things come back to us.'

'It's interesting about higher beings called star children, who have incarnated to help but have been asleep. They are being woken up now by pulses of light being sent through the grid system.'

Zoranda pondered aloud, 'What the Scroll calls the second Great Mystery seems to be the sacred spiritual law of karma that prevails on earth.'

Helen asked, 'How does your understanding of the law of karma compare with what the Scroll says?'

Zoranda considered before he responded. 'We understand that everything sent out by materially based humans, whether it is a thought, word or action, inexorably comes back to them. Sometimes it takes lifetimes to return. Then, as people become more spiritual, the vibrations they send out come back more quickly.'

'It sounds very much the same as the Scroll to me,' commented Tony.

Zoranda and most of the residents nodded in agreement.

'Is that the law of cause and effect?' asked Marcus.

'Yes, that's another way of putting it. If only people realised this they would be more careful of what they did and even of what they thought,' Zoranda said. 'If the Scroll did no more than bring this to the attention of humanity, there would be a huge benefit.'

Marcus was wondering how the betrayal by his ex-girlfriend and boss fitted in. Was it the result of thoughts he had in this life, or actions from a previous existence? He felt the familiar knot of fury in his chest and shrugged the feeling away. 'Why does it take so long to come back?' he asked. 'It seems stupid that there is no relationship between a crime and the retribution.'

A slight gasp greeted his words. He coloured. 'All right I know it's not about punishment and retribution. It's about the soul wanting to make amends. Let me put it this way. It seems unhelpful that there is so long between cause and effect.'

'It disassociates people's actions from the karmic consequence,' agreed Helen. 'So that to most people the just return of karma feels like a blow of fate.'

'It's true,' replied Zoranda. 'That was not the original intention. It was anticipated that humankind would sink into some materialism, but the depth of darkness this planet has sunk to was never envisaged. However, it is simply a question of vibration. Karma means "wheel" in Sanskrit. So everything you send out goes round the wheel and comes back to you.'

'A boomerang,' ventured a resident.

'Quite,' Zoranda agreed 'So if a thought or action has a dark, heavy vibration it goes out from you to the other person like a boomerang and then has to work its way through their vibration before it comes back to you.'

'Can you explain that again,' Marcus asked. 'I'm not quite sure I got the bit about getting through the other person's vibration.'

Helen laughed and Zoranda handed the question to her with a glance.

'Let me give you an analogy,' she offered. 'You throw a nasty thought at someone, and it is like a boomerang. It comes back and hits you. In other words, something nasty will happen to you. That happens quickly if you are out in the open. But if the person you throw the thought at has very negative energy, it's a bit like this: imagine that person is sitting in the middle of a wood surrounded by trees and tangled undergrowth. The boomerang is programmed to hit him and then return to you so it has to work its way through the trees and tangled undergrowth to him before it can come back.'

'So in that case the karma will take a long time to come back!' exclaimed Joanna. 'Thanks, Mum. I never really understood why it sometimes came back instantly and at other times came back slowly. It depends on the vibration of the other person or situation as well as your own.'

'Sometimes it doesn't even come back in the same lifetime,' put in a shy, intense-looking resident with glasses and acne, called Peter.

'It is unfortunate that people no longer understand about reincarnation because, as you say, effect is disassociated from cause,' commented Zoranda in his calm voice.

There were silent nods of agreement.

'The bit about the faster you spin, the quicker the karma comes back to you – is that instant karma?' questioned Joanna.

Tony put on his glasses and read again from the fax, 'Those who are awake will become vortices of light, which spin faster, so that their radiation penetrates matter more quickly and returns more quickly.'

'I guess so,' said Marcus.

'As you become more spiritually evolved, your vibration lightens and the consequences of your actions return to you instantly. So, if you feel you never get away with anything, you are receiving instant karma. It is a good sign.' He smiled at Joanna, as she had asked the question.

'What's this about coming back threefold if you are more spiritual and tenfold if you are very spiritual?' Joanna then wanted to know.

'If you are living only in the material world and are not interested in matters spiritual, then everything you send out comes back to you exactly, no more, no less,' replied Zoranda. 'But as you become awake to spiritual matters this changes. You become a higher vibration vortex of energy, then all that is sent out returns threefold. This means that all the good you do returns as benefits in your life and you get repaid three times, but all the negative thoughts and actions are also multiplied. So your opportunity for spiritual growth or contraction increases rapidly.

'When you live a purely spiritual life, everything is multiplied by a factor of ten. Good and bad return to you tenfold.'

'How do you know this?' Tony asked curiously. 'You obviously knew this before the Scroll told us.'

Zoranda nodded. 'We who live in this community were incarnated in Atlantis. I suspect you were all initiates there, too. At the beginning it was a great civilisation – spiritual, but with very advanced technology, much of which is lost nowadays. They could do things that we now have no concept of. Unfortunately, it gradually became too material and scientific. People controlled other people. Technology became the God and the spiritual values were lost. Finally there was a catastrophe due to the mass of negativity and the continent of Atlantis submerged under the ocean.

'Various groups of initiates escaped, taking with them esoteric spiritual secrets. They scattered and formed twelve groups, which settled in the New World. One was in Tibet. It now seems that the priests who survived recorded the sacred knowledge and stored it in the Scroll with special guidance for the end times.

'We at Kumeka House are a fragment of a group who escaped from Atlantis before the flood. Originally we made our way to Avalon, which is now Somerset, and set about radiating the true spiritual energies. Some of us still retain the memories of those times.'

Joanna and Helen looked at him with renewed respect.

'Wow! That's amazing!' exclaimed Joanna.

'What does the six-pointed star signify?' asked Helen humbly.

'The six-pointed star is made up of two triangles, one pointing downward and the other upwards. This symbolises the bringing down of spirit into matter and the raising of matter into spirit.'

'Will the symbol help with the clearing of the energy lines?'

'Assuredly. We will start focusing on the symbol today, but obviously we need the other symbols and the correct notes in order to return Stonehenge to its true state. That's our first task and I have no doubt we will accomplish it.'

Chapter 20

The communal work at Kumeka House was usually done in silence or sometimes while they chanted or listened to sacred music. But after the first revelations of the Scroll everyone wanted to talk.

Several of them sat round the enormous kitchen table preparing vegetables for the evening meal – a perfect communal task, Helen thought, as she chopped carrots and listened to the conversation ebbing and flowing around the Great Mysteries.

Each of them was consciously watching their thoughts and words.

'I can never get it right,' sighed Joanna. 'If I speak up I feel I'm creating karma but if I bury something and don't say anything, that sends out negative energy, too.'

'I'm something of a suppresser myself,' admitted Helen, and they all laughed in sympathy. 'I think the worst thing is to wallow about something and pretend you're feeling okay. That sends out a really bad energy. It's one of my biggest faults.'

'It's not always easy to get the balance of being aware of underlying feelings and expressing them,' put in a resident thoughtfully.

'I find it easy to convince myself I'm feeling all right about something, when really I'm not,' agreed another.

'I suppose your thoughts give you clues about what's really going on inside you,' Helen responded. 'Then you have the opportunity to be really honest, if you dare.'

'You're a lot better than you used to be, Mum,' Joanna chipped in. 'Thanks to me always telling you.'

Helen laughed ruefully. 'Thanks,' she said with a hint of sarcasm. 'However did I get you as a daughter!'

Marcus grinned. 'My mother always used to say that you're given your family, but you can choose your friends.'

'Illusion!' said Joanna and Helen simultaneously.

'What do you mean?' asked Marcus, taken aback.

'It's all choices,' said Joanna. 'I know in my heart of hearts that my soul chose my parents before I was born. Sometimes I can't think why, but I know I did.' She smiled cheekily at Helen. 'And the Scroll says that all is chosen.'

'It's true,' corroborated Helen. 'I believe our Higher Self chooses our parents because they are the best people to launch us on our life mission and teach us the lessons we need to learn.'

'Bollocks!' exploded Tony so unexpectedly that everyone jumped. His usual composure was shaken and he looked flushed and agitated. 'I've heard people say that before,' he said. 'And I will never believe I chose my parents.' His usually still hands were drumming the table and his jaw was tight.

Joanna glanced sideways at her mother, who said consolingly, 'It doesn't sound as if you had an easy time with your parents?'

'Too right!' Tony was uncharacteristically taciturn.

Helen ventured to add, 'We don't always choose easy pathways and a growth pathway is usually tough.'

Tony's only response was a sarcastic grunt.

'I wonder why I chose my parents?' Marcus was curious and not going to let the subject drop.

'The simplest way to look at it is this: your spiritual task is to overcome each of their worst qualities and embrace their best ones,' Helen told him hastily, trying to ignore Tony, for she hated people being angry. 'So what was your Dad like?'

'Best qualities: charming, good communicator, kind. Worst qualities . . .' he thought for a second. 'Stubborn and inflexible, authoritarian, dogmatic, I suppose.'

'Well,' Joanna said smiling. 'You're certainly charming. I think you're pretty good as a communicator, don't you?' She looked round the table and the others nodded. 'I suspect that's a quality you chose to embrace for your mission. I'm sure you will give out information in some way.' Again everyone nodded in agreement.

'As for kind,' she joked. 'How about making us a cup of tea?'

Marcus grinned, 'That's ingratiating, not kind.' He rose and filled the kettle.

'What about the tendencies you have to watch out for?' Helen asked.

'Stubborn, inflexible, authoritarian, dogmatic. Yes, I have a bit of all of those, I suppose,' Marcus agreed.

'Being authoritarian comes from a fear of the big bad world out there. It's trying to keep everything safe and in control,' responded Helen. 'I suspect the test you've chosen is to face your fears and trust the universe to support you.'

'Do you get a stiff neck?' questioned Joanna.

'Sometimes,' Marcus admitted.

'That's a sure sign of inflexibility,' Joanna told him. 'I've a similar tendency sometimes. I'm trying to learn to relax and go with the flow.'

'I wouldn't say you were dogmatic, would you?' asked Helen.

'No. I like to think I'm pretty open-minded really,' Marcus said cautiously. 'I hope so, anyway.' He paused for reflection and Helen reminded him that there was a good side to being stubborn and inflexible.

'It means that when you decide you want to do something, nothing and no one can stop you. You're like an arrow aiming for a target. So they can be great qualities to inherit but disastrous if you go off in the wrong direction.'

Marcus laughed, bemused. 'It's true. Once I've made up my mind, nothing will stop me, right or wrong. So what about my Mum? She's really nice and everyone likes her, but she tries too hard to please people. She lets people railroad her, especially my father. I think she had a lot of grit, but he wore her down and took her confidence.'

'Well, there are your lessons,' Helen told him. 'Pleasers give their power away and get angry. Your lesson is to be charming, but maintain your integrity and do what is right for you'

'I see,' replied Marcus thoughtfully. 'And don't let anyone beat me down and take my confidence, right?'

'Right!'

'Actually my mother has a lot of good qualities, too.'

'Great,' responded Helen. 'Write them down and know that your life task is to develop those qualities within yourself.'

'Thanks. That's really interesting,' replied Marcus, pleased.

'My mother died when I was three,' pointed out one of the residents. 'She wasn't there to teach me any lessons.'

'I'm sorry. That's really hard,' said Helen with genuine compassion. 'But there are lessons when a parent is absent, whether it's physically – as in your case, because she died – or maybe because one parent was working away or was hospitalised or, more commonly because of divorce. And the soul lesson is to become independent. The same applies if a parent is emotionally absent.'

'What if they are mentally ill?'

'Yes, they would certainly be emotionally absent in that case, so again the lesson is to stand up for yourself in life. That's a tough lesson to choose.'

'My father was so pushy,' put in a rather retiring and diffident young man. 'He wanted us all to be top of the class and successful in everything. I found it very difficult and left home as soon as I could.'

'Again that's a difficult lesson for your soul,' Helen empathised. 'Usually the reason you chose such a parent is to help you achieve your potential. Maybe without that push you would sit back and do nothing. The danger, of course, is that you resist the lesson. Also it's important to stand back and look objectively at what your aim is.'

'I see,' he responded, nodding and pursing up his lips.

'Don't forget his good qualities. Your soul wants you to embrace those,' she smiled.

'Oh, he was loyal, strong and underneath I knew he loved me very much and believed in me, too. I just found it all too pressurised.'

Helen nodded. 'That's brilliant. So embrace those qualities, too, and the sky's the limit for you in this life.'

He flushed and smiled, looking thoughtful.

'My mother was a librarian and my father a lecturer. They were always having deep discussions,' ventured Peter.

'How did they deal with their emotions?' asked Helen.

'Emotions? What emotions?' he replied.

'Exactly. If you have one parent who rationalises and intellectualises everything, your lesson is to get out of your head and in touch with your feelings. If both parents are like that you have a double whammy. Your soul wants you to explore your feelings in this life.'

'Dangerous!' he exclaimed, with such a look of horror that everyone laughed.

'What about an alcoholic parent?' asked Tony, his arms and legs firmly crossed, blocked off and frowning.

We're coming to it, thought Helen, looking at him with considerable compassion. 'That's another very difficult soul lesson because it is such an abuse,' she said gently. 'An alcoholic parent is an absent one, so part of the lesson is to be independent and look after yourself.

But it is much more. People drink to stop themselves from feeling emotional pain as well as from taking responsibility for their lives. An alcoholic parent is also weak and becomes unsupportive and uncaring. So the child of such a parent has undertaken complex and tricky lessons at a soul level – to take responsibility for their own lives. To support and care for themselves. To be strong. To learn to look at their own pain and deal with it appropriately instead of burying it or becoming out of control emotionally.'

'Interesting,' responded Tony in a dry, non-committal voice.

'The commonest ways of denying emotions are obsessive behaviour like being a workaholic, over-eating, over-talking, over-exercising – anything done to extremes.'

'Oh,' Tony looked surprised. 'I suppose I was rather a workaholic,' he admitted. 'But I still can't see why any child would deliberately choose abusive parents.'

'It's not the child. It's the soul or Higher Self that chooses because that's what the soul needs to experience while in the physical plane. I agree it seems horrendous to choose abusive parents.

'One reason could be simply the inevitable return of karma. Then the contract is – I abused you, now I'm going to be born to you and you will probably abuse me so that I can experience what I did to you. The higher aim is that, having experienced it, you will never do it again. But we being humans it rarely works like that.

'But the second reason for choosing abusive parents is this – and I think it's one of the reasons so many old souls are having a difficult childhood. This is the end of the old era, before the Golden Age, as the Scroll calls it, comes in. The final lesson, the ultimate lesson, if you prefer, on earth is unconditional love. Now you can't learn about unconditional love and total forgiveness if there's nothing to forgive. So if you've undertaken that lesson it would be pointless to be born to wonderfully balanced, warm and loving parents. Having abusive parents and moving through it, and forgiving them so that their actions don't touch your spirit, is the greatest lesson on earth.'

There was a digestive silence for a moment. Then Joanna said with a sigh, 'Wouldn't you think a soul coming in would choose one supportive parent, at least?'

'It depends on the lessons they want to learn,' replied Helen seriously. 'Earth can be a hard school.'

'Don't I know it,' grinned Joanna, suddenly lightening up. Her eyes twinkled mischievously. 'Look at the mother I chose. Stubborn, difficult, neurotic, controlling.'

Helen chuckled, bantering back, 'Careful, that sounds like a real mirror of you.'

Joanna laughed. 'You know I love you lots and you're wise and loving and caring and . . .' She paused and added with a grin, 'Too often right, but I'm still glad I chose you.' She waved a beetroot-stained hand at her.

Helen reciprocated by shaking a carrot at her daughter before she chopped it. It was the last one. She got up and washed her hands. Then she stood behind Tony and put her warm healing hands on his shoulders.

Chapter 21

There are some evenings when most people would prefer to be at home by a log fire or even by a central heating radiator, when the wind howls like a vengeful ghoulie chasing black clouds across the moon and trees creak and groan in the dusk.

Such an evening was Wednesday. The moon watched the world like a cool and distant relative, occasionally shrouded in mist, only to emerge again with an icy, baleful stare.

'It's creepy out there,' whispered Joanna to Marcus, as they looked out of a window at Kumeka House.

'I know,' he murmured back. 'I was looking forward to going into the Stones until I saw the weather.'

Helen joined them, wrapped up like an Egyptian mummy. She found herself whispering in collusion, 'I almost wish I wasn't going. It looks awful out there.' A burst of rain beat on the window, as if daring them to venture out.

They jumped like conspirators when one of the residents approached to ask whether there was anything they needed before they left.

'No, thanks. We're fine,' Helen replied in a normal voice, which sounded loud and strange.

'The Kumeka House minibus is waiting. Three of us are coming with you.'

'Good,' smiled Joanna.

'It doesn't look as if Tony is going to make it,' Marcus remarked. 'He thought he'd be back from London in time.'

'Maybe he'll go straight there,' shouted Helen as they battled out into the lashing wind.

'He really wanted to come to the Stones with us, so he'll get here if he can,' Joanna reminded them. 'Something may have come up with the Scroll.'

'Yes, I'm sure you're right,' Marcus agreed. Surely there was no reason to be concerned.

The doctor and his group were waiting for them at the entrance of Stonehenge and perfunctory introductions were performed. The cheery warder counted them, fairly casually, because most of them were a regular group. Then they made their way through the barrier, along the corridor and up some steps towards the Stones.

A shadowy figure following behind them proved to be a tired Tony. Marcus felt relieved to see him, as Tony slipped up to Helen and fell into step beside her.

'How did it go in London?' she asked in a low voice.

Tony nodded an okay and she had to be content with that, as the party was supposed to be walking in silence, following the lantern of the leader.

The Stones looked impenetrably dark in the fractured moonlight and for a moment, she shivered.

But as she stepped over the rope barrier, Helen felt

she had entered a magical world. The wind became irrelevant. It may even have stopped blowing. She touched one of the huge standing Stones. It felt cold and unyielding. She placed her forehead against it and relaxed into it. Gradually the damp hardness faded and she felt it becoming vibrant, alive, even responsive. A humming sensation came from the stone. She radiated love towards it and the humming became stronger. It was a communication of sorts.

Around her she could hear others beginning to *aum* and she knew that each would have their third eye touching the Stone. Gently and softly, she started to chant the sacred mantra. *Aum*. She visualised Stonehenge restored and the network of lines around the planet becoming golden and flowing with light and peace. Her third eye pulsated.

As the *aum*ing died away, she was filled with warmth and peace. She turned and opened her eyes. It seemed as if the circle was awash with light and in the centre stood a vast being, about twenty feet tall. She saw him turn for a moment and smile. Then the vision was gone.

The only light was from the torches of the group as they formed a circle in the middle of the sacred space to perform a ceremony dedicated to peace and light on earth. For a fraction of a second she wondered if she had imagined it. Then the doubt passed and she knew she had not. Deep down inside herself she knew now that, no matter what the cost, the work must go on. Stumbling slightly on the slippery grass she joined the others as they started to chant sacred songs.

*   *   *

Zoranda and the other residents wanted to return to Kumeka House in time for the ten o'clock meditation. Marcus felt he ought to go back with them, but he had been deeply affected by his experience in Stonehenge and wanted to share it. He felt strangely spaced out, a totally unfamiliar sensation for him.

'Come with us to the Jester's Arms,' Joanna said persuasively. 'There's lots to talk about and I'm sure Tony will drop you off later.'

'Of course,' agreed Tony amenably. 'We'll take you back on the way home.'

Marcus needed no more persuasion. He told Zoranda that he would be back later and jumped into Tony's car with Joanna and Helen. They followed the doctor and his two friends to the quiet pub, where they all huddled together like conspirators, talking in low voices.

Joanna had been very much aware of spirits working with them and, like her mother, she had felt a vibration from the Stones and an immense feeling of love stealing over her.

The doctor had been conscious of the ley lines radiating from the Stones, while his wife had felt them streaming out into the cosmos, linking earth to the other planets. They had both sent love and projected the six-pointed star along the lines.

Marcus had never before had a spiritual experience. He told them that he felt completely at one with the universe in Stonehenge.

'I can't describe it in any other way. I felt as if I had been in the Stones many times and I could see them as they were originally, in their full glory and power. It was mind blowing.' He shivered slightly at the awesome memory and was glad that he was with open-minded people, who were supporting him by listening intently and nodding with understanding. 'I'm glad I'm with all of you right now,' he laughed in embarrassment. 'If this had happened a few months ago I would have thought I was going mad. I'd have kept really quiet, I can tell you.'

They chuckled.

'We've all been there,' Helen reassured him. Then she told them of the being of light she had seen.

Neither the doctor's writer friend nor Tony had experienced anything. She was clearly disappointed, but Tony claimed that he had really enjoyed being in the Stones. 'As I stood there I thought about the illusions and then focused on sending out the truths. It felt good,' he insisted, somewhat to their surprise.

When they had all shared their experiences, Tony mentioned casually that Professor Smith had given him more information from the Scroll. 'I think you'll find it interesting,' he remarked in his understated way, as he pulled notes out of his pocket.

Tony told them that Professor Smith and his team were becoming increasingly excited by the Scroll and convinced of its authenticity.

'We know that,' commented Joanna impatiently. 'What did they find out?'

Helen gave her a silencing glance, but it bounced off her daughter like hail off an umbrella.

Tony ignored their interaction, seemingly unruffled. In fact, he found Joanna's directness difficult to handle, so he chose to ignore it.

'They have continued to examine the Great Mysteries and found another symbol. It seems the symbols are very important.' Tony opened up a paper napkin and drew a spiral. From its top came a line like an arrow shooting upwards with a triangle at its top.

In one action they all fumbled for biros and copied it on to napkins or pieces of Joanna's notebook that she tore out and passed round. 'It feels very powerful,' murmured the doctor's wife as she doodled the symbol repeatedly.

'It seems like an extension of the six-pointed star,' commented Joanna, examining it critically.

'I don't know how you get that,' argued their writer friend shrilly. 'It's more like a Catherine wheel shooting off.'

'Yes, you're probably right,' agreed Joanna with her ready laugh.

'Why are symbols so important?' Marcus wanted to know.

Helen responded, 'Symbols are keys. They unlock certain energies so that they can be accessed. Some open doors to our personal consciousness and others unlock spiritual energies available for our use.'

'Like Reiki healing,' said Joanna.

'Yes, Reiki's an example of the use of symbols to draw on pools of healing energy which are available in the realms of spirit.'

'What have they found out about the next Great Mystery?' Joanna demanded.

Tony smiled. 'Okay, but I'd like to know more about

the symbols later.' He lifted a questioning eyebrow to Helen, who nodded an affirmative.

'The third of the Great Mysteries is about focus or attention. The Scroll says that humans were given total control over their lives by being given power over their minds. Unfortunately they have forgotten this and most people's minds are all over the place. In ancient Mystery Schools the initiates were trained to control their minds and focus their thoughts. I presume this is what they practise at Kumeka House.'

Marcus said, 'Yes, they spend two hours a day on concentrated focus exercises. They believe that when they have total control over their thoughts and emotions, they have total mastery over their lives.'

'That is basically what the Scroll tells us,' Tony agreed. 'It says we live in a universe made up of thought. And also that every single thought is an energy or electro-magnetic impulse, which emanates from us and creates things. It adds that words and sounds are even more powerful than thoughts. Actions more so again.

'The Scroll describes this mystery in terms of the primordial soup of energy again. Lots of humans are like bits of flotsam floating around in it, without direction. While their minds are in this vacant, out-of-gear state, other people can control them. However, as soon as we understand that by focusing our thoughts we can move towards any goal we choose, we gain mastery over our lives. Then no one can influence us.'

'Positive thinking,' commented the doctor.

'Yes. Furthermore, when a person is focusing all his energy towards a target, not only will he move towards it, but others will align with his energy and help him to get there.'

'A bit like saying that if you are swimming with determination in a certain direction you will influence others to swim with you and help you?' queried Helen.

'Exactly,' Tony answered, and continued, 'However – and this is important, because we have free will on earth – people can move towards light or dark and take others with them.'

'Is the Scroll really saying that if I focus my thoughts on something happening, it will happen?' asked Marcus.

Tony nodded. 'To a certain extent. If your thoughts, words and actions are clear and focused, you will certainly move in the direction you want to. But there's more. It says that, as with the second Great Mystery, there are three levels. The lowest level is where people spend their lives concerned about money, sex or selfish things. If they are motivated by fear and holding on to jealousy, anger, greed and all the lower emotions, then they are in the dregs of the soup.

'It explains that if you're in thick soup, it is like swimming through mud. It takes a long time and a lot of effort but you get there eventually.'

'That explains why my brother, who fervently wanted his business to succeed, but was incredibly pessimistic about everything, could never get it going,' commented the doctor's wife. 'What about the next level?'

'Yes, I'm coming to that,' Tony replied. 'This is where people have raised their consciousness. They have become more spiritual and less materially orientated. Then they are floating round in the slightly clearer soup.

'To use Helen's analogy, when your consciousness is low, if you want to get to the other side of the wood, you have to hack your way through a thicket. When you become more filled with love and light, the bushes in the wood become thinned out. Then, when you aim in a certain direction, you move more easily as there is less to block the way.'

'I see. I see.' Helen pursed her lips in concentration.

'And at the highest level, when people are living in kindness and truth, taking personal responsibility and doing what is for the greatest good, their aura is clear, so they are moving in clear soup. Or, in Helen's example, across open meadows. They can reach their destination more quickly. In spiritual terms, according to the Scroll, their thoughts manifest immediately into concrete form.'

'So the higher we raise our consciousness the more quickly we can make things happen by mind control and right action,' checked Marcus.

'In a nutshell,' agreed Tony.

'It sounds so simple.'

'According to the Scroll, it is.' He looked down at his notes and read, '"Whosoever hath confused thinking, shall make confusion in his life, for the Mysteries which govern this planet are exact. All is energy."'

'That's fascinating,' said Joanna. 'It makes such sense.'

The doctor agreed. 'I think what tends to happen is that most people focus on what they don't want. So if they don't want to be made redundant, they keep thinking and talking about the possibility of being made redundant . . . and, lo and behold! they bring it about with their energy flow.'

'I'm sure you must see it happen with illness, don't you?' asked Helen. 'Where people give all their attention to the illness they are afraid of having?'

The doctor nodded. 'Yes. People have no idea how powerful their minds are in making them sick. It was one of the reasons I wanted to move into natural medicine, so that I could help to focus people on health and using their minds to heal themselves.'

'So let's review,' suggested Tony. 'The first Great Mystery is that there are specific high vibration portals, where there is a close connection to God. From these radiate a system of communicating lines along which spiritual guidance can pass.'

'But these have been taken over by people's negativity and by vested interests who want control,' interrupted Joanna.

'Yes. And the second Great Mystery is that whatever we give out comes back to us, in exact measure, some-times taking lifetimes. When we live more spiritual lives everything returns to us more quickly and is magnified.'

Tony paused and everyone nodded, so he continued. 'The third Great Mystery is that we have the power to create our lives by focusing on what we want. When we do this for the right reasons, it is facilitated.'

'Yes, as long as we don't waver and send out mixed messages.'

'Got it.'

'When the information is out, what exactly will it mean for humanity, do you think?'

'When we all take responsibility for our lives, we will be happier and therefore healthier.'

'And when everyone cooperates rather than dissenting, there will be enough for all.'

'When we don't give away our power to the church and instead link directly to God for our spiritual growth, surely all the hypocrisy will go.'

'Could make a huge difference!'

'Even more important. When we stop giving power to governments to look after our lives and decide to live in love, there will be an end to wars.'

'Do you think it will happen in our lifetime?'

'I like to hope so,' replied Helen.

'Me, too, and I'm going to start focusing every day on clearing the energy lines and portals, so that the whole planet can move into the Golden Age,' announced Joanna.

'I think we all will,' agreed Tony, and everyone murmured their assent.

'Going back to symbols. Helen, can you tell us a bit more about why they are so powerful?'

Helen nodded. 'It's probably easier if I give you an example. Lots of people are doing Reiki healing now. Have you heard of it?' They all nodded. 'Do you know how it started?'

'Go on! Tell us, Mum,' said Joanna with a grin. 'You were going to anyway.'

Helen gave her a glinting smile. 'Thousands of years ago in the glorious days of early Atlantis everyone was psychic and spiritual. When the social system started to break down, many lost their psychic abilities. They were cast out or used as slaves as they were considered to be lesser humans. That's a total contravention of God's law.

'Certain of the High Priests and Priestesses, who retained the original spiritual values, prayed for help to stop this abuse. The divine sent angels to them with symbols, which as I have already said are keys of energy. When these keys were placed into the energy body of the outcasts and slaves it attuned them to a higher vibration, which restored their psychic and spiritual gifts.'

'I've never heard that. I thought the Reiki symbols came from Tibet?' queried the doctor's wife.

'What happened,' explained Helen carefully, 'as I understand it, is that when Atlantis sank, those High Priests and Priestesses who had been given the symbols, fled to Tibet. They continued to use them for healing and tuning people to a higher vibration. But some of the people to whom they taught the symbols used them agaisnt the will of God. Eventually it was decided humankind could no longer be trusted with the power of the symbols and they were withdrawn.

Thousands of years later some of them were given again to Dr Usui in Tibet, so that he could start initiating those who were ready into the use of the Reiki again.'

'Does this mean that we humans have raised our vibrations and can be trusted with the healing symbols?'

'Hopefully. I have a sense that we are being closely monitored,' replied Helen.

'Crop circles are symbols, aren't they? What are they keys to?' asked Tony, somewhat to Helen's surprise.

'Yes, they are. As I understand it they are energy

keys, which are being strategically placed to open up memories and ancient knowledge that has been locked in the human consciousness. So if we see a crop circle or go into one, a door within us is opened a little.'

'Fascinating,' commented Marcus. 'I've always wanted to go into a crop circle.'

'Ask the powers-that-be and then wait and see what happens,' responded Helen, smiling.

'OK,' agreed Marcus. 'I'll do that.' He received a beaming smile from Joanna as reward for his openness, and was strangely pleased.

'Would anyone like another drink?' asked Tony. 'Or do you think we ought to be on our way?'

'On our way, thanks,' replied the doctor.

'You know,' remarked Joanna. 'I'm beginning to feel the danger is over. Everything has gone quiet.'

'Don't mention it,' Marcus said. 'You're focusing on the danger.'

'Yes. You'll energise it,' reminded the doctor's wife.

'Sorry,' said Joanna quickly. Before long she would have good cause to remember that conversation.

Chapter 22

The weather in England is as changeable as the moods of a toddler, moving from stormy tantrum to sunny smiles quite unpredictably. A few days after the screaming wind of the waxing moon, the sun was hot in a peaceful sky.

Helen and Joanna lounged in garden chairs on Tony's graciously sculpted lawn, admiring the colourful flower-beds and luxuriating in the glorious warmth. The decadent singing of the birds and the occasional splash of a greedy goldfish in the pond completed the idyll.

But Helen felt restless. Even Tony's housekeeper, Bridget, appearing with a tray of coffee, home-baked biscuits and a motherly smile did little to soothe her.

'I'd really like to collect some things from home and check that the house is all right,' she confided to her daughter.

Joanna was deep in a book. 'Mmm,' she responded unhelpfully.

Helen tried another tack. 'You could do with some more clothes now that the weather's better.'

At last Joanna looked up with a grin. 'Mum. Do I hear you say you've got a touch of homesickness and you want me to come with you?'

'Well, yes, I suppose so,' responded her mother.

'Then make your statements clearly,' admonished her daughter with mock severity. 'How long will it take?'

'Maximum of two hours each way. Plus a couple of hours to collect some things. I'd like to pop in and see Miranda and I'd better check on Auntie Peggy.'

'So we'd be back here by six o'clock. No one to stop us and no one would even know we'd gone!' added Joanna mischievously.

'We'd better leave a note for Tony all the same,' responded her mother, jumping up. 'I feel better already. I'm sure it'll be safe. They can't be watching for us all the time.'

'Of course they can't. They obviously lost our trail ages ago,' replied Joanna. 'There hasn't been a squeak from them since we left the holiday house.'

They thanked Bridget for the delicious biscuits. When they teased her that she would be entirely responsible if they put on weight, she was delighted. It suited her to look after people who appreciated being spoilt. But when they told her they were going out, she looked anxious.

'Tony said not to go anywhere,' she reminded them.

'It's okay,' laughed Joanna airily. 'Mum and I are just popping home for some things. We won't be long.'

Helen wrote a note for Tony. 'Please can you give this to him when he gets in if we're not back,' she asked, handing it to a reluctant Bridget.

They jumped into the car feeling rather like naughty girls playing truant from school. They would have been mortified to know that Bridget phoned Tony the moment they left and told him where they had gone.

*   *   *

Feeling almost carefree, they bowled along with all the windows open, enjoying the balmy wind on their faces. Yellow cowslips waved on the grassy banks. Lambs frolicked round staid fat sheep in the fields. Busy birds flapped around with twigs in their beaks. A fox trotted along the roadside in broad daylight, ignoring a farm dog barking behind a gate. In the delight of their freedom, everything seemed happy.

Turning into Helen's cul-de-sac they were pleased to see the pretty house smiling a welcome. There were no sinister strangers lurking in the road. All was well. Each of them heaved a secret sigh of relief and hurried into the house to collect some new clothes, a little summer perfume, a couple of books they wanted to read. Mostly just to feel that home was still there.

Helen listened to the messages on the answerphone and picked up the post. They were in the house for less than half an hour. Then they jumped laughing into the car and popped round to visit Helen's old friend Miranda.

'I thought you were due back from India ages ago,' she exclaimed, hugging them both. 'I've been wondering what happened to you. How was it?'

They brought an overwhelmed and incredibly shocked Miranda up to date with the story of the Scroll. 'My God, it's unbelievable,' she screeched in disbelief, holding her head in her hands. 'Are you in danger?'

'We think they've lost track of us,' answered Joanna. The conversation had made her nervous.

'Anyway the work is more important than the danger,'

said Helen, reverting to her tendency to distance herself from feelings.

'I must give you one of my crystals,' Miranda leapt up suddenly. 'I've had it for ages. I bought it when I went to Mount Shasta in California. Now, there's the most incredible power point! It was quite amazing! Perhaps you can put it on a ley line somewhere to help clear it.'

She flew out of the room and, returning with a quartz crystal, handed it to Helen. 'I know you'll sense where it should be placed,' she said.

Helen took it from her friend. 'I'll do my best,' she promised. 'I'll let you know where I put it.' She wrapped it in a tissue and placed it carefully in her bag.

They left regretfully after forty-five minutes, to visit Auntie Peggy. They hoped she was having a good day and could hear what they said. Bad days were deaf days.

They talked with Auntie Peggy about the weather and the family for some time before the old lady proffered disturbing news. 'There has been a strange car parked down the road all week. Mary next door and Mr Douglas opposite have been keeping an eye on it. Foreign men in it, just sitting there.'

Helen and Joanna went cold and jumped up immediately. 'Sorry Auntie Peggy. We've got to dash.' Without even rudimentary politeness, they left and ran to the car.

No chance. No coincidence. There was a cat by the vehicle. As Joanna bent down to shoo it away she saw a box and wires sticking out from under the car.

'Mum, don't get in,' she shouted as Helen was pressing the knob for the central locking. In a violent reflex action, Joanna threw herself at her mother and sent them both flying across the road. At that instant the car exploded.

The noise was horrendous. Glass flew and they were enveloped in black smoke and hot flames. They lay shocked and stunned as people started running from houses. Kind hands pulled them away from danger. Both of them were bruised and slightly cut, but otherwise unhurt. Helen glimpsed Auntie Peggy's shocked face peering out of her sitting-room window. Already mobile phones were sprouting in people's hands so they knew the police would be there in a moment.

A soothing voice said, 'There, there, an ambulance will be here in a minute.'

'I don't need an ambulance,' argued Joanna.

'Nor do I,' whispered Helen feeling dreadful. She had put them in danger. 'I'm OK.' She could feel the heat of the flames on her face.

'Me, too,' declared Joanna, unaware of her bleeding arm.

The only thing they could think of was to get away before the police arrived. Suddenly a dark blue BMW was pulling up beside them and Tony, stern-faced, called out urgently, 'Are you all right?'

They nodded.

'Then get in.'

To the amazement of voyeurs and helpers alike, both women moved towards the car. A teenager leaning against a wall watched with his mouth open. The black smoke blown by an eddy of wind swirled round them for an instant.

'Hey, stop!' called someone.

'Where do you think you're going?'

'Come back!'

The calls echoed in their ears and they ignored them as they scrambled into the car, which accelerated away.

'How did you know we were here?' Joanna demanded of Tony.

'My housekeeper phoned after you left – luckily, as it has transpired. I dropped everything and drove to your house. A neighbour said you'd gone already and gave me directions to your aunt's house.' His voice was steely cold.

As they roared along the road they could hear police sirens screaming, a note which filled them with terror. Helen told them that the vibration chosen for the police siren in England was the sound that gave rise to the greatest fear in humans. 'It's the alarm call of the universe and it's just another way of spreading fear and chaos.' Her conversational tone disguised her state of shock.

Two police cars raced by in the opposite direction, blue lights flashing and sirens wailing, heading for the burnt out car. Close behind followed a fire engine.

Helen was now feeling sick and faint. 'Why?' she kept repeating and shaking her head. 'Why? They could have killed us.'

'That presumably was the intention,' Tony retorted.

Joanna's shock took the form of anger and she

harangued them from the back seat. 'We shouldn't have run away. Go back and let's tell them about the men.'

No one responded.

'I'm sorry. It's all my fault,' moaned Helen.

'How dare they do that to your car, Mum. You had all your best tapes in it.' Joanna was illogical with shock.

Tony tried to soothe her, but it only made things worse. He realised anger was her coping mechanism, but he did not know how to handle it, so he ignored her.

'How did they find us?' Helen whispered.

'Surveillance on your house,' Tony snapped. 'I guess they didn't have an opportunity to put the bomb under the car there. Too many eyes in a cul-de-sac. Same at your friend's house, I presume, so they waited for you to go somewhere else.'

'What if we hadn't gone to Auntie Peggy's?'

'They would have followed you until there was another opportunity,' said Tony chillingly.

'They're probably following us already.' Joanna's voice had risen an octave.

Tony thought for a moment, decided that it was a remote possibility and did a sudden U-turn in the road. A lifelong, cautious, safe and law-abiding driver, he now executed a series of dangerous and daring moves that he did not know he had in him.

His driving put Helen deeper into shock. He glanced at her and saw with concern how white and shaky she looked. It inflamed Joanna's anger, so she started to scream at him to drive properly. It also shook him to the core.

For the first time he felt personally touched by the

danger and had an inkling of what Helen, Joanna and Marcus had been experiencing.

Tony drove as fast as possible to Kumeka House, which he felt was the safest place. He tried to remain as cool and detached as he could, while Joanna told Marcus and the horrified residents what had happened.

Marcus' face turned grey, his eyes becoming darker and shadowed. He put his arm round Joanna to comfort her. 'You poor thing. It must have been awful.' Her anger evaporated and she crumpled, allowing herself to be comforted.

One of the residents brought them sweet tea and said, 'You're safe. That's what's important.'

'I know,' Helen tried to smile. 'It's not just the car. It's the thought they so nearly caught us.'

He nodded. 'But they didn't. You were being protected.'

Joanna, calmer now, apologised to Tony, 'Sorry I was so awful in the car. Thank you for being there.'

'That's okay.' Tony accepted her apology and patted her shoulder in what he hoped was an avuncular manner. He was somewhat nervous of the angry Joanna.

'You did the anger for both of us,' said Helen.

'And you did the fear for both of us,' responded Joanna, and they both giggled.

Giggling is an infectious virus. Everyone smiled despite the pall of danger lurking over them – except Tony.

'The police will soon trace my car,' he frowned. 'They'll probably be at my house before me. And if they can trace it, so can the others. You three,' he looked at Marcus, Helen and Joanna, 'have got to get out of here.'

Tension gripped them all again. 'What about the work at Stonehenge? I can't run away from that,' Marcus protested. 'And the Scroll.'

'Helen and Joanna have put all your lives in danger,' Tony blazed back. 'If you are dead you can't spread the information of the Scroll.'

Marcus shivered and the faces in the room seemed like a pale blur. He did not even notice Zoranda's approach.

Tony continued, sounding very cool and in control, 'My sister in California will look after you. I'll phone her now. Marcus, go and pack something quickly.' He turned to Helen and Joanna. 'I'll phone my housekeeper and ask her to pack your passports and some clothes. And I'll get you on the first possible flight to San Francisco.'

'But . . .' Joanna opened her mouth to argue.

Zoranda spoke in his quiet, authoritative voice. 'The most important thing is to clear the energy lines on the planet and free the portals for the light. It seems the three of you are instruments for this work. Your safety is paramount.'

'But . . .' Joanna tried again to interrupt.

He held up a hand to silence her and continued firmly, but with compassion in his eyes. 'We at Kumeka House will focus on the work of freeing Stonehenge. I am sure Tony will pass on the information as it is deciphered. Go to America and stay safe.'

'I'm really sorry,' Helen repeated again, feeling like a bad child. 'It was my fault. I didn't mean this to happen.'

'No, of course you didn't,' Zoranda agreed gently.

Tony was on the phone. They could hear him efficiently organising his sister, the tickets and his housekeeper. 'The police have been to my house already. They want me to contact them immediately. Bridget will take your passports and some clothes to her sister's house. We can pick the cases up from there.'

'I'm sorry,' whispered Helen again. She was beginning to feel it was the only phrase in her repertoire.

Chapter 23

John, one of the younger residents, with whom Marcus had formed a special bond, drove them to the airport in the minibus in case the police or those who had planted the bomb were watching for Tony's car. But it slowed them down and time was tight. Tony had insisted on coming, too. He was still tight-lipped and angry. The women were subdued, and Marcus bemused and irritable.

They quickly collected the passports and bags from Bridget's sister. No time for pleasantries. Just perfunctory thanks.

'My sister's name is Boa,' Tony informed them. 'She's completely different from me in every way, looks, character, everything. She'll meet you at the airport and you won't miss her. She'll be flamboyantly dressed with ash blonde hair. And she's a big lady.'

He gave them a piece of paper with her name and address written on it. 'She'll take you to her condo in San Francisco and keep you safe, I hope.'

'It's very kind of you both,' Helen murmured and the others added their thanks.

They lapsed into fractured silence until Marcus asked yet again, 'Why do you really think they blew the car up?'

'It was a warning to frighten us from continuing,' Joanna responded shrilly. It was what she wanted to believe.

'No way. If you hadn't bent down to shoo away the cat, the car would have exploded as you were getting into it. They wanted you out of the way,' Marcus butted in.

'Why? I can't understand why? It wouldn't give them the Scroll.' Joanna was hotly defensive.

'Either they think you've hidden it, so with you dead they could find it at their leisure, or they're aiming to kill everyone involved just to stop the information being revealed,' Marcus erupted, angry with fear.

'More likely, if they killed or injured you two, it would flush everyone else out. Then they would know where the Scroll was again,' Tony suggested dryly. 'They must realise we have a microfilm or believe you saved enough of the Scroll to be a threat.'

John, the driver, said with the quiet equanimity they so admired, 'It does feel as if the universe has protected you so far. I am sure that will continue to happen. Our task is to remain vigilant and careful so that the Beings of Light can help us more easily.'

His calmness restored them. Marcus regretted his outburst immediately. 'I'm just shit scared,' he admitted.

Joanna shivered. 'We all are.'

'I just wish we knew who they were. Is it just the Chinese who know about the Scroll?'

'Maybe only the Chinese know about it right now, but it's the forces of darkness that are trying to stop it.' Helen's sober tone mitigated the drama of her statement.

'What do you mean?'

'The darkness is made up of all those with vested interests in the subjugation of the planet. I presume that they've all banded together on the astral planes to try to stop the influence of the Scroll for freedom. Later each one will fight to be top dog.'

'The astral planes?' queried Tony.

'Yes, the astral planes are where lower entities gather when they are out of their bodies.'

'You mean ghosts.'

'Those, too. But I was thinking of people who are alive. It's where their spirits go when they are asleep. It's where clouds of dark emotions linger. Then evil people like Sturov can manipulate that negative energy and use it for their own ends.'

'Heavy!' Marcus looked to John to refute this fanciful rubbish, but he was nodding affirmation. It stopped Marcus for a full two minutes. Then he said, 'You mean it doesn't matter who is after the Scroll because they will all work together at another level to stop us spreading the information?'

Helen and John nodded.

'Who is this Sturov, I wonder?' said Marcus.

'On earth he seems to be a benign philanthropist. In the inner planes his heart is black. He's very powerful,' warned John. 'We have to remember that light is always stronger than darkness.'

They were crawling now in traffic on the M25. It was the last straw for Tony, who felt personally responsible for getting them to safety. 'You're going to miss the flight. Can't this vehicle go any faster?'

'Not in a traffic jam,' pointed out John so steadily that Joanna had to stifle a giggle. Tony frowned and drummed his fingers on his knee. Even when the traffic flowed again he was strained and watchful.

They reached Heathrow at last. Then they were running with their bags through the corridors to the desk, where their tickets were waiting. 'Be quick. They're closing the check-in,' the girl warned as Marcus picked them up.

Meanwhile, Tony was trying to persuade the woman on the check-in desk to keep it open. She was shaking her head at his bluster. 'You're too late. The flight's boarding.'

Marcus joined him, waving their tickets and smiling persuasively with his grey eyes. 'We've only got hand luggage. We'll be really quick.' She melted immediately. 'Oh, okay, then, as you've no luggage to check in but no stopping at duty free. Go straight through.'

'We promise,' they chorused in relief.

As she quickly and expertly processed their tickets Marcus remembered a story his mother used to tell him about the relative strength of the wind and the sun. The wind boasted that it was more powerful than the sun. It could take roofs off, uproot trees and cause tidal waves. It challenged the sun to a competition. The sun just smiled. Enraged, the wind pointed to an old man shuffling along in an overcoat. He bet that he could get it off his back.

The harder and colder the wind blew, the more it shrieked at the old man, the more tightly the man clutched his coat round him. At last the wind gave up and handed over crossly to the sun. The sun appeared and shone warmly and lovingly on to the old man. Very soon he took off his coat.

Marcus never forgot that story. It had served him well to remember that anger increases people's defences, while kindness and love melt them.

He thought about Tony. It's strange how people think they can make someone change their mind by force, when it's an illusion. Love is always stronger than aggression. Then he laughed. There was another one. He must remember to tell Joanna.

As they said goodbye, Helen was sad to see Tony look so grim and uncompromising. She didn't know how to change that. But the incorrigible Joanna simply slapped him on the back with a grin.

'That's what happens if you will let women into your life. Nothing but trouble, eh?'

He smiled despite himself. 'Sorry. I'm really concerned for your safety.'

'I know. We'll swan around America and you do the worrying for us here,' Joanna's grin was even broader.

'You're impossible,' Tony chuckled. His defences gave way.

He and John watched them through the departure gate until they were out of sight. Tony was still smiling. For the first time since the explosion he started to unwind.

The two men walked slowly back towards the escalator. 'Just a moment,' Tony grabbed John's arm. He was staring at the desk where they had checked in moments ago. The attendant had now closed it. Three men were arguing with her. One was Chinese, a second Indian and the third White. Two of them were trying to get on to the flight but she was adamant it was too late.

Tony went cold all over. It just had to be *them*. He and John watched the trio retire into a quiet space and make several phone calls on a mobile. Then they went to another airline and appeared to be buying two tickets for a flight to San Francisco, which left in three hours' time.

'Oh my God,' whispered Tony. 'What have I done?'

'How do they know?' added John, pale-faced. 'And who are they?'

Chapter 24

Exhausted and oblivious to the new danger, Marcus, Joanna and Helen stumbled through customs in San Francisco looking for a big, blonde, outrageously dressed woman and they saw her immediately.

Tony's sister Boa wore purple – a purple, flowing kaftan, purple scrunchie in her blonde hair, which was extravagantly tied up on top of her head, purple dangling earrings, purple nail varnish and, to finish the effect, matching purple spectacle frames.

'Hello!' she greeted them effusively with hugs, enveloping them in a cloud of musk perfume.

'Let me take that.' She grabbed their trolley and pushed it energetically towards the lift.

'Did you have a good flight? I always travel Virgin myself. I just love Richard Branson, don't you? I met him on a flight once. He came round and shook hands with all the passengers. What a lovely man.'

She rattled on and strode so fast that only Marcus could keep up without trotting. She flung the cases into the enormous trunk of her automobile and talked all the way out of the car park.

It was only when they were floating along the highway, as only an American vehicle can, that she changed tune. Her voice dropped an octave and she was deadly serious.

'I had a phone call from Tony. A certain two men tried to buy tickets for your plane but it was too late. Their flight arrives in three hours.'

They gasped in horror. The feeling of relief, which was beginning to seep through them, disappeared abruptly.

'It's all right, cherubs. Tony told me not to take you back to my house. It seems these guys, whoever they are, have their antennae everywhere. We'll cruise along to a hotel where they'll never find us.' Boa patted Helen's hand reassuringly.

'Now Tony's told me the most extraordinary story I've ever heard. I want you to tell me the whole thing again.'

They talked non-stop for the next three hours about the Scroll. Boa was alternately excited and enraged. She punctuated the story with exclamations of excitement and horror. As the events unfolded she became more and more silent, listening and asking only for occasional clarification. This, they soon learned, was quite unlike her, for her usual pattern was to talk non-stop.

Helen glanced sideways and saw that under the pale skin of Boa's soft flabby jaw was a streak of steely determination reminiscent of her brother.

By this time they were off the motorway and driving through small towns and villages. Boa pulled up at a roadside inn.

'I could do with a pee and something to eat.' She yawned and rubbed her thighs as she hobbled out of the driving seat. 'My goodness, it doesn't do my sciatica any good sitting in that car.'

Moments later her eyes lit up as she pointed to some dresses hanging on a rail outside the hotel shop. 'Oh what lovely dresses. I must try them on.'

Need for tea and pee forgotten, she charged up to the rail, extravagantly pulling off outfits.

'Oh, I love this,' she cried jubilantly, as she held a black, strapless dress against her white skin. 'It would look divine with my jet necklace.' Nano seconds later she was in the changing room. When she emerged wearing it, she held the breathless attention of the entire shop, for it was evidently held up by hope. Unabashed, she rifled through the jewellery display until she found an enormous pair of black earrings. She put them on. 'I could wear this at my little dinner parties. I do love dinner parties, don't you?' she enthused at Helen, who wondered how Boa could think about clothes at a time like this.

The question was in any case rhetorical. Helen had already learned that Boa rarely required a reply.

'No, I don't think so.' Boa retired to cast the dress off and tried on a ludicrously expensive bead-encrusted skirt and top. To wear with it she picked out a gargantuan watermelon tourmaline ring, somewhere between vulgarly gross and tantalisingly gorgeous. After much parading, she bought neither, but acquired a pair of enormous amber earrings.

'My dear, I was so tempted, weren't you? I just love shopping.' She put her arm through Helen's as they tripped into the dining room where Joanna and Marcus were already at a table looking at a menu.

'We might as well make this into a holiday,' Boa announced expansively. 'I'd be so happy to show you the coast route. It's the most wonderful scenery. It gets me right here.' She touched her heart extravagantly. 'Is there anywhere you want to go?'

'Where's Mount Shasta from here?' asked Helen, whose geography was hazy.

'Oh, we can head in that direction, no problem,' Boa replied airily.

'Great,' Helen responded delightedly. 'We can plant the crystal to start clearing the ley line.'

Boa's eyes glazed over. She really couldn't handle ley lines and portals. Her consciousness was with clothes, food, beautiful scenery and, at a stretch, music.

'We can stay here tonight, if you like. The sound of that darling little stream is dreamy and there's a swimming pool. You all look so tired. I can park the car behind the cabins and no one will find us.'

As they looked at each other they individually thought, *America's enormous*. Surely no one would trace them.

'Fine,' Marcus agreed for all of them.

'Good, that's settled,' declared Boa and got down to the serious business of contemplating the menu. She glowed with bonhomie; danger clearly the last thing on her mind.

Marcus watched her across the table. Her hair was ash blonde, and her skin white as alabaster. Her soft jaw and myopic grey eyes made her appear slightly bewildered and even childlike, while her fat arms looked even paler against the dark purple of her dress.

'Tony said you guys were vegetarian,' she said to Helen and Joanna. 'Me, too.' She ordered prawn cocktail with chicken in thick white wine sauce to follow. It transpired she was the sort of vegetarian who adored chicken and fish and was quite indignant when Joanna suggested they were animals. She attacked her meal with relish. All seemed well in her world.

Chapter 25

Later that evening, Marcus, Helen, Joanna and Boa relaxed in the hotel lounge. Boa was luxuriating in the thick cream on top of her coffee. 'It's orgasmic but I'll pay for it later,' she sighed. Suddenly she gasped.

'Oh my goodness. I quite forgot. This came from my brother this morning before you arrived. It's a fax for you. I just grabbed it and ran to get you from the airport.'

She fished energetically in her capacious hold-all and produced a somewhat crumpled, chocolate-stained fax. 'Tony said on the phone that he was sending you two more Great Mysteries. I guess that's what it is?'

'What?' Marcus shouted eagerly, almost grabbing it from her.

'Already?' exclaimed Helen.

'Brill!' Joanna jumped up and looked over Marcus shoulder. 'Read it aloud,' she urged.

Marcus was scanning the fax quickly. 'They've got another symbol,' he announced, his voice loud with delight. 'And . . . oh, great news. They've found the sound keys . . . and, listen to this: "The great secret of materialisation and de-materialisation was ours in Atlantis. Given to us by angels of God for use in the healing, comfort and development of humankind. This sacred information is only to be used for the highest good under the Grace of God and to His glory.

' "We add a warning. Those who used this esoteric information in Atlantis for personal glory and power caused its destruction. They must pay through many lifetimes of suffering and service until their desire once more to serve the Light will give them another opportunity to be tried and tested. Only then will they be allowed access to this information again.

' "Many from Atlantean times, who have not learnt their lessons, will be reincarnating before the Golden Age. You will know them because they put science and technology before spirituality. They will try to repeat the old experiments and use them for their own aggrandisement and control of all on Earth." '

Marcus glanced at Helen who was listening intently. 'I think they mean cloning and experimenting on animals, and transplanting animal organs into humans,' she said. 'Genetically modified food, too. That's all Atlantean darkness.'

'And the hydrogen bomb, and sending things into space, and germ warfare,' added Joanna.

'What about breeding viruses like AIDS to harm people and control the population?' added Marcus.

They looked at one another. 'I'm sure there's lots more.'

'No wonder it warns again and again not to let the Scroll get into the wrong hands or the results could be catastrophic.'

'Don't let's energise the negative any more,' cautioned Helen.

They nodded and Joanna asked, 'Is there anything about the sounds?'

Marcus studied the fax. 'It says there are combinations of notes played or sung at certain pitches which produce the right vibration to free atoms, but this has to be done in conjunction with the symbols and the power-of-thought control.'

He looked up, his eyes glowing with excitement. 'When I was staying at Kumeka House, Zoranda told me that they are now able to concentrate on moving matter in the same way they did when Stonehenge was built.'

'Wow!' said Joanna.

'Wow!' echoed Boa.

'What does it say about the Great Mysteries?'

Marcus read: '"The Great Mysteries are the sacred energies, which operate on earth. These Mysteries are sacrosanct, put into place by the Creator Himself. They cannot be contravened, not even by God. They are absolute. To understand them you must understand the nature of energy. Everything is energy."'

'They said that before,' interrupted Joanna impatiently.

'Shh!' frowned her mother, and Joanna responded, 'Oops, sorry!' and grinned unabashed.

Marcus barely paused at the interruption. '"A human is energy, so is gas or a tree or a bird. All are made up of atoms, some close together so they seem to our eyes to be dense. Others with more space in between so they seem liquid or gas."'

'I see. So they lighten heavy matter such as a stone by creating the sounds which loosen up the atoms. Then they can move it. Is that what happens?' Helen asked.

'That seems to be it,' Marcus replied.

'It makes sense,' agreed Joanna.

'Let me go on: "In the primordial soup, all is moving. Nothing moves haphazardly but all according to the laws of the Great Mysteries.

'"Every thought, emotion or word is magnetic. It either attracts or repels. Thoughts and actions of beauty, joy, love, hope" – there's a whole list of them – "are light and carry a magnetic attracting charge. They draw to them similar energies.

'"Thoughts and actions of lust, greed, anger, destruction, neediness" – again, a whole list – "are heavy and carry a repellent charge. Like attracts like.

'"Within the atmosphere of Earth humans inevitably draw to themselves like energy. This is a unique learning technique designed by the Creator for maximum growth. All is a mirror of Self. To deny is to crack the mirror and repudiate the Great Mystery."'

Marcus paused. 'It goes on to the fifth Great Mystery. Shall I read on?'

'Just a moment,' came from Boa, whose thinking was still in the haphazard universe stage.

'Can you explain that in words I can understand, please?'

Helen replied, 'Like attracts like. Take emotional honesty. If you send out seventy per cent honesty and thirty per cent dishonesty, you will draw circumstances and people into your life to reflect that exact percentage. For instance, if you tell someone you are happy with your relationship when you aren't, that's emotional dishonesty.'

'What if you don't realise you are doing it?'

'That's what the Scroll teaches. Even if you are unconscious of what you are feeling or doing, the exact dishonesty comes into your life as a mirror for you to look into.'

Boa still looked puzzled.

Joanna tried to help. 'Let me give you an example. If you are always trying to please people by being nice and trying to placate them, but underneath you feel resentful and unloved, you will draw into your life people who don't appreciate you. They reflect your frustration back to you.'

'I think I see,' nodded Boa. 'I recognise that one. But how come you guys know this anyway?'

'The Scroll seems to be confirming many awarenesses that have already surfaced,' Helen told her. 'I guess it's wanting to spread the knowledge more widely.'

'I really want to get this principle,' said Marcus. 'Is this right? If someone was really charming to your face but stabbed you behind your back, they would in turn find that people were stabbing them in the back?'

'Exactly right,' nodded Helen.

'And I guess sometimes it is buried so deeply we have no idea we're doing it?'

'Absolutely. And we learn patterns from childhood which cause problems in our lives, so we magnetise situations into our lives again and again until we learn.'

'You mean like my husbands, who all seemed so different when I first knew them but all turned out to be womanisers and weak as water?' Boa demanded.

They all laughed at her expression of disgust.

'You've got it! said Marcus and added firmly, 'Let's look at the fifth Great Mystery now.'

'Yes,' chorused Joanna and Helen.

Marcus cleared his throat and read, ' "The fifth Great Mystery is that energy constantly flows. In the primordial soup there are no vacuums. If the flow stops, something from another direction comes in to take its place. If the flow goes in circles or gets blocked, there is stagnation." ' Marcus paused and looked to Helen for explanation.

'When our thoughts go round in circles we stay stuck in our lives,' Joanna chipped in. 'Some people hoard money and things.'

Her mother nodded. 'And others hang on to dead relationships or boring jobs. It prevents the new from flowing in.'

'The Scroll says if the flow stops, something from another direction comes in to take its place. So if we let go, is there a guarantee that something else will come in?' Joanna questioned.

'If you let it in, I suppose,' commented Helen. 'If you block the flow with a negative belief, the new can't get to you.'

Boa made a big face. 'Well, I've had four husbands. No one could accuse me of holding on. They slipped away as fast as ever they could and another one just arrived. Sounds like I was flowing with husbands.'

They laughed.

Chapter 26

Later that morning Joanna and Helen strolled down to the pool, earnestly discussing the Scroll. Boa trailed behind in a leopard-skin bathing costume, with matching sarong draped over her arm, elegant high-heeled sandals, black bag, hat and outrageous sunglasses. She seemed to have come prepared for all eventualities.

When he saw them, Marcus leapt out of the pool, desperate to talk more about the Great Mysteries. But Boa was holding forth on the subject of her bowels, one of her favourite and most absorbing interests. Nothing appeared to be too trivial or too private to share.

'I've never heard Tony talk about his bowels,' whispered Joanna to Helen.

'He did say he and his sister were different,' she murmured back, and they tried not to laugh.

Boa, either oblivious to their impatience, or ignoring it, continued her soliloquy unabated for five minutes.

As soon as she paused for breath, Marcus mused aloud, 'I wonder how long it will take them to master the powers of the Scroll?'

Boa drawled in her English accent overlaid with Californian, 'Whoever would have thought this little planet was governed by Great Mysteries. I always wondered how things worked but could never make rhyme nor reason of life, so I figured I might just as well enjoy it.'

'But you were never unkind or cruel, were you?' Helen asked, seriously. 'So you must be some way up the spiritual ladder.'

'Mind you,' Boa continued as if she had not spoken, 'I think I can say I've enjoyed my body to the full and not just food.' She winked, and they were forced to laugh with her.

'So,' Marcus addressed Helen. 'I don't really understand how this magnetic attraction works. There are lots of people I meet who are very different from me. And,' he added darkly remembering the betrayal, 'why should I attract in someone like my ex-girlfriend?'

'What I think the Scroll means is this,' replied Helen. 'We humans are like computers and all of our experiences, beliefs etc. are programmed into us. Whatever we put out has to be based on the programmes. If there's bad programming – for instance, low self-worth – we act that out. If our programming is good, like a belief in our ability, we do well. Am I making sense?'

'Yes, I understand that, but how do we attract good and bad to those programmes?' asked Marcus.

'Well, say my programme or belief is "It's not safe to trust men", then my computer will link into everyone else's computer to find a man who is capable of betraying my trust. When I do, we'll have an attraction.'

'Whooa! That sounds nasty,' grimaced Boa.

'It works the other way, too. All the good beliefs or energies link into other people and attract positive things or people to them.'

'I guess you were talking about me,' said Marcus wryly. 'But I did trust women, I think.'

'The Scroll says that everything is the result of energy and that it is exact,' put in Joanna. 'So maybe unconsciously you didn't really trust women and what happened to you gives you the opportunity to look at your underlying belief and heal it.'

'Right,' said Marcus, looking somewhat put out. 'Thanks for the sympathy!'

'We're talking about the spiritual levels,' smiled Helen. 'Of course, on the emotional levels we sympathise. We've all gone through lots of stuff to give us chances to learn and grow spiritually.'

'Mmm, so if I'm ninety-nine per cent honest and one per cent dishonest, at the lower levels it won't matter, but as I evolve I'll attract more dishonest people to me to help me look in the mirror of self.'

'Yes. You could say they were a gift to help you learn!'

'Thanks.'

'So why did the car get blown up?'

Helen thought for a while. 'Maybe we were both sending out such an energy of anger and fear that we attracted that explosion.'

'You know, Mum, I think it was more than that. I think it was the result of a collective energy of anger and fear. The people in India, everyone involved with the Scroll, possibly even those in Tibet who were terrorised by the Chinese. Maybe all that energy came together and allowed the explosion to take place.'

'I think you could be right,' her mother replied

thoughtfully. 'All we know is that energy is exact. Who knows what happened in other lives? That energy may still be active, too.'

'Complicated,' sighed Boa, getting bored. 'Well, guys, I must wear my new gold visor in the swimming pool.' She rose and stepped regally into the water, swimming a slow and stately breast stroke without getting a single hair on her head wet.

'The Scroll says the universe is like a huge great computer,' continued Helen. 'It can keep track and records of everything and arranges our life's experiences according to the energy we send out and our pre-life contracts.'

'Amazing,' said Marcus. 'It makes sense when you think of the universe as a computer. When I was a child I thought there was a little old man on a cloud dispensing judgement.' They laughed.

'It's awesome,' agreed Joanna. 'To think every single thing is so exact. Don't forget the Scroll said that things multiply and intensify as we grow spiritually.'

'That reminds me,' Marcus said, 'all that about flow? Does it mean I can't have any savings?'

Helen laughed. 'At the highest levels it's true you wouldn't need savings because if you flowed properly whatever you needed would be instantly provided. You'd treat the universe as your abundant bank account. But that presumes a very high level of trust.

'Even Joseph of Egypt stored grain for the seven lean years because he knew they were coming. However it does mean that if you have too much for your needs, don't hang on to it. Pass it on.'

'It's what Feng Shui says,' Joanna chimed in. 'Clear the clutter and don't hoard what you don't need. That frees the energy to flow. Basically it allows new and better to come in.'

Helen added, 'It's the same if you hold on to old anger. The emotion blocks your physical body and makes you ill. It stops you enjoying life. The minute you let go of the anger, you feel better and your life improves because the stuck energy has moved so something new can flow in.'

'As I see it, the Scroll basically says we can all be abundant because we receive a direct flow from God. The only thing that stops us getting it all, I mean love, money, success or whatever, is if we block it.'

They considered this in silence.

The next morning, Marcus emerged from his room early and sat with his feet in the icy stream, enjoying the peace and gentle morning sunshine.

Boa soon joined him, looking bright-eyed and bushy-tailed. She plonked herself beside him and sniffed the air, declaring, 'Oh, I do love the silence.' She then proceeded to shred it ceaselessly for the next twenty minutes, until Helen and Joanna joined them.

They looked weary. Boa hailed them with, 'Hey guys, what is it with you? You both look pooped. I hope my snoring didn't keep you awake.'

'It did, as a matter of fact,' replied Helen frostily, while Joanna was more crossly forthright.

Boa felt mortified. She blamed it on the wheat and dairy products she'd eaten the day before.

'Today will be a fruit day,' she announced and Helen quickly pointed out a beautiful bird to deflect her from the conversation about Boa's bowels that she sensed was impending.

There was just time after breakfast for Boa to pop into the shop and emerge with a magnificent topaz ring. 'I do need my shopping therapy,' she told them happily, as she squeezed behind the steering wheel. She had made it very clear that she loved to drive and hated anyone else to drive her.

'Control freak,' Joanna whispered to her mother, raising her eyebrows.

'Shh!' responded Helen, nodding in laughing agreement.

Helen, Joanna and Marcus had only two things on their minds – the Scroll and their immediate danger. Boa, however, had quite a different agenda. She chattered inconsequentially as she drove, frustrating their desire to discuss the Scroll. At first they tried politely to listen and respond to her conversation. It was like watching someone playing tennis against a wall. No partner needed. Evidently Boa did not need anyone to bat the subject back to her. She managed perfectly well on her own.

Eventually they each switched her off in their heads and looked out of the window. Like many non-stop talkers, she was accustomed to this and barely noticed it. Two of her husbands had gone deaf in one ear as a defence against the sound of her voice.

The coastline was fabulously beautiful, the twinkling azure sea framed with glorious glossy green trees and flowers of every conceivable shade and hue.

Somehow Boa contrived to stop in a town, ostensibly for lunch, but in reality for more retail therapy. Infuriatingly, she disappeared into a shop where she spent ages trying on more dresses.

'It's enough to try the patience of a saint,' fumed Joanna. Her mother was less outspoken, but equally irritated. Marcus found a bookshop where he could browse, but Joanna felt too uptight to join him.

'I need to be chilled out to read,' she told him restlessly. 'I'm just tired out after last night and I simply can't cope with that woman's endless talking. I'll be okay when we reach Mount Shasta. I just wish she'd hurry up, for God's sake.'

But Boa was intent on making it a holiday for them. In her own way she thought she was giving them a wonderful opportunity to see California. And she was. But she never troubled to sense that it was not appropriate at that time.

She drove them down a track to a little bay and was gratified by their exclamations of pleasure at its exquisite beauty. Beaming, she announced in true American fashion that her greatest delight was to please others.

The moment they left the main road, they relaxed as if by consent. None of them realised how vulnerable they had felt on the highway. Surely no one would think of looking for them on this little detour.

For the first time Marcus noticed the azure sky and round golden sun, as clear and uncomplicated as a child's painting. They jumped out of the car to feed the perky little chipmunks, which danced everywhere on the rocks. They threw bread to the gulls and marvelled as they swooped effortlessly and accurately to catch it. They paddled in the white-fringed sea and scrambled on rocks.

Joanna unwound so much that she became her old laughing, teasing self. A burden was lifted from them all.

That evening, they found a tiny hotel off the beaten track where they all slept like logs, undisturbed by Boa's snoring, for she was able to book a single room.

They woke refreshed. So much so that they chuckled as they heard Boa approaching the breakfast room, exclaiming, 'The fashion police will arrest me. My greens don't match.' And when she appeared looking rather like an overgrown caterpillar in green shorts, top and sandals, with green earrings and green framed glasses, they laughed and she laughed with them.

Chapter 27

A shock awaited them that afternoon. While Boa popped into a shop, which sold 'simply divine glassware', the others waited for her in a charming little flower-bedecked café. They were soon chatting with a young couple on the next table, who could not wait to tell them that they had a cousin living in England.

The girl did all the talking. She soon informed them that her partner was a new man. 'He does all the dishes,' she told them proudly.

'I thought everyone here had dishwashers,' Joanna whispered to her mother. Helen pretended not to hear.

The girl told them they were camping because they wanted to be near the earth. 'Freddie loves the mountains. He even cried when I suggested coming into town.' She eyed her partner fondly.

Her young man nodded his beautiful long blond curls happily, tears filling his gentle blue eyes. 'The mountains really get to me,' he said, patting his heart.

'Mmm,' said Marcus.

'We're on our way to Mount Shasta,' put in Joanna.

'Mount Shasta!' they squealed in unison. 'You'll just love it. It's so powerful there.'

'I find it hard to stay grounded there. The energy's so high,' confided Freddie.

'You're too sensitive,' said his partner loyally.

At that instant Boa entered the café in her usual flamboyant way. 'Hello, there you are! You must see the most divinely gorgeous little glasses I've bought. Oh, I could murder a hot chocolate with whipped cream.'

As she sat down, parcels erupted from her arms, scattering around her. Marcus and the new man picked them up like true gentlemen. The girl was gazing, bright-eyed, at Boa.

'Hey, I know you,' she said with an air of certainty. 'I've seen you somewhere before.'

Boa eyed her. 'I don't think so.'

'I know your face,' the girl was persistent. Her partner looked up at Boa.

'Yes. It was the photo the man dropped . . .'

His girlfriend interrupted with triumph in her voice, 'Of course. Those guys just now. Before you came in, they were sitting where you are. They were looking at photos and the Chink dropped one. Freddie picked it up and it was you. He was really rude. He just grabbed it . . .'

'Without a thank-you,' put in Freddie, in a hurt voice.

'It was you!' Her statement sent a bloodcurdling chill through each of them.

'What men?' quavered Helen.

'What were they like and what did they say?' Marcus demanded, while Joanna half-rose like a frightened rabbit ready to run.

'One was Indian-looking and the other Chinese or something like that.'

'Yeah, he grabbed the photo out of my hand, stuffed the pile into his back pocket and they walked out,' said Freddie.

They looked at each other in terror-filled shock. How could the men have found them? And where did they get the photos from?

Boa opened her mouth to speak, but Marcus gripped her arm tightly. She closed her mouth abruptly. He thought soberly that she was about the last person he would want with them in a tight squeeze.

'Must have been a friend of ours,' he told the young couple, trying to sound casual. 'We must be going. Nice meeting you.'

Freddie called after them. 'Hey, this fell out with the photo. Your friend didn't realise he'd dropped it.' He held out a white card.

Helen ran back and grabbed it, then paused. 'Thank you so much,' she said graciously and ran after the others.

The card had the letters St V printed in small black letters in one corner. 'Who on Earth is St V?' she wondered.

For all her bulk, Boa moved like a puma and was in the car starting the engine by the time Helen reached it. She had grasped the situation instantly. 'I know just the place. They'd never find us,' she announced. 'A little place in the mountains. I know it well. Let's roll!'

Helen passed the card round.

'St V,' Joanna read aloud. 'Means nothing to me!'

'Could be a company?' suggested Marcus.

'I know what it is!' Helen realised suddenly. 'St V is short for Sturov. St and the last V. My God! That's what the dark forces do. They impersonate the light – making it sound like he's a saint!'

'So, those men are working for him!' said Marcus.

'Yes. We're up against the darkest of the dark!'

Boa sped as much as it is possible to speed on American roads, through open countryside interspersed by long strip towns. As yet there seemed to be no sign of pursuit.

'Where are you taking us?' demanded Joanna.

'The Blue Jay Hot Springs. It's in the mountains. There are hot springs and you can have gorgeous massages. No one will ever find us. What fun to have an excuse to be there.' She laughed with childlike delight as if the whole scenario had been designed for their pleasure.

Marcus decided he had either underestimated her totally, or she simply did not understand the situation. But her chilled attitude and the lack of obvious pursuit took some of the pressure out of a long and fragmented journey.

Boa sat behind the wheel like a chattering automaton through late afternoon and early evening. At six o'clock she stopped for petrol and they picked up a takeaway they could eat in the car. They quickly visited the rest rooms. Marcus saw Boa hurry out of the ladies and disappear round a corner. Surprised, he walked after her and found her leaning against a wall with her back to him, talking into her mobile. Something about it disturbed him, but he couldn't say what. He went back to the car to wait for Joanna and Helen and pretended he had not seen her.

A few minutes later Boa appeared with a satisfied smile and some chocolate for the journey. She refused Marcus' offer to take over the driving. 'I'm stiff but fine,' she said. 'It won't do my colon any good to be cramped up all this time, though. Goodness knows it will have its revenge tomorrow.'

They dozed on and off as Boa drove, but mostly they discussed over and over again how the men could have known where they were. They did not want to mention Sturov again. It would draw his energy to them.

As dawn broke, they passed through the beautiful Naptha Valley. Then they were zigzagging round hairpin bends, sunlight dappling the road. There was still no sign of pursuit. It had been a long scary journey and they were almost at their destination.

Unexpectedly, Boa pulled into an all-night café. 'It's too early to check in at the Hot Springs. You guys get some coffee. My colon is playing me up and I need the rest room. I'll park up and join you.'

She dropped them at the entrance and then went to park. Helen and Joanna walked inside stiffly. If Marcus hadn't stopped to admire the pink early morning sky he wouldn't have seen Boa make a call on her mobile. Then, without a backward glance, she drove out of the car park and back the way they had come.

Chapter 28

Marcus hurried inside, frowning anxiously, to where Helen and Joanna were already seated. His gut was clenched and he hardly knew how to tell them.

'I don't know how Boa keeps going,' Joanna was saying to her mother. 'I'm done in and I wasn't even driving.'

'She's remarkable,' agreed Helen, yawning.

Suddenly Joanna caught sight of Marcus' tense expression. 'Whatever's wrong?' she asked in alarm.

He told them that Boa had just made a phone call and driven off. Then he added that he'd seen her phone someone from their previous stop. Helen and Joanna stared at him in disbelief.

'You mean, she's gone?' asked Helen.

'Yes.'

'But where?'

'What are you suggesting?' Joanna was horrified.

'I don't know,' he responded slowly. 'It's just so strange how the men were in the same café.'

'But she drove through the night to get us away!' protested Joanna.

'How do we know this place isn't a trap?' he flared. 'We don't know that she is who she says she is. She just turned up to meet us and told us her brother had phoned.'

'Hang on. We did have a description of her from Tony. And you can't say she is an everyday sort of person.'

Helen had been silent during this exchange, frowning in concern. She came in quietly, 'I sense that she is genuine. All the same this is more than odd. So are the phone calls. Why the secrecy if they are personal calls? And who could she phone at this time of the morning?'

'I'm going to phone Tony,' announced Joanna firmly. 'Can I borrow your mobile, Marcus?'

'Sure.'

'You can't.' Her mother was aghast. 'What would you say?'

'The truth,' responded Joanna defiantly. 'We're just checking.'

'Let's have some breakfast first,' pleaded Helen. 'There is probably a very simple explanation for all this.'

'Just think of one.'

'Our lives could be in danger,' pointed out Marcus.

'I don't think so. I trust Boa,' Helen stated firmly. 'If there's anything worse than one tired paranoid person, it's three tired paranoid people. Let's get some breakfast. Food puts things in perspective.'

Joanna looked nonplussed, like a cat that has slipped on a rug. Then she shrugged and said to Marcus, 'Mum's probably right. Let's eat.'

Marcus, who prided himself on his ability to judge people, felt confused and cross. He felt torn by his doubts and his trust of Helen's judgement. 'Well, if she's not back soon, I'll phone Tony,' he glowered darkly.

'Right,' agreed Joanna.

'Fine,' added Helen. 'We'll take sensible precautions anyway. Let's sit by the window where we can see who drives in.'

They ate their breakfast staring tensely at the car park. Marcus muttered, 'If there's one thing I hate it's being double-crossed.'

Half an hour passed and there was no sign of Boa. Marcus was fiddling with his mobile. At last he could stand it no longer. He phoned Tony and left a message on his voice mail to phone him back urgently. After he'd made the call and with hot food inside him, he felt much better. There just had to be some plausible explanation. But he was still wary.

Then the familiar violet-coloured auto glided into the car park, with Boa at the wheel. She was alone. Evidently she was triumphant about something.

Marcus said, 'You two stay here. I'm going to talk to her. You keep the mobile.' He thrust it at Helen and got up.

They watched him stride out of the café and heard him call out to Boa, with a steely edge to his voice.

'Hi,' she responded as if it had been the most natural thing in the world to drive off alone.

'Isn't it a glorious sunrise?' She sounded as if she didn't have a care in the world. 'I just love the early morning.' She zapped the car lock as he reached her side.

Marcus was as tight-lipped as an angry lover. 'Where have you been?' he hissed.

She laughed and murmured in a low but excited voice, 'You'll never guess. Come on, I'll tell you all together.'

Marcus barred her way. 'No! You tell me first.'

She was shocked to see the suspicious determination on his face and recognised that it was not a moment to cross him. 'Okay. If you want to know, here it is. There was a tracking device on the car.' She spoke matter-of-factly. 'I've just had it taken off. They can't find us now!'

'What!' exclaimed Marcus.

Boa was evidently delighted by his astonishment. 'I thought there must be something. It was too much of a coincidence the men being in the café. It was going round and round in my head. When we passed through the last village I remembered my friend Sebastian who lives there. He's in the police – some special branch. I phoned and he told me to get the car straight over there.' She spread out her arms in an expansive gesture and laughed with relief and delight.

Marcus felt ashamed. More, he felt embarrassed. He could hardly meet her eyes. Boa pushed past him and joined Helen and Joanna who looked at her with suspicious anticipation.

'Hey, guys. I haven't got the pox,' she joked, expansively.

'Tell them, Boa,' ordered Marcus.

'You tell them. I'm pooped,' she said, sitting down heavily.

Marcus said abruptly, 'There was a tracking device on the car. That's how they followed us so accurately. Boa suspected something and called a friend in the police. That's why she went off just now.'

'We passed my friend's house in the last village. That's when I thought of him,' put in Boa.

'It's been like some James Bond thing. Those men following us so accurately. I couldn't get it out of my head. And I suddenly thought: ask Sebastian. He'll know. So I stopped here and rang him. He said to come round immediately. So I took off.'

The women stared at her. 'Why ever didn't you tell us you were going?' Helen asked.

'It sounds stupid now. Firstly because I thought it might be nothing and secondly because I thought there might be another bomb under the car on a timer or something,' replied Boa. 'And I felt you guys would be better out of it.'

Joanna opened her mouth to speak but thought better of it. She closed it abruptly.

'Boa, you are a stupid, crazy, wonderful woman,' said Helen. 'Thank you.'

Boa smiled. 'Can someone get me a coffee?'

'Coming right up,' responded Marcus. 'With cream and two sugars. I'll get a takeaway. They must know we've found the tracking device. They'll be searching for us so the sooner we get out of here the better.'

They were in the car again within minutes. Despite her evident exhaustion, Boa stubbornly insisted on driving. They flooded her with questions. 'What did Sebastian say? When was it put on the car? How? How did they know that was our car?'

'Yes, it was weird.'

'But when did they do it?' asked Marcus.

'Either at my house before I left for the airport or in the airport parking lot.'

'But how could they know who was collecting us? It doesn't make sense.' Joanna argued.

'Unless . . .' said Marcus and paused.

Boa nodded. 'Yes. Unless Tony's phone is bugged and they knew who was collecting you.'

They gasped in shock.

'There's something I didn't tell you. There was a break-in at Tony's house while he was taking you to the airport,' Boa told them.

'They've known where we were all the time!'

'I guess so.'

Silence fell.

'They could have killed us any time.'

'Yes. They must think we can lead them to the Scroll itself.'

'Surely they think it was destroyed in the fire?'

'If Tony's phone is bugged they must know there is a microfilm.'

'Perhaps they are waiting for us to be sent the codes of power. They'll translate that after the Great Mysteries.'

'Then they can use it.'

'And use us as hostages to get all they need?'

Impenetrable silence greeted this. They must get to the Blue Jay Hot Springs and hide.

Chapter 29

The Blue Jay Hot Springs lay at the end of a wooded valley, tucked into a fold between two hills. They stopped
at the reception building and all trooped in. The girl
behind reception was new, which was just as well. Once
met, no one ever forgot Boadicea or her name. Without
turning a hair, Boa signed in under the name of Zelda
Zimmerman, managing to imply that Helen was her
sister and Marcus was Joanna's partner. She filled in
a wrong car number, asked if there were any garages,
and was given a key.

Their three-bedroomed chalet was set back among
carefully tended emerald lawns, tropical flowers and
trees. Everything hummed in the glorious sunshine.

'They can't find us now. I defy anyone to discover us
here,' Boa sang gaily. Exhaustion vanished and exuberance returned. 'Let me tell you who it was I phoned last
night.' Her eyes glinted with humour as she looked at
Marcus, who had the grace to blush.

'Who did you phone?'

'I phoned to book you all a massage as a surprise . . .
my gift to you. Two of us at eleven o'clock and two at
twelve o'clock. And I'm having one with Chiwawa. He's
divine. Mary-Lou is excellent, too. But Chiwawa, he's
drop-dead gorgeous.'

She was duly gratified by their exclamations of delight and thanks.

Joanna looked sideways at Boa and grinned. 'This is definitely a place for diamanté sunglasses with your purple kaftan.'

She replied, 'I might not be able to get into it much longer. They sell wonderful chocolate here. It's truly orgasmic. It's just not very good for my . . .'

'Colon,' the others shrieked, and Boa appeared surprised when they all laughed.

Marcus threw his case on to his bed and gazed out of the window, which overlooked the hillside covered in trees, shimmering a million shades of green in the sunlight.

There will be great walks through the forest, he thought and then found himself wondering what Joanna would look like in a bikini. As he was about to disappear into a male reverie, he heard her voice coming from the room she was sharing with her mother. 'I can't wait for my massage. And just look at the view from here! Isn't it glorious?'

He could not make out Helen's murmured response. From the third room issued the sound of Boa's voice. 'Oh, I've chipped my toe nail on my suitcase. I'll have to do a repair job immediately.'

Marcus smiled to himself and couldn't help shaking his head in disbelief. There was a short silence and then Boa's voice floated out again, as she talked to herself. 'Now what shall I wear? Shall I put on blue or orange?'

She emerged in a vast orange sarong with matching

sandals, bag and sun hat, sensuously rubbing cream into her white skin. 'I can't wait to lie in the hot pool,' she announced.

'Don't you want to sleep after you drove all night?' Helen asked solicitously.

'Absolutely not. I'll snooze out there. We've just got time for a dip before our massage. Come on!'

They all trooped to the pool area, where the water was a scintillating turquoise. 'Look,' Boa pointed excitedly. 'Isn't it gorgeous? I love it here. See there's the cool pool for swimming. Really, it's beautifully warm. The little round one is glorious. It's bath temperature and the hot pool really is hot. Then there's a very hot pool over there with the cold plunge.'

Bodies were strewn everywhere, big, small, young, old. Everyone seemed to be carefree and relaxed. Boa rubbed her hands in glee. 'It's so lovely to be here.' She threw down her bag on to the deck and flung off her sarong with an extravagant gesture, revealing her orange and white striped bikini. She was confidently, flamboyantly huge – hedonistic, voluptuous and sensual.

Oblivious to anyone else, she walked carefully down the shallow steps into the blue waters of the hot pool. She sat back in the water and held her face up to be kissed by the sun, a vision in an orange sun hat, matching lipstick and long dangling earrings.

In other circumstances it would have been an idyllic day, Marcus thought. He had drifted idly from cool pool to warm pool to luxurious hot pool and relaxed into the expert massage. The biggest decisions he had to take were what factor sun cream to wear or whether or not he was hungry. But he felt restless.

For a time this was assuaged when he and Joanna played with two little girls in the pool. Marcus had always been a magnet for children and these two, who it transpired were twins, would not leave him alone.

Children were not encouraged at the Blue Jay, for it was a place for business people to chill out. All the same, they livened the place up enormously. They both clamoured for rides on his back because he was stronger and faster than Joanna. They shrieked with delight when he threw them into the water and he found himself forgetting the Scroll and relaxing into the fun of the moment. He and Joanna were quite sorry when their mother called them back.

After lunch he and Joanna wandered along the sundappled forest trail, enjoying the glorious scent of the pines. However it was too hot in the middle of the day and by mutual decision they returned to the pools. Pretty soon he was bored with sunbathing.

'I'm going to get my book from the chalet,' he told Joanna.

'Don't disturb Mum. She's gone back for a snooze,' she reminded him.

As he strolled across the lawns he tried to focus on the planetary grids being free and flowing with light. Then he thought he would focus on Joanna fancying him, but decided not to. He didn't want her to pick up his thoughts and be put off by it. I am changing, he realised wryly.

Walking up the chalet steps he wondered for the

umpteenth time why he had attracted the betrayal by his ex-girlfriend and his boss. Even now he had an unpleasant feeling in his solar plexus when he thought about it.

He found Helen quietly resting in the cool sitting room. He decided to ask her for any insights.

She smiled and said, 'I wondered when you were going to ask me that. It is quite simple. You have a belief in betrayal.'

'What?' he stuttered, surprised. Then he frowned. 'What do you mean?'

'Unconsciously you have a belief that you will be betrayed. Look what happened when Boa went off. You didn't think that there might be a simple explanation. You immediately assumed that she was betraying us. That's because you have an unconscious belief that you will be double-crossed. You even said, "I hate being double crossed."'

Marcus was silent for a moment, digesting this. 'You mean that is enough to bring someone who betrays me into my life?'

'Absolutely. That's how it works. Remember what the Scroll said? If you fear something it comes into your life so that you can look at it.'

'Doesn't it get worse and worse then?' Marcus wanted to know.

'Very often it does. Take, for example, your fear of betrayal. It will get worse and blight your life until you look at it differently.'

'Look at it differently? That woman two-timed me and my boss really did the dirty on me.' Marcus was angry now. 'Besides it hasn't happened before, so I don't think it applies to me.'

Helen was unperturbed. 'It's never happened to you before?' she repeated.

'No!' He paused and thought. Unbidden memories of small betrayals came to him. The fact that he could never trust his sister not to tell on him. Another girlfriend who had gone off with a good friend. He had told himself it didn't matter as he didn't really care. The time his mother said she would watch a school match and didn't turn up.

Helen was watching his face. He told her of these memories and more that came to him as he talked.

'So you see, it was like a time bomb waiting to explode into something big and draw your attention to your belief.'

Marcus nodded. 'But where could it possibly come from?'

'Remember that anything unresolved in another life comes forward to be looked at in the next one.'

'So you think I was betrayed in another life?'

'Quite likely. Possibly more than one as it's quite deep. Or that you betrayed someone and are calling back the karma.'

'How do I find out and how do I get rid of it?'

'First, it isn't essential, but it is helpful to look at and understand the past lives that impact on us. If you don't do that, when you are ready, your soul will find another way for you to clear the beliefs.'

'Can you help me?' he said suddenly. 'You could do it, couldn't you?'

'Sure,' Helen smiled. 'Now? 'Close your eyes,' she directed, 'and take a deep breath. Relax.' She helped him to relax by guiding his breathing.

Then she leant over and touched his third eye, the space between the physical eyes, lightly with her fingers. 'Go back to the source of betrayal and let a picture or feeling emerge,' she commanded.

Marcus felt a swirling sensation in his forehead. Then a vivid and clear picture of a man on a camel came to him. He told her what he saw.

'Do you recognise the man?'

'Yes, it's me. I'm an Arab. I'm with a man. He's my brother. We're in the desert. On camels. He's coming up behind me. Oh no!'

Marcus felt shocked and distressed. He clutched his chest involuntarily.

'What's happening?' Helen's calm voice floated to him.

'He's knifed me. How could he? He called me and I turned and he stuck a knife in my chest. Blood. I'm bleeding. It hurts. He's killed me.' Marcus was groaning.

'Do you know the reason?'

'I'm the eldest. He wants to inherit.'

'Is he anyone you know in this life?'

'My ex-girlfriend. The bastard.'

Helen soothed him and helped him to understand and reconcile what he'd seen. Then she said, 'Now go back further. There is something else.'

It was not so clear this time. He had an impression of himself as a young woman. 'I feel I've got a younger brother and sister. We're on a boat on a loch. It's round. I shouldn't have taken them out. The wind's coming up. The boat's capsizing. I try to help them but I can't. Oh God. They drowned. It's my fault. I let them drown.'

When he opened his eyes Marcus felt very shaken. He told Helen that the girl was his sister in this life. 'It was the eyes I recognised.'

She nodded.

'No wonder she was always angry with me and I didn't trust her.'

'Possibly it was yourself you didn't trust!' Helen suggested.

Marcus nodded thoughtfully.

'What about the brother from that life? Do you recognise him in this one?'

Marcus hesitated. 'Yes. I think it was my ex-girlfriend again.'

'Oh, you two really did have stuff to deal with.' She asked him to close his eyes again and they did a forgiveness exercise.

'It's unbelievable, I feel so much better,' he commented, when it was over.

'Well, as long as you truly forgive her and yourself, the karma is complete. You need fear betrayal no more.'

'That's wonderful,' Marcus said. 'What a relief. That was quite unbelievable. I feel shaky, but as if a whole load has lifted from me. But what about other people? You were here for me, but I'm just lucky.'

She raised an eyebrow and he blushed.

'I forgot. I attracted you in.'

'It's the same for everyone, Marcus. You were ready. When the student is ready the teacher will appear. Let's join the others.'

As they walked back to the pool, Marcus said, 'I think I must have imagined it all.'

'Images come from your soul,' Helen told him. 'And don't forget how your ex-girlfriend served you. By drawing your attention to your belief, she enabled you to look at it and release it.'

'You're joking!'

'I'm not. What happened between you was probably a pre-life soul contract, so that you could learn and grow.'

'I never thought of it like that,' said Marcus.

Chapter 30

That night Marcus slept the deepest and most profound sleep he had ever slept. He dreamt he was sitting on a rock with huge balls and chains attached to him. A woman came in and cut them off with a sword. She clapped her hands and slaves appeared and carted them away. Suddenly the rock disappeared and he grew to twice the size. Then he woke up.

Joanna and Helen laughed when he told them over breakfast.

'Something major was cleared yesterday when you did that past-life healing with Mum,' said Joanna.

'Your dream is telling you that you've been freed up to expand,' Helen confirmed.

'Do all dreams have a meaning?' asked Marcus curiously.

'Yes. They're all coded messages.'

'I dreamt soldiers were chasing me,' Joanna complained. 'It was horrid. I managed to hide in a beautiful cave, which was all blue and green, but it wasn't really safe there. I woke feeling I needed to escape but there was nowhere to go.'

Immediately Helen looked very serious.

Boa, partly comprehending, tried to mollify her. 'Well,

the baddies certainly have been chasing you, cherub. But you're safe here.'

Helen said nothing, but she was disturbed by her daughter's dream. Joanna was so intuitive that she often had pre-cognitive dreams, revealing the future. Presumably the beautiful blue-green cave was the Blue Jay. But were they really not safe here? Was the dream just expressing Joanna's fear or was she being given information from another dimension? She felt a surge of anxiety in her stomach.

'And I always thought dreams were incomprehensible rubbish,' Boa commented. 'Mine are always about trying to push boulders through underground passages.'

Joanna turned a laugh into a cough and gurgled, 'I think that's a message from your bowels.'

'Do you really?' Boa pounced on this in delight. 'How amazing. It's just how I feel sometimes.' She disappeared into her own private thoughts long enough for Marcus to slip in quickly.

'My father used to say dreams are meaningless clap-trap.'

Helen said, 'That's an illusion. Wise ones throughout time have known that most dreams are direct messages from the Higher Self about the way we are handling our lessons on earth.'

'But . . .' Marcus was interrupted by a knock at the door. They froze. In the silence a clock ticked loudly.

Marcus got up slowly. His palms were sweating as he quietly slipped on the chain and opened the door a crack, ready to slam it shut. The five-year-old twins stood there, grinning like two cheerful pixies. 'Hello, Marcus! Please can you and Joanna come out to play?' they chorused hopefully. They were totally amazed when Marcus unchained the door and opened it wide; the grown-ups inside were all laughing. Moments later their mother, full of apologies and out of breath, arrived at the door.

'I'm so terribly sorry. Did they disturb you? I don't know what possessed them.' She turned to the children. 'You're very bad disturbing these kind folks.'

To Joanna and Marcus she added, 'They so loved playing with you lovely people in the pool yesterday and they've been talking about nothing else. It's just not a children's place here. We only come because my parents are part-owners, so we don't have to pay and they love to see the kids. And I'm so busy with the babies I hardly have time for these two.'

'Yes, I've seen you with little ones,' interjected Joanna. 'Aren't they twins, too?'

'Yes,' she laughed. 'They're eleven months and they take all my time and energy.'

'Two sets of twins!' exclaimed Helen, appalled. 'I could hardly manage one at a time.'

'I know. It's hard work. My husband's looking after the babies now, but these two just slipped away.'

'We've nearly finished breakfast. We'll be up at the pools in ten minutes and we'll play with you then. How about that?' Joanna said to the kids.

'Great!' they beamed.

'Will you give me a piggy back ride first, Marcus?' squealed Amanda.

Laughing, he promised he would.

'See you later.' And they ran down the path behind their mother, as happy as skylarks.

Boa announced that she was going to have a salt scrub, which was absolutely divine. 'They rub salt all over your skin and then hose you down in warm water. It pulls out all the toxins and you feel simply wonderful,' she explained to Helen. 'Would you like one?'

'Sure,' answered Helen. 'I really fancy a mud bath though. That looks fun.'

'It's orgasmic,' replied Boa, predictably.

'Not as orgasmic as chocolate, surely,' slipped in Joanna, looking at her with a sideways grin. Boa laughed.

'By the way, Mum, did you realise you got another illusion?'

'Oh yes,' said Helen. 'About dreams.'

'Mmm. It's illusion that dreams are meaningless rubbish. The truth is they are messages from our souls.' Joanna wrote it down as she spoke.

'What about recurring dreams?' enquired Marcus.

'A dream contains a message and if you ignore the first one, it is sent again until you get it,' said Helen.

'I used to dream that a little child was locked in a bare room with a telephone and she dialled for help but no one ever answered,' Boa told them. 'I still have that dream sometimes. Does that mean anything?'

'Sure,' Helen nodded. 'Dreams use symbols to give us information about feelings we are not in touch with. Boa, you're the only one who can truly interpret your dream, but it sounds like a part of you feels you are trapped in a situation you can't get out of. It feels empty. You try to get help but no one responds.'

An unexpected tear slid down Boa's face.

'You know,' Helen told her gently, 'when you were a child, there may not have been anything you could do if your parents didn't hear your needs. But now you are an adult, you can do something about it.'

'Can I?' Boa leant forward eagerly. 'I hate feeling this way.'

'Your adult self can answer the call and listen to what that child has to say. She's still locked away inside you waiting for you to listen to her cry for help.'

'Wow! That sounds good.'

'It feels it's about time, doesn't it?'

Boa agreed.

'Why are dreams coded?' asked Marcus. 'Why not simple, direct, clear and straightforward?'

Helen and Joanna laughed.

'You sound quite indignant,' Joanna teased.

'Yes. It seems stupid. If your soul's got a message for you, why not make it obvious?'

'Put it this way. Dreams are telling you about feelings you have not dealt with in your life. You haven't dealt with them because you are afraid to or don't know how to. Most people don't want to recognise their fear or rage or greed or whatever, so they suppress the feeling into the unconscious. They lock it away into a compartment with a bolt on it, where they can ignore it.

'Remember if you could have dealt with it you would have. Your soul wants you to look at it, but whenever it sends a clear message, you just bolt it away more firmly.

'So, your soul – or, if you prefer, the computer within you – presents you with coded information in dreams about what's locked away inside you. It is hoping to get the information to your conscious mind without you rejecting the message.'

'Fascinating,' nodded Marcus.

'How do you uncode the symbols?' Boa wanted to know. 'When you explained about my dream, it seemed obvious but I would never have got it on my own.'

'When you start to get interested in understanding yourself, you find out more about the power of dreams. But the simple rule is this. Write down your dream and *become the symbols*. In other words, if you've got a breaking branch in your dream, close your eyes and imagine you are the breaking branch. That will tell you about the feelings the symbol represents.'

Boa looked puzzled.

'Do it now. Be the breaking branch. What does it feel like?'

Joanna closed her eyes. 'As that branch I feel hurting and in pain.'

Marcus said, 'Oh, I get it. As the branch I feel power-less and angry.'

'Go on, Boa,' Joanna urged. But Boa could not get into it.

'Anyway,' said Helen, 'it just shows how we can't really interpret someone else's dream symbols, though sometimes they seem obvious.'

Joanna was looking at her piece of paper. 'I think that illusion should read: "It's illusion that dreams are meaningless. The truth is they are coded messages from our souls."'

'You're right,' said Helen. 'That's much better. And I'm ready for a swim.'

Joanna jumped up guiltily. 'Those kids will be wondering what's happened to us. Come on, Marcus. Let's go.'

They played energetically in the pool with the twins for an hour or more. Then their grateful parents collected the two little girls. 'What energy,' laughed Joanna. 'I'm absolutely whacked.'

'They're like tornadoes,' agreed Marcus, throwing himself down on a towel near Helen and Boa, who had been enjoying a morning of luxurious indolence. Inevitably, within moments they were discussing the Scroll, what could be happening in England and just who Sturov was.

Boa was lying like a seal on the deck, soaking up the sun. She was snoring, dead to the world, and Marcus could see that people were either irritated or amused by it.

Then the mobile rang. They all jumped. Boa returned immediately from some other galaxy. They stared at each other. It could only be Tony.

'Don't forget his phone is bugged!' warned Joanna unnecessarily. 'Be careful what you say!'

'I know,' responded Marcus tersely, picking up the receiver. 'Hello?'

'Hello! Tony here! How are you all?'

'Fine.'

'Are you all right?' Tony asked sharply. 'Are you sure?'

'Yes. How are you?' Marcus batted it back to him. One of those banal and inane conversations was developing as Marcus tried to think how to warn him that his phone was probably bugged. He saw the women looking at him with anxious eyes. Tony ignored the question. 'I've got some more news for you about the Scroll.'

'Oh great, we're a bit busy now. Could I phone you back later?' Marcus knew this sounded ridiculous.

There was a pregnant pause. Then Tony said tentatively, 'I'll be here all evening.'

Marcus replied meaningfully, 'Or maybe somewhere else?'

Marcus could almost hear Tony's brain click. Would he get the message? Then the older man added slowly, 'But I may go over to Kumeka House for the ten o'clock meditation.'

'Right. Thank you. I'll phone just before ten.' Marcus shut off the phone and looked at the others.

Suddenly Joanna mimicked, 'Oh great, we're a bit busy now.' She collapsed with laughter.

'I didn't know what to say,' Marcus spluttered.

'Obviously!' Joanna was off into peals of laughter again.

'He realised that something was up?' checked Helen.

'He realised that something was up!' Joanna shrieked holding her middle, which was hurting from laughing. 'I should think he did. He's got information about the

Scroll and Marcus says, "Oh great, we're a bit busy now."'

Helen was infected by Joanna's hilarity and soon they were all laughing. 'If Tony could see us now he'd think we were mad.'

It was Boa who said, 'I can't wait to hear what he's discovered. When will it be ten o'clock in England?'

Marcus sobered immediately. 'Three hours. Let's get back to the chalet now and have some lunch and a shower.'

Boa rummaged in her hold-all. 'Would you like an organic dried apricot?' she proffered. 'It keeps you regular.' She could not understand why they all started to laugh again. 'I take my bowels very seriously,' she told them earnestly.

At that moment there was an announcement over the tannoy giving a car number and asking for the owner please to report to reception. Boa sprang up.

'That's my car!' she shrieked. 'What the hell's going on?'

Chapter 31

The sound of the tannoy reverberated in their heads. They looked at each other in bewilderment and fear. Who knew the car number? Had it been stolen? Had they been traced?

'I'd better go and see what's the matter.' Boa's lips were pale.

'But your car's in the garage,' Marcus frowned.

'And you gave a false number for it,' puzzled Joanna.

'Besides, they would never tannoy you if they needed you,' added Helen. 'They'd call the chalet and then send someone from reception to look for you at the pool. The tannoy's too intrusive.'

'It's the first time I've heard it. I didn't even know they had one,' agreed Joanna. 'I don't like the feel of this.'

'Nor do I.' Helen shook her head.

Boa started to get up but Marcus suddenly commanded, 'Don't go. It's a trap. They're trying to flush us out.'

She sat down abruptly. Her eyes had lost their colour. 'Whatever shall we do?'

The approaching sound of light scampering feet distracted them for a moment and the twins, bearing wide grins, appeared beside them. 'We're back!' they yelled together.

Marcus groaned inwardly. What a moment! Their mother was close behind, inevitably apologising for the intrusion.

'Hi,' Joanna called to her. 'What's going on? I've never heard the loudspeaker before.'

'Noisy, isn't it?' the young woman replied. 'There's a couple at reception, complaining that as they drove past the main gates a woman in a violet car bumped into them and drove straight into the Blue Jay without stopping. They took the number and followed.'

They stared at her.

Amanda, the outgoing twin, now piped up, 'They were Indian.'

They went cold and stared at each other. 'And there was a man with a funny face staring at us,' screeched the irrepressible Amanda. 'He looked horrid.'

'There was an Oriental gentleman in reception,' their mother apologised again. 'Sorry. The twins don't understand about political correctness. They think different is funny.'

'Mummy,' shrieked Amanda accusingly. 'You said he gave you the creeps.'

Her mother flushed crimson

'Look, I can see them. They're coming this way,' the other twin called from her vantage point up a tree.

Instantly Boa jumped up, scrambling to collect her towel and bag. 'Quick, bring your things and follow me,' she commanded urgently.

'What!' exclaimed Joanna, who had frozen in horror.

Boa pushed her. 'Hurry!'

She marched to the furthest corner of the pool area

and into the Therapeutic Mud Zone. The others followed, oblivious to the disappointment of the twins and the surprise of their mother.

Boa was magnificent. 'Hi, Star! Is it okay if we do each other?' she called out with easy familiarity to the bronzed, long-haired old hippie in charge of this area, who was engaged in stroking therapeutic mud over a plump, recumbent form on the couch.

'Sure you can, Boa. Help yourselves. You can use the white and red clay to decorate yourselves.' She smiled a generous, inclusive smile. 'I've nearly finished here. I'll be with you in a sec.'

'Great. That's wonderful.' Boa was typically enthusiastic. She stripped off her bikini top and had already plastered a handful of mud over her head, covering her silver hair. She looked completely different already. 'Come on, guys. Get your cossies off. Let's do each other.'

Even as she spoke she was stroking the lovely, oozing brown clay over Helen. It felt cool and soothing. In other circumstances it would have been divine, Helen thought and noticed wryly that she was already catching Boa's terminology.

In their frantic fear, it took surprisingly little time to cover each other in the dark oozing clay.

Star called out, 'Hey, you guys. You're too quick. You're meant to relax with this.'

Boa laughed, 'Sure thing. Let's slow down or we'll be too lumpy to decorate.' She winked through the clay mask at Joanna, who giggled nervously.

'Give yourself a little time to dry,' Star advised, as she finished off her client and joined them.

They looked completely unrecognisable, only their eyes gleaming through slits in the clay.

At that moment two grinning faces peered over the fence. 'Can we come in?' pleaded the twins. 'You look weird.'

'Are they with you?' asked Star.

They all said, 'No!' with such vehemence that Joanna was in fits of giggles again.

'Don't make me laugh. The mud's cracking.' she spluttered.

'Sorry, kids,' Star smiled at the twins.

Their little faces fell and Joanna walked over and streaked mud down their noses and across their cheeks and foreheads. They squealed with delight and ran off to show their parents.

'Now,' asked Boa, 'who wants to be decorated first?'

'Go on, Marcus.' Helen pushed him forward. As they watched her at work, they stood round laughing and chattering as if they were carefree holiday-makers. Indeed, Boa's puppy-like exuberance was so infectious that for whole seconds they forgot their fear.

Boa painted a star on Marcus' chest with white clay, with rays spreading in all directions and then smaller stars in red clay in other strategic locations. It looked superb. She was clearly no novice at this art. Boa revelled in their admiration.

'Now me!' she demanded like an overgrown child. 'I want bondage gear. Start with fishnet tights.'

For a nano second they all hung back, startled, but she was on a roll, adding, 'And a tiny bikini and whip!'

'Good God,' muttered Marcus.

But Star's erstwhile sleeping client leapt off the couch, cracking his clay and offered to decorate her. He introduced himself as Chuck and proved to have a huge laugh to match his size.

Amidst bawdy comments and hysterical laughter, the two of them became a comedy act, while everyone else threw in comments and creatively decorated each other's bodies.

When the Indian couple walked by, peering intently at everyone, they didn't give a second glance to the exuberant group. They were seeking nervous, frightened fugitives.

When they were all done, they sat and waited. No one wanted to hose off the clay. It is good for the skin, they reminded each other. They lingered. In limbo.

Then the incorrigible twins peeped over the fence again. 'It's us again.'

'We know!'

'Those people have gone. They just drove away.' They had the intuitive knowledge of young children that something was wrong.

Joanna felt giddy with relief. Helen realised how tight her solar plexus was. Marcus felt his shoulder muscles relax, but Boa hardly looked up from her engaging conversation with her erotic decorator. She was either curiously switched off or a consummate actress.

Danger past, they started to hose each other down. Star relented and allowed the twins to come in and help. Relief and the wild enthusiasm of the children made it fun.

As they left the Therapeutic Mud Zone, feeling cleansed

and, as Boa put it, 'shimmering with purity', they met the twins' mother, struggling along with the eleven-month babies. Joanna's offer to carry one was gratefully accepted. Marcus was already carrying his inseparable shadow, Amanda, on his shoulders.

'We'll take them back to our chalet until you're ready to collect them,' Marcus offered.

And so it was that Marcus and Joanna happened to look like any young couple with a family as they strolled back to their chalet.

They did not see the Chinese man watching everyone intently from a quiet corner. Nor did he recognise them, as they did not fit the picture he was seeking. In this way the universe rendered them invisible to him. Kindness earned its just reward.

Nor did he notice Helen when she passed him ten minutes later, pushing the other sleeping twin in a buggy. She was dismissed, unseen, as a grandmother with a child.

Only Boa remained drinking at the bar with Chuck, her new friend, eating nuts and crisps and ignoring all warning messages from her bowels.

Later, long after the Chinese man had left, Boa floated out of the pool area with her new admirer. They wandered together to the garages and she checked that her car was safely there, untouched, as she had left it some days earlier. Relieved, she left Chuck and joined the others at the chalet.

It would be ten to ten in England.

Marcus phoned Kumeka House. Tony was already there

waiting for their call. Marcus explained briefly what had happened.

They could sense Tony's tension and sense of violation when he understood his phone might be tapped. His horror at their danger was apparent, but they reassured him quickly that they were all right. They wanted to hear about the Scroll.

'Zoranda and the other initiates have been practising the sounds and they also have another symbol. They intend to go into Stonehenge the night before the full moon and start to restore the energy.'

'What exactly do you mean?'

Tony paused. 'They hope they will be able to move one of the Stones back into position using the information from the Scroll.'

'Wow!' Marcus felt a light sparking inside him. He told the others, who danced for joy.

'The Light is winning. The Light is winning,' sang Helen.

'Any more of the Great Mysteries?' Marcus asked Tony.

'Indeed. There's some more. It's . . .' The meditation gong sounded.

'I must go.' Tony automatically lowered his voice, though it was not necessary. 'I'll phone you in an hour on the land line.'

'We'll be waiting.'

Marcus told them what Tony had said.

'I think we need to link into their meditation,' said Joanna at once, sitting cross-legged with her eyes closed and instantly looking at peace.

'Yes,' agreed Helen. 'We must.' She joined her daughter. So did Marcus.

They settled into quiet meditation and it was just as well. The fear and frenetic energy they had been transmitting was drawing danger close to them.

Now, as they sat in quiet harmlessness and peace, it enabled them to receive a wave of light directed towards them from Kumeka House. For the time being they were totally safe, protected by a bubble of cosmic love.

Chapter 32

Zoranda phoned them exactly one hour later. In his deep, calm voice he told Marcus that they were too important to the cosmic plan to place themselves in danger by sending out fear.

'It is vital that you meditate on radiating peace and harmlessness,' he reminded them. 'Please place divine protection round yourselves constantly and have total faith in it. We can and will support you from this end, but you alone have the power to do this.'

'I know,' said Marcus humbly.

'We have been too focused on our work,' admitted Zoranda. 'We have not sent a projection of peace and safety to you. From now on we will do this.'

'To all of us?' Marcus checked. 'Boa, too?' It felt important that they should all be included.

'To all four of you,' Zoranda confirmed. 'If you do your part you will be safe.'

They were crowded round the phone, and even though they could not all hear what Zoranda said, the waves of confidence and harmony that he automatically transmitted gave them immediate confidence.

Zoranda continued, 'We have work for you to do. Tony told you we are going into Stonehenge to start the work of regaining the portal for the light, as instructed in the Scroll. We'll be there in the Stones on the day before full moon. That's next Thursday, six days from now. We'd like you, if you can, to be at Mount Shasta to hold the light. It's the most sacred vortex near you, so we want you to send energy from there down the ley line to Stonehenge.

'We've asked groups of light-workers all over the world to be at sacred sites on that night to send energy to Stonehenge and to clear the grids. You are the only ones who know the full importance of what we are doing. So your part is to clear the illusions we have discovered by focusing on the truth.'

Marcus blinked.

'I'll pass you to Tony now. He's got information for you.'

'Thank you,' murmured Marcus automatically, his mind whirling.

Joanna and Helen were grinning with glee and giving each other the thumbs up. Boa, however, seemed pre-occupied. Clearly her thoughts were elsewhere.

Tony took the phone and told them that the next Great Mystery had been translated. 'I'll dictate bits of it to you,' he said, clearing his throat and lowering his voice. '"All is sacred within the primordial soup of energy. Young and old, dark and light, big and small, all is sacred. All is honoured. All respected. Dark cannot do anything to light unless light asks. Big cannot do anything to small unless small asks. Old cannot serve young and young cannot serve old unless permission is gained and granted. Soul to soul all is respected. Neither angels nor devils can approach humans unless asked.

' "The radiant ones are forced to stand by and watch with love and compassion as their beloved children on earth cry with pain. They cannot help unless asked. Many scream for help, many howl in anguish and cry or demand or rage or threaten. That is not asking. That is trying to manipulate the energy of the divine.

' "To ask is to centre yourself in the radiant light and project your clear divine thought into the mind of the Great Radiant One. When your thought vibration aligns with the cosmic thought, that is asking. The divine current must answer and pull you into itself so that the situation moves and transforms.

' "To ask in such a way is always to receive a response from the Godhead. So be clear and ready to receive before you formulate your request. Mountains move and seas run dry to accommodate such prayer." '

Marcus was scribbling down the words of the Scroll, while Joanna was holding the paper still for him. Their minds were bursting. They wanted to discuss it, but Boa insisted on talking to Tony first.

'He is my brother,' she said with finality.

It transpired that Tony and Boa had not communicated for four years until the night he phoned her from England and asked her to look after them.

'You never mentioned it before!' Marcus was amazed. Boa shrugged.

'And you dropped everything to look after us!' exclaimed Helen in wonder.

'Why?' asked Joanna.

'He asked me to,' answered Boa simply.

'That's what the Scroll says. Whatever help you need, you must ask,' pointed out Marcus.

'Yes, but you've got to ask with the right energy.'

'Obviously Tony did,' Helen said. 'Boa certainly moved mountains for us.'

'What's that about dark cannot do anything to light unless asked? I don't understand that. What do you think it means, Helen? Surely no one asks to be burgled or have violence done to them?'

Helen paused and sighed. 'I guess no one does at a personality level, but we send out thoughts that align and flow with dark currents as well as light. According to the Scroll that constitutes an unconscious form of asking.'

'It seems to be another way of describing like attracts like, doesn't it?' asked Joanna.

'You've lost me.' Boa sounded petulant and even bored.

'You're right, Joanna,' replied her mother, ignoring Boa. 'What we send out, consciously and unconsciously, creates the attraction and repulsion of circumstances. And this Great Mystery is about how we can override that to draw in cosmic energy.'

'I think I get it.' Marcus sounded excited. 'If a child demands and screams for something, his energy is not aligned to the energy of what he truly needs. So he doesn't get it. On the other hand, if he asks sensibly, the parents know he is ready to appreciate it and so it is given to him.'

Boa was with them again. 'I see that, but I've seen parents give in to wilful children.'

'True. Then that is two egos clashing in a learning experience that blocks the flow of harmony. It puts a rock in the river. You remember what the Scroll says about abundance. The Divine wants us to have our heart's desire. It's our ego desire or our fears and limitations that put a block in the flow.'

'The universal energy doesn't grant what isn't appropriate.'

'It's complicated,' Boa frowned.

'No, I don't think so,' Helen replied. 'But it does help to recognise which Great Mystery we're keying into.' She turned to Marcus. 'Can you read that bit about asking again? Something like, "It's when your thought aligns with the divine thought".'

'Okay. I've got it. "To ask is to centre yourself in the radiant light and project your clear divine thought into the mind of the Great Radiant One. When your thought vibration aligns with the cosmic thought, that is asking. The Divine Current must answer and pull you into itself so that the situation moves and transforms. To ask in such a way is always to receive a response from the Godhead."'

They contemplated this for a moment.

'I see.' Joanna frowned with concentration. 'Before we ask for something we must consciously align to the cosmic current.'

'Take my redundancy, for example,' said Marcus. 'I think it means I invited it into my life by aligning my thoughts and beliefs to rejection. That was certainly unconscious, but I can see now how I did it. However, as I become more aware of my thoughts, I can access the cosmic help available. So if I want to draw something to me, I must ask in the right way and the divine current will bring it to me.'

'Yes, as long as the intention is right.'

'Sure.'

'And you've got to be sure you're really ready for it.'

He nodded.

'So,' said Joanna. 'Asking is prayer. Rote isn't really prayer. When you pray for something and really believe it will be granted, your energy links to the divine current and the universe sends a response.'

'Absolutely,' agreed her mother. 'Then the faith you have is what aligns your request to the universal current.'

'I always thought that prayers were a ridiculous waste of time at school,' commented Marcus, 'and they probably were because it was either rote or we were fervently asking for things we never really thought we would get.'

'It's such a waste of energy, isn't it?' agreed Joanna. She grinned wickedly as a picture came into her mind. 'I can just see you in short trousers and long socks, desperately asking for a new bicycle.'

'No, I used to ask to do well in my tests and for my parents to come to visit me at school.'

'That's sad.'

Boa suddenly woke from her reverie and burst in, 'I think I understand the other Great Mystery about attracting things. Is this right? It's an illusion that if we hate someone they are our worst enemy. In fact, we invite them in with our energy to teach us lessons.'

'You're right! That's brilliant, Boa!'

She flushed.

Helen added, 'They say that often the people we clash with are our best friends in spirit who love us so much at a soul level that they come in to teach us lessons.'

'I can't quite get my head round that one,' Joanna said ruefully. She had taken out her notebook and was adding the illusion to her list: 'Illusion. Those we hate are our worst enemies. Truth. Our enemies are soul connections helping us to learn lessons.'

'It just shows you can never judge anyone,' remarked Helen.

Boa coughed and a slow flush crept over her fat white cheeks. She started to speak, stuttered slightly and sounded quite different from her usual brash self. 'As a matter of fact, Helen. I felt you disapproved of me at the Mud Zone, when I was being decorated. It felt like judgement.'

Helen blushed crimson and looked really uncomfortable. 'I'm so sorry, Boa. You're quite right. I did judge you. I suppose it seemed inappropriate to bring sleazy sex into the situation.'

'I was trying to lighten things up. Get everyone to laugh.'

Helen was contrite. 'Bondage isn't in my world. I suppose I don't know anything about it.'

'Nor do I,' answered Boa. 'That's why I did it for a laugh.'

'I'm sorry,' Helen repeated, feeling awful.

'Hey, Mum. Don't beat yourself up for not being perfect,' Joanna chimed in. 'You always used to tell me to accept others as they were but to discriminate about what was right for me. Perhaps it's about that, too.'

Helen threw her daughter a look of gratitude and felt a warm rush of love towards her.

'Anyway, back to the Scroll.' Joanna steered the conversation back to calm waters. 'I suppose we've invited these people who are trying to stop the Scroll into our lives with our fears. If we align to Divine Harmony they will lose our trail.'

'Do you think that's possible?' asked Marcus.

'It's what the Scroll says,' answered Joanna. 'If we remain harmless we don't invite them into our lives.'

'How come you were there in the first place when the monk was killed?' asked Boa, riled by Joanna's show of solidarity with Helen.

'Probably a destiny thing,' replied Marcus. 'Our souls invited the situation in to test us or else it was a job we undertook before we incarnated.'

'The latter, I suspect,' said Helen. 'But I'm sure it's true that our fear has kept it alive and chasing us. Let's stop now and radiate harmlessness, and ask the universe to help us with our quest.'

They did this together and all felt curiously comforted, safe and happy. Surely everything was going to change.

Chapter 33

Boa was up with the lark. 'You know, my colon feels much more comfortable this morning,' she announced to Helen. 'I feel it's turned a corner. The niggle in my side has gone.'

'Good,' Helen replied graciously.

'And I'm asking the powers-that-be for this list of things in my life,' Boa informed her happily. She read out a list of wants, all of them material. Helen sighed but said nothing. She did not want to sound judgemental.

It was left to Marcus to lean over Boa's shoulder and remind her jokingly that there was no point in asking for a palace if she had a semi-detached mentality.

'I thought it was too good to be true.' Boa pouted crossly. 'What can I ask for then?'

'Anything your consciousness is really ready to receive and believes it can have.'

'You can always ask for qualities like patience or peace of mind,' Joanna teased.

'How boring!' Boa replied, abrupt as a thwarted child. She tore up her piece of paper in disgust.

She decided she did not want to go to Mount Shasta, complaining that all the driving made her constipated. 'You guys can take the car if you want to,' she offered generously. 'You can pick me up on your way back.'

'That's very kind of you,' Marcus thanked her. 'But that would mean you're stuck here. We'll hire a car. I feel it's time to move on, don't you? They've clearly lost our trail.' He looked at Helen and Joanna who nodded in unison.

'Yes, I'd like to get to Mount Shasta,' agreed Joanna eagerly. She was bored with sunbathing and, despite Marcus' reassurance, still fearful of discovery. Furthermore, she could not stand another day of Boa's eternal chatter.

Minds made up, they were packed and awaiting delivery of their hire car by lunch time. Boa emerged from her room to say goodbye to them, in a creation in lime green and turquoise, which flowed generously over her contours.

They felt touched that she had dressed up to say goodbye to them until Chuck turned up to drive her into town for lunch. Then they realised she had another motive. She lowered her voice an octave as she greeted him huskily, positively oozing charm and seduction.

'Hidden agenda for staying!' whispered Marcus to Joanna, his eyes glinting.

'Number five?' Joanna mouthed back with a grin.

Marcus raised his eyebrows. 'Probably.'

They waved goodbye enthusiastically.

'I've grown quite fond of her,' murmured Helen.

'Mum, that sounds patronising,' put in her daughter and Helen flushed, looking fragile.

Marcus jumped to her protection. 'Come off it, Joanna. That's not patronising. I feel like your Mum. I'll miss Boa, and yet be relieved that she's not around.'

Joanna felt uncomfortable. 'You're right. I'm sorry.'

'That's okay,' Helen accepted her apology and felt instantly better. Suddenly she shrieked, 'I won't miss her bowels. I feel I know them intimately, every bend and kink, like and dislike.'

They agreed, laughing and lapsed into companionable silence. It was broken an hour later when Joanna mused, 'I wonder how Boa's getting on with Chuck.'

'Famously, probably,' Marcus replied. 'They really seemed to hit it off.'

'Did you notice his shorts had lime green stripes, the same colour as her dress?' Joanna commented.

'I expect they'll take that as a sign they are suited,' quipped Helen.

'Maybe they are,' said Marcus quietly.

Mount Shasta was magic. The glistening snow of the pure white mountain towered in front of them, reflected in the clear blue of the lake. Their hotel comprised of cedar cabins hidden in oak trees and silvery poplars. A fat cat lazed in the flowerbed in front of their cabin, peeping out of a riot of regal, bright-blue delphinium, yellow dahlias, orange marigolds, blue, white and purple lobelias and yellow, happy-faced pansies.

They felt soothed by the steady drone of distant insects, calmed by the beauty, and lulled by the warmth. Joanna pointed to a hawk circling in the blue sky above them and they watched it until it dropped like a stone from the sky on to some unsuspecting creature and disappeared from view. It is easy to float relaxed in a still, quiet pool, bathed in golden sunshine – impossible in a turbulent, rushing river.

While he was staying at Kumeka House, Marcus had learned to meditate. Within the peace of the community he had felt infinitely serene and quiet. Out in the turbulent world again he had never been able to recapture the sense of stillness that he had experienced there. Now they were at Mount Shasta, he wanted to practise what he had learned, so that he could enter that state of meditation at will.

He recalled a conversation with John, the initiate who had driven them to the airport. John reminded him that prayer is talking to God while meditation is listening. 'The purpose of meditation is to still the chatter of the mind to enable you to enter, if only for an instant, the infinity of God,' he had told Marcus. 'It is during those moments that the divine can directly communicate with you.'

When Marcus confessed that he never 'heard' anything, John had laughed.

'No. It's not like that. One person in a million may receive a direct revelation or vision. Most communication is telepathic, so it comes as a thought or impression, which people often dismiss as coming from their own minds.'

John had explained that divine messages are often like seeds, which are planted in the mind. Meditation prepares the soil so that it is in perfect condition to sow the seeds. Then from these seeds, thoughts, new ideas or different understandings come up later.

Marcus had nodded and John continued, 'So, basically,

meditation prepares the mind to receive the seeds. It aligns your consciousness to the divine consciousness. That's why it is so important.'

Joanna told him that when people are together their brain waves synchronise, which is why it helps to meditate with others. Then even beginners can sometimes float into the silence with beneficial effects on their health and also their lives and destinies.

It all made sense to Marcus. He knew that he felt calmer and more centred when he meditated and smiled wryly when he thought of the stressed and striving person he had been less than six months ago. The Marcus he had been then would have laughed at the idea of meditation.

'Meditation is for nuts and fruitcakes,' his boss said to him once, and he had laughingly agreed. His sleek and immaculate girlfriend with the needy, greedy, hungry eyes was equally disparaging of people who meditated.

'It's a crutch, like religion,' she had said once in her Barbie-doll voice.

Marcus realised that he had thought of them both without pain or regret. It was as if they were from another world. He wished them well and had no desire to participate in that way of life again. I really have changed, he thought, surprised.

The Scroll stated that you attract in mirrors of yourself. His new mirrors were Joanna and Helen, Tony, Zoranda and the men from Kumeka House, who were of very different understanding and consciousness. He felt a sudden warm glow of appreciation and gratitude. He might have lived his whole life in that competitive world without realising that there was another way.

Marcus finished his meditation, stretched and went out into the sunshine feeling centred. But he found that the effects of the meditation soon dissipated and within half an hour he was full of restless energy again.

He decided to drive to town to purchase some necessities. As he did so, he kept thinking about Thursday. What if the Stone really did move? The consequences of Stonehenge being re-instated to its true power and glory were awesome. Surely the knowledge of what the human mind really could do would free all people from the prison of ignorance and limited thinking. Marcus frowned in deep concentration as he considered some of the mind-blowing possibilities.

The medical repercussions alone were breathtaking. They could levitate people with burns to allow healing to take place. If people had a visible demonstration that their minds were so very powerful, they would use that power to heal their bodies. Presumably, then, the stranglehold of the medical use of drugs would lose its grip. He knew that more people were currently in hospital as a result of medication than for any other cause.

Even before his awakening Marcus had become uncomfortably aware that the pharmaceutical industry was literally controlling the people. He fully accepted that drugs were right in many circumstances, but he was somehow not surprised when Helen explained that drugs, medical or otherwise, shut down people's chakras, preventing their spiritual growth. Chakras, she told him, are the spiritual energy centres within each person.

God! The world would change when the Stones moved

A dinner-party conversation from years ago surfaced. A scientist sitting opposite him asserted that humans now had the knowledge to propel vehicles without the use of fossil fuel and we need not pollute the world. He claimed that vested interests made sure the knowledge never surfaced in a way that made it a viable proposition.

At that time Marcus had laughed scornfully. Now he was not so sure. It was strange how that conversation never quite left his mind. Doubts lingered. With the moving of the Stones and return of the light, surely things must change. The power of Sturov must diminish.

If there was such a visible demonstration of the power of the mind, surely enough people would focus on peace and cooperation in the world and bring it about. If there could be an end to war, the money and energy used on weapons could be used to feed people. He realised he had thought 'if' and changed it to 'when'. When the Stones move . . . when.

In sudden stark contrast to his mood of expansive optimism, a memory intruded unbidden. As a young teenager, he had been debating the subject of war with some friends at one of their houses. His friend's father had walked in and told them that wars were a result of power-hungry people fermenting situations so that they could make money from the battles that ensued. 'Britain's biggest earner is guns,' he had said. 'The

West has a big investment in keeping the world in disharmony.'

His voice sounded so harsh and angry that Marcus had been profoundly shocked. He slunk home from his friend's house and the sense of despondency that overcame him lasted for days.

Suddenly he realised that there was a huge unexpected force trying to prevent peace on earth.

Fear is control. Peace is freedom, he thought. Keep people everywhere in fear and you have control of them. When people are at peace, they become individuals and explore their full potential. That is dangerous to the establishment.

He shook his head as if to dismiss the current of these thoughts. Whatever the opposition, the Scroll could bring peace to the planet. It was just a matter of time. He just hoped the Stone moved on Thursday.

Thoughts were still chasing each other round his mind when he parked in the generously wide main street, which ran through the centre of Mount Shasta city. He switched off the engine, leaned back and closed his eyes.

Suddenly, in front of him appeared a picture of humanity chained to banks and investment houses that charged hefty interest on illusory money, keeping humanity in debt and therefore in prison.

A picture of millions of schoolchildren followed. Their right brains were shut down and locked, blocking their creativity, their uniqueness and personal connection to God. At the same time their logical left brains were fed information and other people's ideas. This turned them into stultified, shadow people, lost and unfulfilled. It closed their hearts so they perpetrated cruelty without feeling another's pain. They were puppets of the establishment.

Next he saw a light appear and schools changed into education establishments aimed at empowering children and helping them to expand into spiritually aligned adults. They became individuals, not a herd. They became free thinking, wise and fearless. He watched the lights in millions of children becoming brighter.

Finally, in his vision Marcus saw the hearts of billions of people opening and love flooding into the planet, raising the consciousness of everyone.

There was no need for guns or drugs. People took control of their own minds. All that which kept the world in thrall simply dissolved. He opened his eyes and his stomach lurched suddenly as he thought of the responsibility he had been given. Then he remembered that the higher forces of the universe were protecting him and putting him in the right place at the right time. He must trust that. There was so much to do. By himself he could do nothing, but with the universe behind him, he would succeed. He must never give up until the world was free or he died first. That was his mission.

Marcus recalled Helen's words about Sturov's elite group of people who ruled the world; those who obliquely controlled the establishment and had a vested interest in keeping power. He wondered if these really were the people who were trying to get the Scroll. Was it a branch or faction of the Elite?

If it was so, no wonder they had been traced so

accurately. It was said that they had worldwide influence and resources, which was a terrifying prospect. Then he remembered his mission statement. No matter what, he would never give up until the message of the Scroll was released to the world. With a great feeling of determination, he jumped out of the car.

Chapter 34

Marcus reflected that the city of Mount Shasta was like a wild-west town, with its wide central street flanked by shops and houses with wooden balconies. Some looked like saloons out of a movie and he half-expected a cowboy to step out of the doors at any moment.

Purple petunias, bright-red geraniums, blue and yellow pansies and flowing white, pink and blue lobelia burst out of window boxes. People stopped to greet each other. It was like a village in a city.

He entered one of the shops to buy a film. With his ready smile and cheerful grace he was soon talking to a middle-aged couple, who were choosing a frame for a photo of their granddaughter. To his discomfort, they complained extensively about the cost of everything. The woman, rotund, with pink-tinted hair and lines of discontent etched on her face, confided that they were locked into their mortgage.

'We'll never be free,' she grumbled to Marcus.

Marcus blinked. He had a sense of black pincers reaching out from the lending house holding them in thrall.

He paid for his film and said, 'Have a good day.' As he did so he thought, The universe is drawing something to my attention. Then he smiled ruefully. He was even *thinking* like Helen and Joanna now. All the same, it was peculiar. In his whole life he never remembered talking to a stranger who told him of her mortgage problems. How interesting it should be now when he was thinking about people chained by debt.

For no reason, he suddenly wanted to buy a little gift for Joanna and Helen. He had no idea what to get. Then he remembered the Scroll saying that there were many helpers in spirit, but you must ask. He stood still for a moment and asked that he be directed to perfect gifts for the two women.

Well, he thought, let's see how that helps.

He soon discovered a shop full of crystals, books, chimes, singing bowls and all the wonders of the Golden Age. He knew instantly he would find what he wanted in here.

Within moments he was in conversation with the sales assistant, an enthusiastic woman with a perfect toothpaste smile, and a long-haired youth, whose girlfriend was vastly and unhappily pregnant. The young man was moaning about his job. 'I work all hours for next to nothing. It's not worth it. It's all right for some. They go to college. I never got the chance.'

The sales assistant murmured sympathetically.

His girlfriend complained about the heat when she was pregnant and their 'bad luck' with their awful landlord. 'And we've got to get out by the end of the week. We've nowhere to go. He chucked us out just because we have a smoke now and then with some friends.

'And he objects to the dogs. They're no trouble but he says it's against the lease.'

The Silent Stones

The sales lady turned to the pregnant girl. 'I know just how you feel. I was sick all through my second pregnancy and my husband left as soon as my son was born. The bastard.'

'Oh you poor thing,' trilled the imminent mother-to-be and instantly they were off on a downward spiral of blame, recrimination and negative talk. A dark cloud hung over them.

Marcus felt dispirited somehow. Their low energy affected him and he wandered round the shop trying to shake it off. Suddenly he realised, It's someone else's negative cloud and I've taken it in. Helen had taught him to picture the cloud and then blow it away and seal his aura. He did it as he stood behind a pillar and instantly felt much better.

Almost at once his eye was caught by a display of Buddhas. He chose a prettily carved one in rose quartz for Joanna and then an amethyst pyramid for Helen. Just anticipating their delight in receiving these surprises fully restored his sense of well-being. The low-consciousness couple had left by the time he took the gifts to the counter and he was able to direct the conversation to the beauty of the crystals. This restored the good humour of the sales lady, too. Marcus smiled to himself as he walked briskly back to the car.

All the same, his trip to the town had been a nasty reminder of the negativity of mass consciousness. It would be a huge job to lift it. Then he realised that this was simply not the case. No! It's just an illusion that change is difficult. The truth is that light instantly transforms darkness. Of course, he thought.

You only have to switch on a light and the darkness disappears.

He couldn't wait to tell Joanna he had found another illusion and drove quickly back to the hotel.

Marcus was deeply gratified by Joanna and Helen's delight upon receiving their gifts. He had even forgotten that Joanna collected Buddhas and Helen loved pyramids. As they hugged and thanked him, he wondered if his helpers in spirit really had directed him to choose presents they would like. Mentally he thanked them.

'And,' he announced, 'I have another illusion.'

'Let's have it, then,' Joanna squealed in anticipation, taking out her notebook and pen.

'Illusion. Change is difficult. Truth. Light instantly transforms the darkness.'

'Brilliant,' responded Helen and Joanna together, and the latter added it to her list.

'I wonder how quickly and easily change will come to earth,' mused Marcus.

'Very quickly,' replied Helen promptly. 'After all, there's the hundredth monkey, old souls being born, the Scroll, a speeding up of lightbursts into the planet and . . .'

'Wait a minute. Hang on. Can you run that by me slowly?' laughed Marcus.

'Of course,' Helen said, smiling. 'Have you heard of the hundredth monkey?'

'I've heard the term, but I'm not sure what it means exactly.'

'Briefly, then: scientists were doing experiments on an

island in the Pacific. They fed the monkeys by throwing yams into the sand. That meant they were gritty and unpleasant to eat. One day a baby monkey dropped its yam into the water and when it fished it out, it was clean of sand. Next time it picked up a yam from the sand it did the same thing again and washed it in the water. Eventually the mother copied and then other young monkeys followed suit. Then more mothers. Finally the males did it, too.

'When a critical mass of perhaps a hundred monkeys had learned to wash their yams, suddenly all the monkeys could do it. But here's the stunning thing – researchers found that at that critical mass moment all the monkeys on all the other disconnected islands in the Pacific also did it. In other words at the point of critical mass the consciousness spread to all.'

'That's fascinating,' commented Marcus.

'Isn't it just! And there have been lots of other similar observations where this has happened. For instance, tits learned to peck the silver foil off milk bottles in Scotland. When a certain number got the hang of it, in an instant, tits all over the country were doing it.'

'Right,' said Marcus thoughtfully. 'So consciousness merges and when a certain critical number of people switch on their spiritual lights, in an instant, everyone does.'

'Absolutely,' agreed Joanna. 'And it's happening more quickly than we realise. Just imagine the impact of the Scroll. As the power points are restored to the light and more people send positive energy along the ley lines the change will speed up.'

'And don't forget,' added Helen. 'More of the babies being born now are wise evolved old souls who are already awake and aware. They are automatically raising the consciousness of their families and those around them.'

'What was that about lightbursts?' Marcus wanted to know.

'Oh, at one time bursts of high-frequency light were pulsed to the planet once or twice a year. Remember – light contains spiritual information and knowing. It also contains love. Naturally it unsettles people as it wakes up their consciousness. Well, they say these lightbursts are now coming in monthly and sometimes fortnightly. Everything is speeding up. Change is inevitable.'

The energy was infectious. They felt optimistic and even jubilant. Their hopes were pinned on Thursday and the moving of the Stone.

Chapter 35

As the days passed, Marcus, the doer, became more impatient and restless. He wandered round like a grumbling bear, grizzly and restless, waiting for his honey. In this frame of mind, he could not access the healing powers of meditation he had acquired at Kumeka House. He knew he was annoying Joanna and irritating Helen.

The more often Helen reminded him in her soothing voice, 'We need to be calm and centred', the more frustrated he felt.

Joanna told him sharply to stop being an irritating idiot and do something useful. His eyes became dark and hooded as he observed that there were parts of her that he did not like.

At last, on Thursday morning they received three of the symbols, each e-mailed separately from a different place and sent to three different hotels for safety. Marcus travelled miles to pick them up. In his agitated state he was relieved to do so.

Zoranda had decided to e-mail them because these symbols were all in glorious colour. How the colours – in all their vibrancy – had remained impregnated in the material, they did not know. But it demonstrated to them yet again that the Atlanteans had powers and skills long since lost to modern humans.

Marcus wanted to know why the earlier ones they received had been black and white and was told quite simply that it was because they had been faxed. It also appeared that the professor was somewhat reluctant to tell them of the colours, possibly because it was beyond their comprehension and they wanted to do more research. Only when Tony visited him and saw the originals did he realise that the symbols were all intact in their original magnificent colours. Then he persuaded the professor to part with the colour pictures.

Nothing had prepared Marcus for the impact their vibrancy had on him. He'd bought felt-tip pens in anticipation that the symbols could be copied and tinted, but the range of colours he had available now seemed inadequate. He felt alive, lit up and buzzing with excitement as he raced back to the hotel.

He could not wait to show them to Joanna and Helen. They sat round the table in their cabin and pored over them, drawing them again and again as if to impress them into their minds. Each came with an explanation of the door it opened in the consciousness.

One was beautiful, like a swan, and was to open the deeper mind and expel karmic debt. It glowed iridescent peacock blue and green. A second was a triangle, filled with deep blue, one side green, one blue and the third pink. This was a key to align the heart and connect thousands of souls to an energy that would open the grids. It was incredible. They could feel the power as they drew it and then sat back and pictured it in their minds.

The third was a heart-shaped sapphire in a flame, which was to bring friendship to all lonely people and light up the beauty of the earth.

'Wow!' exclaimed Joanna. 'These are quite stunning.'

'They're unbelievable!' agreed her mother.

Marcus glanced at Joanna, watching for a moment her delicate, sensitive face and long dark hair, which fringed her face as she concentrated. It must have been a difficult and frightening time for her, too. He admired her containment and cursed himself for being so openly impatient.

She looked up and, reading his mind instantly, smiled. He felt a great deal better.

Zoranda had suggested they find a quiet place on Mount Shasta at two o'clock to synchronise with the seven o'clock vigil at Stonehenge. So they were sitting under a huge pine tree, below the snowline, looking out over a magnificent view of trees and lakes long before the due time.

Marcus contemplated the divine plan to send spiritual information and knowledge through the portals to spread it through the ley lines round the planet, with the intention of manifesting heaven on earth. It could have been such a wonderful place if only humans had not used their free choice negatively.

He reflected that Satanists and humans of evil intention had always tried to harness the power of the full moon to corrupt the ley lines and take over the portals. Then, inevitably, many people were sending fear along the lines, which spread confusion and panic. Marcus realised these were the ideal conditions for take over and control. It was no wonder that most countries were already masterminded by control freaks, for whom personal power or sensual satisfaction were of paramount importance. He suspected that Sturov and his force were one strand of this dark umbrella.

At two o'clock they started to visualise Stonehenge in its perfect state. They used all their powers of concentration to project to Stonehenge the truths and the symbols they had received. Then they visualised it spreading along the ley lines, lighting up the planet.

Several hours later they received a call from Tony, which sent them into a buzz of excitement. They hugged, ecstatic with delight.

Marcus made a phone call to an old schoolmate, Tom Tyler, before he went out to buy a bottle of champagne. Then they celebrated.

The currents of life move some people gently through the years with scarcely a wave to disturb the even flow of their existence. Day after day their sun rises and sets over the same horizon. Others, the lucky few, though they rarely feel so at the time, are picked up one day by a tidal wave and their lives inevitably change.

On Thursday night, driving wearily home from a late assignment, Tom Tyler was unaware that he was about to become one of the few. The impossible was beyond his comprehension. Had he been able to glimpse the future his attitude would have been one of cynical disbelief.

The damp, murky evening, an elusive ground mist rendering visibility patchy, presaged no such shift. It merely made driving uncomfortable. Tom's plump, well-groomed and slightly hairy hands held the steering wheel efficiently.

Once he had been sharp and ruggedly handsome, with alert blue eyes. Then he had been excited by life and ambitious – altruistic even. After ten years as a journalist, his spirit had deflated and his body had inflated correspondingly.

Disillusion had darkened his eyes, indulgence softened his jaw and too many beers of dissatisfaction bloated his stomach. Tom was soul weary, though he would not have understood the expression.

His car phone rang. 'Tom Tyler,' he said automatically, his voice lacking lustre or expression. Crackly reception indicated the call was from a poorly placed mobile. Damn, he thought sourly.

He noted with surprise and a tug of the gut the controlled excitement in Marcus' voice at the other end.

'Do what?' he responded, belligerent in his surprise. 'What on earth for? It's out of my way!'

Marcus repeated the request with such breathless urgency that Tom's curiosity was aroused at last.

'Hey, Marcus, what . . . ?' he started to ask, but the line cut out.

'Damned if I will,' he grunted irritably, and inevitably thought about Marcus, who had been his junior at school by a year. Marcus was a linguist; Tom an artist. Marcus played rugby, Tom cricket. They had been in the same house, but there was no natural point of attraction or interest between them and they had neither met nor thought of meeting in the ten years since he had left. Until six months ago, that is.

Then they had been seated opposite one another at an Old Boys' fund-raising dinner. Tom was the not-quite-successful journalist with a young child and failing marriage to a bored and boring wife. Marcus was the rising star in a city firm with an elegant girlfriend and the promise of a brilliant future.

Tom had felt his inadequacy keenly and battened his defences down tight. Sardonic comments were his attack. After the dinner, they had, for some reason, exchanged cards, formal politeness, no more. He assumed they would never meet again.

As he answered the phone during his late drive home that night, Tom did not know that during the six months since that dinner the tidal wave had already picked Marcus up, shattered his structured, elegant and successful life and carried him into the unknown.

He only remembered that at the Old Boys' evening Marcus had been as good looking as he had been at school, with the same laughing grey eyes and a manner that was surprisingly relaxed, considering the strong, capable shoulders and square, determined jaw.

Mostly Tom recalled, almost grudgingly, how genuinely likeable Marcus was. Beneath the surface conversation about careers and family, he felt the guy really understood and cared, moreover that he was interested in him personally. To his surprise, he had found his defences crumbling. That unsettled Tom. Marcus did not fit into his cynical picture of a city type.

Perhaps that was what decided him. That, and the

bizarre information Marcus had just given him. At the next roundabout, he deflected from his route home and turned towards the A303, which passed Stonehenge.

What on earth did the guy mean? he wondered. It had better be good. He glanced at the clock. Almost midnight. He'd be at Stonehenge in a few minutes.

The clouds suddenly parted like dark velvet curtains and the moon, a giant floating pearl, illuminated the landscape. In its light the Stones of the henge appeared black – even sinister. Privately he could not think why anyone would want to visit a bunch of higgledy-piggledy fallen rocks, even if they had been an ancient sundial. He had read somewhere that they were built according to calculations not available to scientists even now. He could not imagine why druids or a rabble of hippies would want to dance round them. The gentle qualities of tolerance, acceptance and open-mindedness had yet to filter into Tom's personality.

For years he had driven past Stonehenge with barely a glance and had always been surprised at the number of tourists who paid good money to see it from a distance. At a point where they became clearly visible, he glided off the road and switched off the engine, peering towards the strange silhouette. What had Marcus said? Something about the Stones moving. Wearily he thought, I must be crazy to listen to that gobbledegook. He felt suddenly angry with Marcus and with himself.

Then he realised that the structure looked different. Impossible! How? What was it? The place was deserted.

Suddenly his eyes lit up and his body vibrated as if a

lightning bolt had recharged him. He made two calls on his mobile. Then he was out of the car and running across the road. The tidal wave was picking him up.

An hour later, when Tom's mobile rang again, he responded very differently to Marcus, who had now transformed into the old mate who had given him his scoop.

'What's it about? How did it happen? What's the background? How did you know?' The questions tumbled out. And then, 'Where are you? What's your number?'

Marcus declined to give it. 'I'm in America. You tell me first. What's happening there?'

'One of the lintel Stones has been lifted and placed in its original position. No trace of how. It's a mystery.'

Marcus knew this already from Zoranda, but he was giving thumbs up to Helen and Joanna all the same.

'How did you know?' Tom repeated.

'What's the press coverage?' Marcus countered, ignoring the question.

'No one else here yet. It's my scoop, thanks to you. Photographer's on his way, though I've taken some pics through the confounded mist. The dailies will have it tomorrow.' Tom changed tone, sycophantic now in his desperation for information.

'I'm terribly grateful to you, Marcus, old chap. Thanks for thinking of me but can you give me any more information?'

Marcus almost laughed. 'Listen carefully.' He gave Tom a drastically edited version of the story of the Scroll, naming no names.

He wanted the world to know about the Scroll and to understand the importance of Stonehenge. Even more important, he wanted people to know about the power of the mind. He didn't want this to be sabotaged by vested interests.

Tom was dumbstruck. 'Are you pulling my leg?' he demanded.

'No!' responded Marcus. 'I've got to go. I'll phone you back later.'

'Wait,' shouted Tom, but Marcus had switched off. Tom was left cursing and sweating.

Marcus phoned back Tom at what would be the early morning in England.

'What's happening now?' He omitted any charm preamble.

'Hey, give me your number,' Tom pleaded. 'I may need to contact you urgently.'

Marcus hesitated. 'You must give it to no one. No one at all.' There was a hint of a threat in his voice and Tom remembered another side to Marcus. He recalled how he had taken on and thrashed two bullies twice his size, who had been terrorising a younger boy. No one messed with him after that. Tom promised. He was good at numbers. He'd keep it in his head.

'Now tell me what's happening?' Marcus repeated.

Tom's news was disturbing. 'The place is swarming with police. The photographer's still here, too, though they're not letting in the rest of the press at the moment. They've cordoned off the Stones and the road, so it's bedlam. Lots of rumours of alien interference. There's no sign of human intervention. It's extraordinary. There's just the dent where the Stone was and suddenly it's a lintel across the other stones again. Even some talk of the army coming in, but that's just rumour. There's no question of national security.'

'Did you mention the Scroll in your article?'

'Sure did, but it may be cut. The editor wasn't too happy about it.'

'Damn,' Marcus cursed under his breath.

'I just hope they don't gag the press,' Tom muttered gloomily.

'Can they do that?' Marcus frowned, astonished.

'Wash behind your ears, Marcus.' Tom's voice was sarcastic. 'They can do anything.'

'Damn,' repeated Marcus. 'Get it out everywhere you can, Tom. This is more important than you have any concept of at the moment.'

'I'm beginning to realise that,' the journalist replied. 'If it was anyone other than you, Marcus, I'd think I was dealing with a nutter.'

There are times when the universal powers-that-be step in to create miracles. The heavy mist and fog rolled back so that the early edition of the *Daily Mail* splashed a spectacular picture of the changed outline of Stonehenge against a gloriously rising orange sun. The headlines blazed: MYSTERY OF THE SILENT STONES.

Later editions of all the papers carried similar pictures. The headlines shouted: ALIENS INVADE, MOVED BY SOUND, IMPOSSIBLE!

Speculation was rife. Only one paper mentioned the

Scroll. Several referred to a sect, which claimed to have moved the stone by the power of sound.

A po-faced government minister appeared on television and said, 'There's a perfectly reasonable explanation for it. We're looking into it.'

To those with closed minds and cramped hearts, unknown is suspect and mystery equates with danger. The police cordoned off Stonehenge. The A303 was closed and traffic diverted, causing fuming delay to hundreds of motorists. For three days the different factions had a field day. Every group of cranks and intellectuals offered a theory, often presented as fact – aliens, angels, the devil, even God moved the Stone. Crop-circle experts gave their opinion. The mystery Scroll received a cursory mention.

The human capacity for creative invention is enormous. The desire to rationalise the irrational seems to bypass truth. Interviewed for the news, two local people were happy to swear they had seen vehicles with heavy lifting gear travelling down the road to the site. The driver of a passing car came forward to say that he had seen men at work at Stonehenge in the middle of the night. People saw space ships, lights in the sky and even heard humming.

The Scroll was dismissed. Zoranda appeared on breakfast television to talk about the power of mind control and telekinesis, but the interviewers derided him and would not let him get a word in edgeways. The only benefit of his appearance was the high-frequency light he radiated by his very presence to those who watched the programme.

A few days later a bed-hopping scandal knocked Stonehenge out of the news. The story was dead as cold pudding.

Chapter 36

We all receive constant guidance, though most people are unaware of this. When we ignore our gut feeling, we reject the prompting of our soul. When we know something will lead to trouble and misery but we do it all the same, we resist the messages from our higher self. Guidance often comes in the form of intuition and when we honour it, we swim with the current of life.

Marcus knew it was unhelpful to be so angry with the media for deriding the Scroll and with the authorities for closing Stonehenge, but he felt powerless. He walked around like a grumbling volcano.

He knew it would be impossible to raise the frequency of the Stones while the low vibration of the police and other interested parties kept such a presence there. He repeatedly said so.

'There is a higher purpose in everything,' Helen reminded him, but at the moment he couldn't and didn't want to see it.

At last Joanna warned him crossly, 'Your attitude will break down our protective bubble of harmlessness.' That cooled him for a while.

They decided to meditate together for guidance, but he could sense nothing. Helen repeated that meditation is rarely a time of illuminating flashes, but rather the preparation of a seedbed in which higher ideas can be planted. But Marcus continued to feel out of sorts.

It wasn't until the following day, when Joanna said sharply, 'Frankly, you're a danger to us and I don't want you around,' that he pulled himself up. He knew that she meant it and from what he knew of Joanna, she would simply leave no matter what the consequences.

She was very clear on her bottom line and her boundaries. It was one of the things he admired about her. He also found it difficult to cope with. Most of all, he admitted to himself, he was behaving like a prat. After all, it was not her fault and he did not want to risk her leaving.

He decided to walk up the mountain through the pine trees. It was a wise decision. The strenuous exercise and sheer beauty of his surroundings put him back in a reasonable frame of mind and returned things to some sort of perspective.

When he returned to the cabin that evening, he apologised for his grumpiness. Helen smiled graciously while Joanna rumpled his hair and said lightly, 'We all go over the top at times.'

Her brown eyes were full of understanding laughter and he felt relieved that she wasn't going to hold resentment against him.

Helen announced, 'I've just realised another illusion.'

'Go on, Mum. What is it?'

'The illusion is this: if you worry about someone it shows you love them. That's rubbish. You worry about someone either out of neediness or control. The truth is that true love is absolute acceptance and harmony.'

'Nice one,' exclaimed Joanna. 'I can see that. Worry is really lack of faith, which you project on to others.'

'Right . . . and I was just thinking,' went on Helen, 'what most people consider to be love is actually neediness. And love and hate are the polarities of a co-dependent relationship.'

Marcus put in, 'From what the Scroll says about flow, true love is a non-growth relationship?'

'I suppose so,' agreed Helen. 'That's why so many people are getting into co-dependent relationships. It thrusts them into self-examination. The divorces and separations that Churches and politicians call breakdown of society are wake-up calls from spirit.'

'Hang on a mo. Let me get it right,' said Joanna, getting out her biro. 'You're saying it's an illusion that if you worry about someone you love them. Yes, I go along with that. The truth is that true love trusts the other person to do what is right for their highest good.'

'That's a great way of putting it!'

'And,' added Marcus, 'it's an illusion that divorce and separation are failures. The truth is that they are wake-up calls or learning experiences.'

'Great! Two illusions together,' said Joanna, and, putting her notebook back in her rucksack, she rewarded him with a brilliant smile. 'I can't wait for the last Great Mystery.'

Joanna and her mother went to bed early, so idly picking up a book that had been left by previous guests, Marcus settled down to read.

He read with a sense of wonder and growing excitement about Machu Picchu, the lost city of the Incas, hidden in the forest-clad mountains of Peru. According to the Scroll it was another of the two-way inter-dimensional portals on the planet.

The Scroll said that the universe arranges synchronicities to remind us that we are on the right track. The next morning Helen and Joanna both reported vivid dreams.

'I dreamt we were at Machu Picchu and a rain of golden flowers fell into our hands,' Joanna related. 'What do you think that means?'

Her mother looked at her, stunned. 'I don't believe it!' she exclaimed. 'I dreamt about Machu Picchu, too. Wait till you hear mine. First there were dark shadowy forms round the sun gate, which is the entrance to the sacred city from the Inca trail. Then hundreds of people in white, with shining light round them, appeared and placed rings of pebbles on the ground and in the etheric, and – wait for it. There were angels circling above Machu Picchu.'

They looked at each other. 'What a fabulous dream,' exclaimed Joanna. 'And what synchronicity!'

'What's the etheric?' Marcus demanded.

'It is the aura of the place, the ethers around it,' Helen told him.

'All three of us connected with Machu Picchu last night in some way!' Joanna exclaimed. 'I wonder what that means.'

Marcus was in no doubt. 'It means we've got to go there.'

'But it's in South America, isn't it?' frowned Joanna.

'Peru. We can fly to Lima and from there on to Cuzco,' Marcus told her, with his newly acquired knowledge. 'You can walk the Inca trail right into Machu Picchu.'

'Just a minute,' interrupted Helen apologetically. 'Apart from the Scroll mentioning that it is one of the portals of light, I'm afraid I don't know very much about Machu Picchu.'

'Nor do I,' affirmed Joanna. 'Can you tell us a bit about it?'

'Sure,' agreed Marcus, delighted. 'I was reading about it last night. Sounds a fascinating place. First let me tell you a bit about the Incas, who were the indigenous population. It seems that they were a highly structured Indian civilisation, living in the Andes. The whole of central Peru consists of rugged mountains and jungle. That meant that for the most part the Incas lived in remote mountain villages and they cut terraces into the hillsides to farm their crops. I've seen some pictures and it was an amazing feat. They were incredible. They built advanced aqueducts, forts and cities in impossible places.'

'Amazing!' agreed Helen.

'They also crafted magnificent adornments in gold, so by our greedy Western standards they had fabulous wealth. Of course, the Spaniards wanted it, so they invaded in the 1530s. It was a bloody massacre. Horrendous by all accounts.' Marcus shook his head, as if in disbelief at the barbarity. Joanna shivered and the hairs prickled on her arms.

Marcus continued, 'Thankfully the Spaniards never found Machu Picchu, which was known as the lost city. It had been depopulated or abandoned before the conquest and even the Incas didn't know of its presence or they would certainly have told the Spaniards. The book I was reading said that everyone at Machu Picchu may have died of plague or maybe there was no rain so they starved to death. No one knows for sure. It's a mystery.'

Helen was frowning slightly as she concentrated on what Marcus was saying. What he was telling them did not really feel right to her.

He resumed, 'In 1911, Bingham, an American explorer, discovered Machu Picchu. He thought it was the last refuge of the Incas. There was none of the fabulous gold he was expecting to find, but he plundered it of artefacts anyway.'

'In those days people seemed to think it was okay to steal,' Helen commented.

'Yeah! Well, Machu Picchu has so many religious buildings that they think it is a site of spiritual and ceremonial significance – or a giant sundial!' Marcus paused. 'First Stonehenge and then Machu Picchu. They think everything's a sundial. Little do they know.

'One of the most fascinating things is the way the huge Stones that make up the ceremonial buildings are fitted together. Those huge Stones fit so snugly you can't get a razor blade between them.'

'Incredible!' said Joanna. 'That's quite something. I wonder how they were built? Was that telekinesis, too?'

'I wonder,' replied Marcus. 'Anyway, back to Bingham. Later he discovered the Inca highway, which is now called the Inca Trail. Apparently it's an incredible paved highway of neatly fitted Stones. There are giant steps and you pass through a series of ritual baths. In those days it was the only way to enter the city so you had to go through them. Oh, and they built an aqueduct which still provides spring water to the ceremonial baths after all these years.

'Amazing isn't it? And to think we Europeans had the cheek to call them savages!'

'So!' said Helen. 'Machu Picchu was built in the middle of nowhere, an incredible sacred city and it's really an inter-dimensional portal. Oh, I'd love to go there! I'd love to help restore the light.'

'Well, I intend to go,' declared Marcus, with a determined look. 'I want to walk the Inca Trail and enter Machu Picchu through the Sun Gate, just like they did in the olden days.' He had half-risen from his chair, as if he was already on his way.

'I wonder why they abandoned the city?' mused Helen. 'It must have been something major or else they would never have left their sacred task.'

'Yes, presumably the people who lived there were guardians of the portal,' agreed Joanna.

'Absolutely. If everyone who entered the city had to go through ritual baths, they would be purified before they entered the sacred energy of the place.'

'It doesn't make sense to abandon it,' frowned Helen.

'Oh, and I read that almost all the skeletons of people left there were women!' added Marcus.

'That's weird, too.' Joanna looked puzzled. 'There's obviously more to the place than books can tell us.'

'Only one way to find out,' declared Marcus, 'and that's to go there and see if we can free the portal.' He paused. 'I don't know if I can do anything on my own but I just feel I must go there and try to spread the teaching of the Scroll.'

'Beware of the darkness,' warned Helen, and he immediately felt a surge of anxiety.

Joanna joked, 'Mum said there was a higher purpose to the blocking of Stonehenge. Clearly it was because you were meant to go to Machu Picchu.'

'I'm sure you're right!'

Grinning, Marcus threw a cushion at her and she retaliated with a kitchen roll. Life felt exciting again.

Chapter 37

Marcus and Joanna walked together quietly along a tree-lined track. The rich blue sky was reflected in the lake they glimpsed occasionally through the pines. A hawk hovered, watching with gimlet eyes, and butterflies danced and spiralled together over the glorious flowered bushes, magnets to a million humming creatures. They breathed in the fragrant scent of warm pine and Marcus reflected on his dilemma.

He hoped to persuade Joanna to come with him to Peru without asking her directly. He wanted the suggestion to come from her. At last he broke the spell of silence and waxed eloquently about Machu Picchu, trying to make it sound like an opportunity not to be missed.

She spoke equally enthusiastically but did not mention going with him. At last he was forced to concede defeat. 'It'd be great if you could come to Machu Picchu with me.' He was annoyed with himself when he heard the pleading tone in his voice.

She shook her head, laughing. 'No, this is your part of the work. Anyway, what about Mum? I couldn't leave her stranded here.'

'Both of you could come.'

Joanna was still laughingly dismissive and his face fell.

They started to retrace their steps in silence. Marcus took a long glance at her, looking radiant and relaxed in light blue shorts and white top. Her long limbs were suntanned and her hair gleamed in the sunlight.

Her ability to distance him constantly stunned and depressed him. Females had always fallen for his easy charm. Joanna was an enigma. He yearned to hold her and she read his mind instantly. With a wide smile, she turned the conversation to attachment.

'The Scroll says that if you are attached to something, you stop the flow,' she reminded him with laughing eyes.

'What do you mean?'

'If you are attached to anyone or to anything taking place, you put a block on it happening in a perfect way.'

Marcus was nonplussed for a moment. Was that a rebuff or was it Joanna's defensive tactics? Suddenly he decided, What the hell!

'Come here,' he murmured, 'I don't care if I am attached to you.' He drew her to him firmly and she didn't resist. He kissed her and she wound her warm brown arms round him and held him close. He was aware of her fragrance. She was aware of his. In the middle of the forest time stopped as they moved into another dimension.

Much later, they wandered homeward, hand-in-hand. It was strange how the leaves had halos, and the bird song was sweeter. Everything the other said appeared to be light and funny. Old hurts fell away as if they had never been. They were both happy and sparkling. Marcus knew he was invincible.

They chattered inconsequentially, but Joanna was firm about not going to Peru. His attitude had changed, however.

'You're probably right,' he agreed amiably. 'And I'll be back soon.'

Approaching the chalet, they turned a corner and bumped into Helen. She smiled when she saw the scintillating aura around them. At last, she smiled to herself. At long last!

Marcus drove into town to buy his ticket to Lima, looking abstracted, cheerful and excited.

Helen eyed her daughter fondly. 'You'll miss him, won't you?'

'Of course I will,' responded Joanna cheerily. 'So will you!'

Helen chuckled. 'Not quite the same, methinks. But I'm glad you two are an item. He's a great guy. You look good together.'

'Mum, it's early days,' responded Joanna, alarmed.

'Sure it is,' replied Helen and changed the subject. 'How about we get our tickets to Peru this afternoon?'

'You're joking!'

'No. I'm not. Of course we must go.'

'Can we afford it, Mum?'

'Some things you just have to afford,' replied her mother. 'If we miss this opportunity, just imagine how we'd feel when we pass over.'

Joanna gave her a hug. 'Why didn't you say before?'

'I just have this feeling Marcus has got to walk the Inca Trail alone. I'm not sure why. I just know he has to.'

'I think you're right,' Joanna agreed thoughtfully. 'Though I must say I'd love to walk it, too.'

'Well, it's your choice. Do what you think is right.'

'I'll think about it, Mum. But I've a feeling what you said is right. He's got to do it by himself and if we tell him we're coming, he'll persuade me to go with him.'

'Yes,' agreed her mother.

Joanna felt extraordinarily happy that afternoon.

Marcus returned within a couple of hours, elated that he had his ticket to Lima with an onward flight to Cuzco. He was to leave next day. Helen and Joanna kept quiet about their plans. Both rather enjoyed keeping the secret.

Marcus phoned Kumeka House and told Zoranda of his decision.

'I'm going alone,' he declared.

When he put the phone down Zoranda called a meeting and told the community members of Marcus' intention.

There was a brief pause.

'Can we afford it?' One of the members spoke for all.

Zoranda replied, 'There are some things you just have to afford. It is our destiny. Therefore the money is already there. That is universal law. Seven of us need to go.'

Together they did an invocation and gave thanks to God for the money to travel to Peru. Then they took action, phoning the bank as well as friends and relatives.

It is universally recognised that loans are impossible to arrange quickly, but when it is the will of spirit, money comes through instantly. Within forty-eight hours they had bought their tickets to Peru.

Marcus phoned Tony to tell him he was flying to Machu Picchu to do what he could to free the portal for the light. Tony wished him well and promised to stay in touch by email.

Then Tony put down the phone and thought hard. Ten minutes later he phoned his travel agent.

Helen and Joanna drove Marcus to Redding airport. He looked very different from the Marcus who had caught the plane to India all those months ago. His eyes were eager and full of light and he walked with the confidence of a man with a mission. Though he had no idea what lay ahead, he had no doubt that he would be guided to the people who could help him and the places he needed to go to.

However, as he hugged Helen and kissed Joanna goodbye, none of them had any idea of the awesome events that lay ahead.

Chapter 38

A few days later, Helen and Joanna retraced their journey to Redding airport, but this time they were booked on the flight to Lima.

The flight to Peru is long and sometimes tedious. They found themselves squashed next to three very large women, who talked in the strident voices that certain Americans seem to value. First the trio complained about the rubbish strike, then seemingly revelled in describing all their ailments and those of their family, friends and neighbours. Throughout dinner they vilified their workmates before they plunged into an orgy of criticism of the medical services, pollution and government policy.

As the fat ladies started, with relish, to embark on the horrors of car accidents, Joanna rolled her eyes and muttered to her mother, 'How come we attracted them?' She felt saturated with their palpable negativity.

Helen grimaced. 'Perhaps it's a reminder of how we used to be.'

'Were we ever that bad?' Joanna was aghast.

Helen considered. 'Possibly, before we were aware.'

'Do you think they are showing us our negative side?'

'Could be a warning not to be negative. Or maybe it's presenting us with an opportunity to shine light and love on to them.'

'Yes, let's do that. It can only help.' Joanna was glad to take positive action.

They closed their eyes, opened their heart centres and poured love on to the three women. A strange thing happened. Within minutes they stopped talking.

'It's worked!' exclaimed Joanna.

'I know. It never ceases to astonish me,' smiled her mother.

'Let's focus love on that crying baby!' cried Joanna eagerly.

'Okay,' Helen responded. 'Poor little thing feels ungrounded up here. Ground it by visualising roots connecting it to earth and then we'll enfold it in love and ask its angel to hold it.'

They quietly focused on their intention and within minutes the baby settled and slept.

Joanna was really enjoying her power. 'Let's try it on that woman over there.' She pointed out a passenger who looked angry and tense and had complained several times to different air hostesses. They focused for a long time but nothing happened. Joanna sighed, feeling a failure.

'We mustn't be attached to the result,' her mother reminded her.

'I know,' her daughter agreed. 'But it would have been nice if it had worked.'

They were still discussing it when a thin, middle-aged man of Hispanic appearance walked down the aisle and paused beside them. 'You've done some good work,' he murmured quietly in a Spanish accent.

They were startled. 'What do you mean?' stammered Helen, taken aback.

'I've been watching the energy. You calmed the baby and an angel came in to hold him. Those three,' he indicated the sleeping women, 'they have been drawn into a bubble of peace – but you couldn't get through to her.' He pointed to the stressed, angry lady who seemingly hadn't been affected by their work. 'She's got armour plating round her but the light you sent is hovering around her waiting for an opportunity to enter her energy field.'

'Oh,' gulped Joanna, breathless and looking at Helen with her brown eyes alight with joy. 'Thank you for telling us.'

Just then someone wanted to pass down the aisle and the man quickly smiled. 'Bless you.' He returned to his seat at the back of the plane.

'Hey!' exclaimed Joanna. 'That's amazing!'

'The universe is giving us validation and proof already,' Helen laughed, buzzing with delight.

'It's so interesting what he said about that cross woman. The love can't get through yet, but it's waiting.'

'Fascinating, isn't it?' agreed her mother. 'I guess that if it doesn't find a way in, it will take itself somewhere else where it can be accepted.'

'So it's never wasted! That feels brilliant.'

'I wonder if it was the baby's guardian angel who stepped in to cradle it, or a different angel?' mused Helen.

'Does it matter?' laughed Joanna. 'The great thing is knowing that when you ask for an angel to take care of someone, it works.'

'You're right. The Scroll says everyone has help in spirit. If only we all knew that. The world would soon change. Love truly is the power.'

Feeling contented and excited, they both sat back and closed their eyes. They dozed.

It was only later, when they talked about it again, that they wondered who the man was. He looked very ordinary, the sort of man you would never notice in a crowd. They wanted to ask him some more questions and Joanna walked up and down the aisle looking for him, but she could not recognise him again.

Chapter 39

There are times when one feels on top of the world. Despite the thin blue air and his heavy backpack, Marcus felt wonderful as he strode along the Inca trail, paved centuries ago by the agile Incas as a sacred pathway to Machu Picchu, through the mountains of darkest Peru.

It felt extraordinarily familiar, as if he had walked this route a million times. He seemed to know the gaunt and hostile peaks, which stretched as far as the eye could see. His boots clanged against the neatly cut stones and in his mind's eye he could see a river of Indians in their hats and colourful ponchos laying them with careful symmetry.

Among the cactus and scrub at the start of the way, ruined Inca houses littered the route. Higher up, he found himself touching the stones of the incredible terraces, as he passed them.

What extraordinary people they were to build with such precision in such precipitous terrain, he thought.

Later they passed ancient ceremonial baths, which were purification stations for the priests of ancient times, as they arrived at the sacred site. He found himself carrying out a spontaneous ritual, washing his hands in the trickle of water available. He was aware of the local porters, who were carrying the food and some of the baggage for the group, watching him – simply observing, without expression.

He felt separate and apart from the party of back-packers, who were panting and good naturedly groaning about the steep climb.

Two days ago he had been jostling with the rest of teeming humanity, taking the train along the breath-takingly beautiful Urubamba river which torrents through the Sacred Valley. Locals boarded the train at every stop and tried to sell them goods.

He was one of a party of eight who had booked the tour in Cuzco. Like almost every other tourist before them, they discussed their travels and shared coca leaves, which numbed the tongue and helped the effects of the altitude sickness. Most of all they talked of their expectations of Machu Picchu. In his usual easy-going way, he soon got to know the others and at the same time befriended some locals, though they only spoke the local Quechuan dialect. Lack of common language never bothered Marcus.

His grey eyes alight, he communicated in finger lan-guage with a man in an orange and blue poncho. His wife wore a top hat and carried a red and yellow sack on her back, from which emitted the plaintive cry of a totally hidden baby. They grinned with him as he bought something and his fellow travellers were in hysterics at his expression when he tasted it and realised that it was dried meat. He laughed loudly at himself.

But his interactions with his travel partners were eclipsed now by the wild and steep mountainside. He wanted to be solitary. On the second day, after a night in a flimsy tent, he stayed back from the rest of the group and walked alone. The others sensed his mood and no one tried to call him or wait for him.

He walked tall and straight, a priest of old, a wise one walking the Inca trail to Machu Picchu. And then it happened. A speck appeared on the horizon and wheeled towards him, followed by a second, a third, a fourth and fifth. Five condors, huge birds, wings outstretched, silhouettes against the blue sky, sailed on the air currents above him.

He was transfixed. They floated closer until they were above him – white ruffs clearly visible, vast wings outstretched.

You might see one condor in the Andes, a pair at a pinch, but five was inconceivable. One at a time they dropped to ten feet above his head. Each took it in turn to float over him, incline its head from side to side, as if in silent acknowledgement of his presence, then rise and glide away.

He stood still. Entranced. Five condors! The party ahead had turned and was watching, silently, in awe.

As the last one floated away, the group ahead burst into spontaneous applause, cheering and pointing, calling out, 'Did you see that!' The wave of their excitement hit him as he approached them and he found himself grinning inanely. He wanted to be silent and dignified, but delight and wonder burst inside him like a balloon and he was laughing with sheer exhilaration. How he wished Joanna had been here to see it.

Even the porters were smiling, excited and chattering among themselves. They had never seen anything like it.

They eyed him with something akin to reverence, all the more extraordinary considering he was foreign.

Before long they turned together and, with Marcus in their midst, plodded upwards, upwards, along sheer cliff edges, upwards, feeling as if they could fall from the fragile path into the abyss below. From time to time he caught their looks of amazement and it felt good. Elation added wings to his boots.

The next morning, Marcus rose early, in the dark and ran to the Sun Gate, the entrance to Machu Picchu. He knew he had to be there at sunrise. His rucksack weighed a ton, his head pounded, his heart burst as he ran, but he was just in time to watch the orange sun glide, brilliant in its glory, above the mountain, pouring its rays on to the ancient city of Machu Picchu.

He stood, entranced, silenced by the wonder of the lost city, hiding in the palm of the mountains, afire in the orange light. The sight of the ancient city exceeded his expectations. At the other side of the sacred place he could see the Moon Mountain, rising sheer and stark. Below him lay the remains of the beautifully built temples and lower still the cruder houses of the artisans. All was laid out like a spectacular jigsaw.

As he watched, pearl-coloured, iridescent butterflies, the size of birds, rose and fluttered around him. The scenario was magic. Marcus laughed aloud in jubilation.

Too soon the others joined him and they marched soberly through the Sun Gate and down along the track, through the butterflies, through the lost city. They had seen many Inca ruins along the trail and the others were disappointed. They thought of it as just another ruin, on a larger scale. To Marcus it was the most spectacular place he had ever seen.

They left their rucksacks at the entry kiosk, where a guide, speaking passable English, joined them and conducted them round the highlights of the city.

The temples and houses of the priests were built with engineering precision. Each giant stone was placed almost seamlessly. It was truly amazing to find such buildings among vast mountains, which could only be approached by a precipitous, narrow trail, days' journey from any quarries.

No wonder rumours abounded about extra-terrestrial help with the building of Machu Picchu. When someone asked him the question, however, the guide bridled at such a suggestion.

'Of course our ancient people had the knowledge to move such stones,' he declared scornfully. 'They were advanced peoples.'

He intrigued them by telling them that when Hiram Bingham had discovered Machu Picchu in 1911, almost all the bodies found at the site were female. He suggested it might have been a temple of the Virgins of the Sun, or it might have been a citadel, used to defend the region – but from whom? Was it a major agricultural market? The terraces could produce more food than was needed to support the people who lived there.

Marcus sat by the great central stone known as Intihuatana and reflected deeply. The guide explained it was an advanced sundial and they all accepted that explanation. Marcus felt it was more, much more.

He sensed great spiritual ceremonies were held there, but what was the purpose? To protect the two-way inter-dimensional portal, of course. But why had the protectors left?

He was soon given the official explanation. As he pointed out the sixteen little baths, set in a cascade, probably used for religious purposes, their guide informed them that the city had been abandoned because of lack of rain, which meant they could not grow crops and they all starved or left.

'There is no other explanation,' he told them firmly.

Marcus frowned, deeply considering the guide's words and thought of the legacy of incredible aqueducts that the Incas had left behind them. And a year of drought had driven them out! It did not sit well with him.

He wanted to sit there and contemplate but the relentless guide moved them on. Reluctantly he followed the party further down the hill to the prison. Here their guide showed them the giant stone in the shape of a condor and told them it guarded the entrance of the prison. They saw the cells where the prisoners were held. Something didn't feel right to Marcus, but he didn't know what it was. He was glad when the tour was over.

Moon Mountain beckoned. It was so beautiful, rising abruptly like a sentinel. Marcus approached it alone and started the steep climb to the top. On one side of it, a subterranean temple had been discovered, containing an observatory. It was closed to the public, so Marcus scrambled up the narrow vertical path to the top and sat on one of the huge rocks overlooking Machu Picchu from the opposite side to the Sun Gate. He surveyed the city.

He was alone. High priest of his kingdom. But not for long.

A tiny thin man, with a deeply lined, weather-beaten face scrambled up the hill and stepped nimbly over the rocks towards him. He stood in front of Marcus and peered at him through deep, dark, unfathomable eyes as if he knew him.

'So, you come!' he grunted. 'Just in time.'

'What?'

'Machu Picchu been waiting for you! Condors are sacred guardians of this place!' Now Marcus understood.

It transpired that the man was a shaman, a wise medicine man, and he had a fascinating story to tell Marcus about what really happened at Machu Picchu.

Chapter 40

The elderly shaman squatted by Marcus on the rock. His shoulder-length black hair flowed from under his woollen cap, and he wore a poncho despite the heat. Marcus had the same uncanny feeling he had experienced when he met Helen, that she looked through him, but this time more so, much more so. This man's eyes penetrated his soul.

He started without preamble by telling Marcus in broken Spanish that Machu Picchu was the most sacred place on earth.

'Here is the gateway to God!' he announced, poking a dark bony finger at him to emphasise his words. 'Many places connect to the heavens, but this is the most important.'

Little hairs started to stand up on Marcus' body. He knew something important was about to happen. He told Marcus that God had placed this secret gateway to earth in the middle of the mountains of Peru where no one would find it. Only those who were initiated were allowed to live in the city. No one else would want to come here anyway. These divinely chosen priests protected the gateway to Heaven with special ceremonies.

The place was always kept pure. No one could approach except by the Inca Trail. This took three or four days and was a sacred journey. Ceremonies took place regularly on the route and there were seven ritual purification baths. This was to prepare those who approached this sacred city. It raised their consciousness until they were ready to enter. This was not just the high priests and priestesses, but also the worker priests. All made vows to dedicate themselves to the protection of this portal.

'What is the purpose of the portal?' Marcus wanted to know.

'It was to allow angels of light and wise beings from other planets and galaxies to enter, bringing messages of inspiration and information from the universe. The task of the guardians of Machu Picchu was to send these messages round the world through the ley lines. That's a system of energy lines, like telephone wires. Originally these were laid around the planet from sacred place to sacred place.'

Marcus gasped. It was the same esoteric information contained in the Scroll. He could hardly believe it.

'What's an angel?' he checked.

The shaman chuckled. 'A high spiritual being. One who has never incarnated in a human body. They are intermediaries from God. We humans are surrounded by them, but they are invisible to the average person because their vibrational frequency is so much higher than ours. They are out of your visibility range.' He paused and glanced sideways at Marcus. 'Your guardian is very beautiful and evolved. He stands very close to you and is shimmering with many colours. There are others near you, too, awaiting direction.'

Marcus opened his mouth to ask questions but the shaman, his eyes glittering with mirth, held up his hand to stop him. He continued, 'Angels are sent to earth to help us but they cannot do their work when we ignore them. They have to step down their vibrations to enter the heavy atmosphere of earth. And it is easier to enter where there are special portals of light.'

'Such as Machu Picchu?' Marcus raised a questioning eyebrow.

'Yes – and others. But here is most important. This is a two-way portal. Trained priests sent their spirits out into the galaxies to communicate with beings from other stars. They took messages out into the universe and brought back information.'

The shaman was silent. A dozen questions tripped through Marcus' mind but he remained quiet. At last the shaman sighed, shaking his head, brooding. 'Now the portal has been taken over by the dark forces. Dark angels enter here. Bad aliens. They bring trouble and dissent to the world.'

'How did it happen?'

'The people who lived at Machu Picchu were very pure. They dedicated their lives to harmony, peace and ceremonies to protect the entry point of the angels. The ultimate aim of everyone who lived here was to ascend.'

'What's that?' interrupted Marcus, curious.

'It's what happens when you have learned all the lessons offered by earth. You serve the planet and then you can ascend above the suffering of this world. After that you don't have to come back. Nowadays it is different.

After you ascend, you can stay on earth and serve God. In those days, when someone ascended, they took their physical body with them. It turned into light. But I must tell you only the greatest of the great, the purest of the pure, the most noble, were able to ascend.' He turned his dark brown eyes on Marcus. 'It was the culmination of a lifetime of initiations and dedication to truth.

'There!' He pointed down to the prison guarded by the stone condor. 'They say that was a prison!' His voice was contemptuous, as if it was beyond comprehension that anyone could believe such a thing. 'A prison, in an Ascension City. No! No! There were no prisons. They did not need prisons. Everyone was dedicated to God. The stone condor was the symbolic guardian of the initiation chambers. There is water there for purification before the rites of passage. And the sound of running water raised their vibrations.

'They do not realise, even now, that there are chambers deep in the earth. The initiates went down into these chambers to be prepared. They must conquer their minds so that they could walk unharmed through a pit of snakes. That was the final initiation. Then they were taken to the Temple of the Moon for retreat. Only then were they allowed to take part in the Ceremony of the Sun. They were sun priests.'

'But why did they abandon Machu Picchu? Why leave their sacred task of guarding the portal?' Marcus pressed him. 'What happened?'

'They ascended,' the shaman replied simply. 'They thought they had done their task. They believed Machu Picchu would never be found. Before the final ceremony, worker priests were allowed to leave under oath of secrecy.

'Those priests who were ready for ascension, assembled at Intihuatana.' He pointed way down to the great central slab of rock, where ant-sized people were gathered even now. 'There they meditated deeply and prepared themselves for the Ascension Ceremony. The priestesses assembled here at the Mountain of the Moon where we are sitting. Their task was to support the priests with certain incantations and prayers.

'As the sun rose, it touched Intihuatana and at that moment the priests ascended en masse. They turned into light. They disappeared. The priestesses, too, had completed their life purpose. Their final offering was to help the priests ascend by holding the vibration steady. They returned together down to the temples, where they lay down and waited for death.'

'Hence the reason most of the bodies found were female?'

The shaman nodded. Marcus looked over Machu Picchu and imagined the scene. Then he frowned. 'But why did they leave without protecting the portal?' he persisted.

The shaman sighed. 'They thought it was protected. Sacred symbols of protection were strategically placed throughout the site. They believed that was enough. They never thought the portal would be found. But when the American discovered the city, he pillaged it. He stripped Machu Picchu of the sacred protecting symbols and took them back to America. With the protection gone, the dark forces started to enter through the portal

– dark angels, evil aliens, entities of bad intention. Many light-workers have come here to try to stem the tide of evil but it has not succeeded.'

He turned to Marcus. 'That is why you were sent. The condors are the guardians of Machu Picchu now. They have been waiting for you. They came to greet you and welcome you. They did not approach anyone else. They waited for you to be alone and blessed you.'

Marcus felt surreal. This man seemed to know everything. Again he wanted to cry out, 'Why me?' He felt totally utterly inadequate. What could he do?

The shaman read his mind. 'You do not have to do anything. You carry a certain light. That is enough. It is unconscious. It was your destiny to bring it here.' He smiled at the confused young man. 'You are bringing others with you.'

Marcus shook his head, 'No, I'm not. I have come alone.'

The shaman smiled, knowing more than Marcus did. 'Any questions?'

Marcus knew Joanna and Helen would want to know how Machu Picchu really was built. Was it extra-terrestrials? Was it muscle power?

The shaman chuckled at the question. 'The angels built it,' he replied, watching Marcus' expression.

'The angels toned certain sounds to lighten and de-gravitate the rocks. The vibration of sound was also used to cut and shape them perfectly. Then they used their thoughts to move the slabs and place them together in a way that is beyond the capabilities of humans even now.

'The sound and light they produced here was so

incredible that it drew holy ones from all over South America. Those who were ready were guided by God to this place and they became the sacred guardians of the portal.'

'Not all of Machu Picchu was built by the angels, was it?' Marcus asked, feeling foolish even as he uttered the words, yet curiously accepting them.

'No. It is clear which sacred places were built by the Light Ones. The houses of the lower orders of priests were built by men. The difference is obvious!'

Marcus agreed.

He noticed that the shaman had become restless. The old man had started to move his head from side to side.

'Danger,' he muttered. His eyes were half-closed as if seeking information internally. 'Two women seek you. In danger.'

Marcus went white. Something must have happened in America to Joanna and Helen. He should never have left them.

'The protection was stripped away from them,' the shaman mumbled. Suddenly he opened his eyes and pointed down to the city. Two distant creatures were walking innocently through the ruins towards the base of the Mountain of the Moon.

Marcus put his binoculars to his eyes in disbelief.

'Joanna! Helen!' he shouted.

Then he saw that a man was stalking them, watching them from the protection of a stone wall and creeping along in its shadow. As he was forced to move into a patch of sunlight, something glinted in his hand. It was a knife.

Chapter 41

Marcus yelled but the sound was lost in the air. He rose and raced down the hill, crashing recklessly down the steep and dangerous track. His legs moved automatically. He could hear the older, more agile shaman behind him.

'Joanna! Helen! Be careful,' he screamed in his head. 'What are you doing here?' He must get to them. He slid unheeding through dark tunnels in the rocks, tearing his shirt and almost breaking his ankle a hundred times on the rough stones. His breath was rasping. 'Oh God, let me be in time,' he pleaded.

As he emerged from the undergrowth into the open, Joanna and Helen were walking slowly towards him. The man was close now. He saw Marcus and instantly started to run towards Joanna, the knife poised.

'*Nooooo!*' Marcus screamed, jumping through the distance. Joanna turned abruptly. The knife missed her back and plunged into her side. Blood spurted everywhere as she screamed, and the man pulled out the knife, stabbing again.

Marcus hurled himself on to the man like a snarling tiger, knocking the weapon from his hand. The man sidestepped and slithered like an eel. Marcus fell heavily, winded. The attacker ran to the edge of the cliff and disappeared among the rocks and trees. After what seemed like eternity, a young male tourist chased after him.

Joanna lay, white as death on the ground, the shaman kneeling beside her and Helen, almost as white as her daughter, holding her hand and whispering her name in anguish.

Marcus was distraught. For an instant he thought Joanna was dead, but then the shaman was giving instructions to local people who appeared from nowhere. Expertly he pulled the wounds together and bound them with a strip of cloth from his own shirt.

'Get her to hospital.' Helen's voice was barely audible.

'No hospital. My house,' the shaman contradicted in Quechuan. But she knew by the shake of his head that Joanna was being taken somewhere in his charge.

A cry went up. 'Police.'

'Keep them away!'

Somehow a diversion was created. Marcus could hardly believe his eyes. In an instant two poles were converted to a stretcher and, moaning, Joanna was laid on it and tied securely.

Four men ran with the stretcher, lightly, smoothly. The shaman ran beside them. Another sprinted ahead, obviously with instructions from the shaman that preparations be made for Joanna. Forgetting Helen, Marcus raced behind them.

Tourists scattered in front of them. People shouted, some curious, some wanting to help. A couple from Marcus' group who walked the Inca Trail rushed over.

'My rucksack!' he shouted.

'We'll bring it,' they called back.

'Wait for me,' Helen called, but firm hands held her.

A local guide said kindly, in poor English, 'We will take you to her. She is in good hands.'

'Don't worry,' said a well-intentioned American tourist. She wanted to scream 'Shut up', but instead she stood up shakily and walked blindly, quite unaware that she too was covered in Joanna's blood.

How strange, she thought, that policemen appeared to be chasing through the undergrowth near the cliff edge. Weren't police meant to help the victims?

Feeling weird and unreal, she let herself be led by strangers, where she knew not. It was as they were walking out of the main gates that the most extraordinary, surreal thing happened.

A man, neatly dressed, hurried towards them. She knew him, but through her faint haze she couldn't place him.

'Helen!' He called her name. 'Helen! It's me. Tony! What's happened. Are you all right?'

'Thank God you're here,' Helen managed through nerveless lips, coming out of her trance.

'Jo's been stabbed. Oh Tony, I think she's going to die.'

Chapter 42

When they reached the shaman's stone-built, straw-thatched hut, Joanna was lying on a pallet on the floor. Her eyes were closed and she looked like death.

The shaman had re-bound her wounds in bandages soaked in herbs and given her a secret concoction to drink, to take away the pain and to promote healing. Marcus, grey and drawn, was sitting by her, holding her hand, while a young native woman appeared to be filling the room with aromatic smoke.

The shaman came out to greet Helen and Tony and various others who had followed them.

'Your daughter will be all right,' he told Helen gravely. 'Knife miss vital organs. She has lost blood but she okay.' His English was broken, but she understood what he said.

'How do you know?'

'I have the sight. I see inside body where injuries are. She will be okay.'

'Thank you,' Helen said in a faint voice.

The shaman took her hands and looked into her eyes. 'It is our sacred duty to make her well and return her to you.'

Helen felt the power in his eyes, yet her knees shook and Tony put his arm tight round her in a deeply comforting way. Strange, she had forgotten how supportive a male presence could be. He led her into the hut and she sat on the earth floor beside Joanna, stroking her arm tenderly. Her daughter's eyes flickered open for a second with recognition and then she closed them and fell into profound sleep.

Dusk fell and when Helen went outside, a group of old men sat in consultation round an oil lamp. Tony sat with them. The couple who brought Marcus' rucksack had long since left. So had the stray tourists.

Tony fetched a rickety wooden chair for Helen to sit on.

'Have they caught the man who did it?' she demanded. Her voice quavered.

Tony hesitated. He took her hand and said gently, 'He threw himself over the cliff when he was cornered.' He paused. 'He's dead.'

'Good,' said Helen, without one shred of spiritual feeling, only a kind of numb satisfaction. And a stirring of anger.

Tony squeezed her hand, with a half-smile. 'It's nice to know you're human.'

'Hmm!' Helen responded. 'I'd have killed him with my bare hands if I'd got hold of him.'

Just saying that made her feel better. Tony was reminded of a tigress protecting her cub. It was strangely reassuring that Helen's basic instinct was definitely on top right now.

'It was the Chinese man who has been following us, wasn't it?'

Tony nodded. 'We think so. He was obviously work-ing for Sturov. He is still trying to stop the Scroll changing the world.'

'He won't succeed,' Helen grunted.

Tony was watching Helen with concern. 'Look, Helen, you're exhausted,' he continued. 'Why don't you get a good night's sleep in your hotel tonight. You can't do anything here. Marcus will stay with Joanna and she's in good hands – though I still think she should be in hospital,' he added firmly.

To his pin-striped perspective, the mumbo-jumbo world of healing was still inconceivable and he felt obliged to make his point. He had always equated health with the clinical, sterile and drugs. However, a window in his mind was beginning to open after the events of the past weeks, and he was starting to realise that Joanna was receiving perfect treatment here, despite the dirt and the chickens and children everywhere.

For a moment he thought Helen would refuse to leave Joanna. Her exhausted face had the look of a child about to mutiny. She hesitated and for a second he wondered if she might even insist on Joanna being taken to hospital.

The shaman was watching her. He touched Helen's elbow and told her that the air in the hut was blue with healing light. 'Every breath your daughter takes here is a healing breath,' he reminded her. She sensed he was right, and she knew Joanna was in the best place and that Marcus would guard her with his life.

Yet she wanted so much to stay with Joanna. For a moment she felt she was in free fall. I mustn't go to pieces, she thought, digging her nails into her palms. She breathed deeply to centre herself. Common sense prevailed and she realised she would be fit for nothing tomorrow if she was exhausted.

She looked up at Tony and nodded.

Gently he asked her where her hotel was. She flushed and confessed, 'It's a dive in Aquas Calientes.' Aquas Calientes was a thriving village set around hot springs and the railways station to Machu Picchu. Indeed stalls selling everything from chickens to vegetables to clothes were clustered along the tracks. The crowds only moved off the rails when a train lumbered through. It was a town catering for low-budget travellers and she really did not want Tony to associate her with staying there.

I'm becoming a snob! she thought through her woozy head.

Tony seemed to know instantly what she was thinking. 'Right,' he said, masterfully. 'Your belongings will be fine down there, but tonight I'm getting you a room in the Machu Picchu hotel.'

To his surprise and her own, she acquiesced without a murmur. In fact, she felt eternally grateful. Only Tony could organise a room in a hotel that was permanently full.

'Look after her,' she murmured to Marcus, and he nodded and half-smiled in response.

Tony and the shaman supported her faltering steps out of the hut and helped her into the shaman's nephew's bruised and battered car.

In the back of the car, Tony put his arm round her shoulder and held her comfortingly. What a kind and caring man he was, she thought gratefully. Then, for the first time, she became aware of the blood on her clothes.

'I can't go into the hotel like this,' she gasped in distress.

He reassured her, 'Don't worry. I'll look after everything.' Helen surrendered.

When they reached the hotel, Tony left her in the car while he talked to reception. He appeared a short time later, carrying a thick woollen cloak, which she was able to wear over her blood-stained clothes.

'I just explained you had been in a bit of an accident. They were very understanding,' he told her. He did not add that rumour had reached the hotel about the incident. He hoped fervently that they left her alone. He was not taking any risks, however, and led her through a side door and up some back stairs to his room. She did not realise he could be so resourceful.

'I can't get a second room, but you can have mine.'

Helen wouldn't hear of it and started to become distressed.

'Helen,' he spoke gently, 'you're in shock. Have a hot bath. I'll order some tea and something to eat and we can talk about it.' Once more she acquiesced, without demur, surprising him and herself.

Later, bathed, fed and wearing Tony's shirt, which was ludicrously large on her, she lay back against the pillows of one of the twin beds. He sat on the edge of the bed and gently stroked her head. He was healing her, though he wasn't aware he was doing it. He just felt very tender to the vulnerable Helen and wanted to soothe her. As he did so, safely and kindly, and without knowing it, he pulled out layer upon layer of emotional pain.

With no thought in his mind other than to care for this woman whom he admired, his heart opened and the blocks of his childhood started to dissolve. *When we give, we receive*.

He tenderly stroked her to sleep and then, as they had previously agreed, he slept in the other twin bed.

Chapter 43

Despite her injuries, Joanna was sitting up next day, propped against piles of large red, blue, black, white and violet cushions. It hurt to move, but she had a little pink in her cheeks.

Marcus, on the other hand, looked terrible after a sleepless night on the hard floor with his rucksack for a pillow. He had not shaved since he left Cuzco and he looked ill and haggard. Tony conducted Helen into the hut, where she sank down on the floor beside her daughter and held her hand. She was shocked to see how pale Joanna still looked and could hardly bear to look at the gaunt and hollow-eyed Marcus.

The shamans who had gathered were about to perform a healing ceremony. Tony, who was feeling out of place and uncomfortable, offered to fetch Helen and Joanna's belongings from their room in Aquas Calientes.

He touched Marcus' arm. 'Come on, old son. It would do you good to have a wash, shave and some sleep,' he encouraged in a kindly voice.

Marcus shook his head numbly, but Helen and the shamans urged him to go. He would be needed later, they said.

And so it was that Tony and Marcus were driven

down to Aquas Calientes in a rusty and battered old truck held together by wire and hope. Round and round the hairpin bends they looped, steeply down the forest-clad mountain until the familiar Urubamba river frothed white and noisy beside them.

The driver of the truck, in his red and white woolly hat, knitted by his mother, turned out to be one of the shaman's numerous relatives. He hooted his way through the bright mêlée of people and squealed to a stop in the car park. Tony and the driver jumped out of the truck, while Marcus climbed out stiffly. Then they dodged amid the throng of drab tourists and colourful locals across the railway line and through the congested market stalls, manned by stout pigtailed women in bright ponchos and hats. When they had battled through the crowds they toiled up the steep, narrow road to the hostel.

By good fortune the lady who ran it was standing at the top of the wooden steps outside her front door, arms akimbo, gossiping loudly with a neighbour. Their driver called up to her volubly in Quechuan. Like everyone else, she had already heard about the condor man and was agog to see him. She had also heard that a tourist had been stabbed and was horrified to learn it was the young girl who had been sleeping in her house.

She was soon persuaded to let them in to collect Helen and Joanna's belongings. She wanted to re-let the room and the train would be disgorging the next clutch of tourists shortly. While Tony collected and packed the women's things, Marcus lay on one of the beds and fell into a deep, sound sleep.

The chink of coins purchased a few hours' rest for Marcus, and the matter was obviously settled very happily, for the landlady was beaming when Tony left the house. *The condor man was asleep in her house!* Tony told her he would return for Marcus in a few hours and she promised to tell no one he was there.

The shaman's cousin disappeared, promising to return soon. Tony wandered idly down the hill, examining with half a mind the prettily crafted silverware, leather goods and unique pottery which crammed the shops, while his thoughts floated between Helen and Joanna and the Scroll. In the meantime, the landlady scuttled up the hill to share the news of her mystery guest with her best friend and daughters.

Marcus was dead to the world for four hours. His spirit was far away and it returned to his body feeling refreshed and regenerated. He leapt off the bed and hurried out to find the landlady, who had returned and was delighted to provide the condor man with boiling water to shave.

Showered and shaved, he felt human again and was anxious to get back to see how Joanna was. The landlady brought him a cup of coffee, which he drank sitting on a wooden bench in the communal downstairs room. As he sniffed the aroma of coffee, he could see noses pressed against the window. With no idea he had become a local celebrity, he waved and smiled.

With impeccable timing, Tony arrived as he drained his coffee, fetched by an emissary of the landlady. Shortly afterwards their driver turned up. With many handshakes and waves, they left the landlady and her family, who appeared in droves from nowhere to glimpse the hero.

To their bemusement the truck was laden with iron bedsteads and some tacky mattresses. The driver grinned and tried to explain that they were expecting visitors, who were arriving on the next train! Tony and Marcus eyed one another, wondering what kind of visitors were given beds in a two-roomed Peruvian home. They left Helen and Joanna's belongings in the cab of the truck and mingled with the expectant mass waiting for the train to come in.

Marcus was becoming impatient. He wanted to get back to Joanna. His discomfort was exacerbated by the number of people who pointed to him, and stared with awe and worship in their eyes.

'Why?' he asked Tony.

'Well, the condor business was more than remarkable, you must admit. The shaman told me about a legend that fortune will smile on the people when the condors appear to greet the saviour. I think they were expecting a native shaman, someone revered by the local people, not a young white tourist. That's why they are bemused and are holding back. But make no mistake, the rumour is spreading like wildfire.'

Marcus listened and frowned. He was not sure that he liked or understood what was happening to him.

Then they could hear the train rumbling down the valley. Foolhardy people bustled across the track, vendors selling their wares jostled for a better position, landladies with empty rooms waited with determined expressions. And then the train disgorged its daily quota of passengers, hundreds of them pouring off the train like ants out of a log of wood, seeking friends and family, accommodation and excitement.

Tony and Marcus saw them together.

'My God!' exclaimed Tony.

'What the . . . ?' shouted Marcus, but he never finished. He was running through the crowds towards the cluster of seven men with shaved heads, who emerged from a carriage near the end of the train.

They stood out from the jostling hordes as they stayed together, very still and quiet, like an island waiting for the rushing torrent to pass.

'Zoranda!' Marcus yelled. 'Paul, John! Oh, wow, and Pete and Henry!'

As one, they turned and greeted him with broad smiles.

'Fantastic to see you! What on earth are you doing here?' Marcus demanded, eyes shining with delight.

'We came to support you in freeing the portal,' Zoranda replied in his deep brown voice, smiling at the young man's surprise. Then Tony was with them, shaking all their hands. Marcus, grinning with joy, threw aside his Western ways and hugged them.

A huge feeling of relief flooded him. Suddenly he felt everything was going to be all right.

'It's great to see you but how weird that we were at the station when you arrived,' he remarked.

'I don't think so,' replied Zoranda, nodding towards the shaman's cousin, who was standing by his laden truck, grinning awkwardly.

'You mean you are the people he was sent to meet?'

Marcus was amazed. 'The shaman said there were people coming. I never thought of you.' He hesitated. 'Do you know about Joanna?'

'No.' They were instantly intent, knowing from his expression that something serious had happened. Buffeted by travellers and blasted by the noise of the place, he told them the news and they were horrified.

The driver was standing back. He had taken off his woolly cap and was twisting it awkwardly in his hands. Now he caught Zoranda's eye and spoke. 'Uncle sent me. We are expecting.' And he held out his hands in a gesture of welcome.

Zoranda glanced at Tony, who told him that this was the shaman's cousin and they were evidently expected to stay as guests in the village.

The young Indian signalled for them to follow, and they walked behind him off the platform to the car park, where two long-haired youths with dark watchful eyes were lounging by a second battered truck, waiting to drive them to the village.

'Thank you. Let's get in,' Zoranda accepted in his dignified way and they threw their cases over the side and climbed agilely into the back of the truck. Marcus leapt in with them, while Tony sat in the cab with the driver. They rattled up the snake-like road in incongruous convoy, one truck loaded with rusty old bedsteads and mouldy mattresses, the other carrying European men, most of whom had shaved heads.

The light and the dark were preparing for battle.

Chapter 44

When the rickety old trucks roared into the village and stopped in a cloud of dust outside the shaman's hut, a motley crowd had gathered to greet them. Small children in bright bobble hats, in slings on their mothers' backs, peeped over their shoulders. Their older siblings peered from behind their skirts. Men and women had stopped work to glimpse the condor man and the seven strangers, who they had heard were English shamans.

Marcus jumped out, ignoring the crowd. He hoped that the sight of Zoranda and his men would engage their interest and deflect it from him. It did. Everyone was staring at the shaven visitors. He hurried to see Joanna. She was lying on an iron bed in the middle of the hut and looking a great deal better, though still feverish. She greeted Marcus with a faint version of her old grin and something immediately lifted within him.

The shaman had 'seen' the seven men from Kumeka House on their way to Aquas Calientes and had prepared for them in what he presumed was European style – with proper beds. The iron beds and thin mattresses were soon placed in several of the village huts and there was no doubt the visitors from Kumeka House were to be treated as honoured guests.

'I told you,' the shaman chuckled to Marcus, tapping

his brown wrinkled finger on the young man's chest. 'I said that you were bringing people with you to help.'

'So you did,' nodded Marcus in wonder. 'And I didn't understand you.'

The shaman smiled knowingly. 'I know many things. Right now from everywhere people are coming to help free the portal.' He did not add that representatives of the dark powers were also gathering.

Joanna was relieved and delighted to see her old friends from Kumeka House. They gave her healing, after which she slept deeply.

The men sat round a fire, communicating in whatever way they could and meditating. Together they invoked the people, spirits and angels who could help to reclaim the portal for the light.

'All are on their way,' the shaman repeated.

In the morning Joanna's fever had dropped. The shaman said that the infection had healed already. She was now on her way to recovery.

Only then did Zoranda announce that although they did not yet have the Codes of Power, they had brought the Seventh Great Mystery with them. Everyone buzzed with expectation. They carried Joanna's bed into the sunshine so that she could listen.

He pulled a paper from his money belt and unfolded it, then looked round solemnly at the expectant faces and read: '"Every planet, galaxy and universe has a separate plan. The Great Divine Experiment is unfolding on earth and we reveal this for the Blue Planet."' He glanced up at their intent faces. '"All is a hologram. As within, so without. As above so below. The key to heaven is balance. This reveals *all*. This is the code for the plan of God in the plane of duality. *All* is love. All is *One*."'

The bald man paused for a moment so that they could digest this. Then he continued., '"Light contains love. Anything not seen as love is an illusion. Duality is only on earth. As you release illusions and take mastery, you become co-creators with God to bring your own heaven to earth.'

Marcus thought about the man who had stabbed Joanna. How could he become one with him? Zoranda was continuing.

'"Everything sees only itself. You can see only your shadow and your magnificence, your fears magnified, your joys enhanced. There is nothing else. On earth all is self. Everything just is. It is what self imposes on *is* that creates. Balance is acceptance of *is*. Truth is whatever you see it to be."'

'You mean that murderous swine is part of me!' glowered Marcus silently to himself. Without realising it, he had moved impatiently and Zoranda glanced over at him before continuing.

'"Whatsoever opens the door to the human heart, opens the door to the heart of God. Therefore do as you would be done by. Be true to self and do not be controlled by the will or expectation of others. Be your unique self. This is the simplicity of the Creator."'

Zoranda folded up the piece of paper very slowly and carefully and returned it to his money belt.

His eye caught Helen's.

She burst out uncharacteristically, 'I know all about

love is forgiving. Right now it feels a load of rubbish. Maybe when Joanna's better I'll feel more charitable.'

'You are always saying you can't force forgiveness,' Marcus put his hand on her arm. 'I feel just the same right now.'

Helen smiled gratefully at him. Her head was full of how she ought to feel. Her heart was full of bitterness towards these people who had hounded them and now injured her daughter.

Zoranda stood up suddenly, very tall. He quoted slowly. ' "All is love. Anything not seen as love is illusion. Duality is only on earth and as you release illusions and take mastery you become co-creators with God to bring your own Heaven to earth." ' Then he continued, deliberately addressing Helen and Marcus. 'The truth is we are all one. As I see it, your souls are calling in the ultimate lessons of unconditional love. And someone has to volunteer to offer you this lesson. For Marcus and Helen this is, can I love someone who harms my loved one? For Joanna it is, can I love someone who harms self?'

'And by love, you mean acceptance as the person is, not anything sentimental?' checked Tony.

Zoranda nodded. 'Unconditional love not emotional love, of course.'

Joanna said softly. 'I really want to get it in this lifetime. The stabbing just *is*. It has brought me fear and pain and anger, but it has also brought me healing, support and friendship. I have felt vulnerable and also very strong. Most of all I have never felt so loved in my life. I didn't realise so many people really cared for me.'

A tear slid down her cheek and Marcus squeezed her hand tightly.

She went on, 'When I think of that man I feel hate and rage. That's my shadow and I am in hell. When I see you guys I see my magnificence and I am in heaven. Then I want to forgive him. I really want to feel that love all the time.' She grinned and closed her eyes, exhausted.

Tears were running down Helen's cheeks and Tony went and stood behind her and gently massaged her shoulders. She received it gratefully.

Marcus shrugged his shoulders in despair. 'I don't understand. The monk in India said I had a destiny. Here the condors greet me and they call me the condor man. It's all so weird. I'm just an ordinary bloke and I feel so inadequate. I don't feel at all forgiving.'

Zoranda laughed. 'The key to heaven is balance. Yes, you are an ordinary "bloke", a human with human failings and inadequacies, and you are also special. But you're not perfect. You are simply unique. Don't try to be anybody else.'

John punched Marcus on the arm, 'Hey, I'd give my teeth to have had your experiences.'

'Me, too,' murmured several of the men, and Marcus was amazed to detect a hint of envy.

'I wouldn't mind feeling ordinary or inadequate if those things happened to me,' muttered Paul, 'because I'd know inside that there was something important going on.'

'*You*'ll always get the help and support you need,' advised Peter. 'Everyone knows that.'

Marcus grinned suddenly. 'I always thought you guys

were really special and holy and devoted and goodness knows what else – and now I discover you're human, too.' They all cheered.

Then they were carrying Joanna's bed back into the hut. The shaman was giving her more herbal brew and she was beginning to protest at the taste, which he indicated was a good sign.

Helen laughed and said it was an extremely good sign.

'That's our old Joanna,' she said happily. But her daughter could not retaliate – she was already asleep.

Helen looked fondly at her sleeping daughter and said to Marcus, 'I do know it's an illusion that anyone has power over us or can do anything to us. We actually do control our energy field and emotions, so he couldn't have stabbed her unless she had let him into her aura.'

'I suppose not,' Marcus agreed.

'I've just been holding on to anger towards him because it's a coping mechanism. I think I'd have collapsed if I hadn't been angry.'

Marcus smiled. 'I know. I felt a bit the same. I really thought she was going to die. Now I know she's going to be all right, I can see the spiritual perspective again.'

'I still feel a bit angry and unforgiving, though,' added Helen cautiously.

'Me, too! Hey, I'd better write that illusion down for Joanna. We can tell her when she wakes.'

He found a biro and wrote on a scrap of paper: 'Illusion: other people have power over you or can do anything to you. Truth: You have control over your energy fields and emotions.'

'Good one, Helen. She'll be pleased with that one.'

That night they placed a dome of peace and light around the village. It was just as well, for Sturov and the forces of darkness were gathering outside.

Chapter 45

Four days later the moon was full. Each day Zoranda and the shaman had consulted together for hours through a guide who spoke Quechuan and some English and Spanish, trying to decide on the best course of action. Clearly each held the other in great deference and respect and much of the time they seemed to communicate telepathically without need for words.

Everyone got used to the incongruous sight of the big bald white man and small stocky South American in his knitted hat, as they walked together or sat and talked earnestly to one another and to the growing number of shamans arriving at the village from all over South America.

They were to hold a special ceremony in the sacred city, while the moon was full. During this ceremony the seven symbols from the Scroll would be placed in the etheric of Machu Picchu, above the Intihuatana Stone. The shamans would use incantations to seal the gateway to the darkness and raise the vibration of the portal so that only light beings could enter. Then new protection would be placed around the city.

As they waited for the full moon, they held daily ceremonies, blessing certain stones and crystals as well as special artefacts. They invoked the Great Ones to fill these with the power of light and protection. That which had been plundered must be replaced. Each was to be placed in a particular spot. Nothing was haphazard. All was carefully calculated by the Wise Ones. This must be a ceremony of the greatest purity and power if it was to do its work.

Although not all of the information from the Scroll was available, they felt hopeful that they could tone the particular sounds that would send out the clarion call into the universe to bring help to the planet. These they practised meticulously. At the same time, they chanted the notes designed to spread truth and purity along the ley-line system around earth.

'This is a great responsibility,' pronounced the shaman to Zoranda, on the morning of the full moon.

The taller man nodded. 'We are ready. We have prepared for years for this. Lifetimes, I am sure.'

The shaman nodded, soberly. 'We will all do our best. Even without the Codes of Power, which we need to free the minds of humanity, we can still retrieve the portal.'

'I agree.'

'There must be thirty-three of us. Seven of you plus Marcus and Tony is nine. And twenty-four shamans from Peru will come.'

Zoranda felt that Helen and Joanna should be included. However, he had to respect the local culture, so he deferred to the wise man. And it was certainly true that Joanna was still very weak.

'Thirty-three is the most sacred number,' he agreed sagely. 'The powers of the universe will use us for the highest good.'

'But we must be vigilant. Sturov, the greatest high black magician and his acolytes will try to stop us. I feel them drawing close. We must not let them penetrate the force field of light.'

They nodded in sober agreement.

'We may need to put our lives on the line,' said Zoranda. The shaman closed his eyes for a moment, then changed the subject.

Night fell, cold, clear and cloudless. Even Marcus and Tony commented that the universe seemed to be on their side. Low mist would have rendered the whole ceremony more difficult.

Joanna and Helen were bitterly disappointed to be excluded but, after talking to Zoranda, had hidden their upset well. They agreed to relinquish their desire to be present if that was for the highest good. They would sit in the hut and meditate to add their energy to the ceremony, just as the priestesses of old had done. When we detach from our ego and hand the outcome over to the highest power, new possibilities enter. And so it was on this occasion.

Tony, Marcus and the seven initiates from Kumeka House were ready. Only twenty-two shamans had arrived, all wearing their brightly coloured ceremonial jackets and caps. At the appointed time, thirty-one men waited to perform the most important ceremony of their lives. All had agreed that there must be thirty-three participants. Helen and Joanna stood a little distance away, watching.

Zoranda looked at the shaman. The shaman stared back at him. Both turned simultaneously and beckoned to the women. Without hesitation Helen and Joanna stepped forward and joined the group.

All knew and accepted that Joanna would need help. Two at a time they carried her in a chair at the front of the procession. She accepted their attentions gracefully.

As arranged by the shaman, they were spirited through the gates of the sacred city and walked in threes to the appointed places where they were to plant the artefacts, stones or crystals, all blessed and containing the energy of protection. This was accomplished in silence by the silver light of the moon. They walked in an anti-clockwise spiral, round and round each place, winding up the energy, making sure each symbol was perfectly placed.

They washed their hands and faces in the pure water of the ceremonial baths, a symbolic purification.

At last they gathered round the Intihuatana Stone. A strange ground mist was starting to rise and it became bitterly cold. Then the wind rose and clouds, black clouds, scudded across the moon, darkening the world. There was a weird and sinister feeling.

Helen knew something was wrong. So did the others. The shamans increased the force field of light and love around them. They could feel the love and peace pulsing. As long as they maintained the circle, all would be well.

Zoranda started to draw the symbols – given to them in the Scroll – in the etheric above the Intihuatana Stone. They all toned the sounds to invoke the light but these were being lost in the wind and swirling dark mist.

Suddenly there was a clap of thunder and a tall, dark bearded man in a long black cloak appeared out of the night and walked up to the circle. He pointed a stick at Joanna, who fainted as a terrible pain shot through her. Then he walked through the space she had occupied and faced Zoranda. It was Sturov.

More cloaked figures appeared, silhouetted in the moonlight as it shone between the clouds. They surrounded the circle. Helen rushed to Joanna and held her. The circle had been broken. The evil ones filtered into the circle. Marcus felt rooted to the ground.

Zoranda was silently calling on the Powers of Light; Sturov, the Powers of Dark. An evil stench wafted through the circle, more foul than any of them had ever experienced.

The shamans, the men from Kumeka House and Marcus were pulling light in from the universe. The silence was intense.

Sturov stood over six feet tall, erect and formidable, one arm raised. With an arrogant gesture of defiance he threw back his hood, so that moonlight fell on to one side of his face. His features were sharp, with a large aquiline nose and the deeply creased lines of one who is used to absolute authority. As he moved slightly, his ice-blue eyes glittered with sardonic humour. The moon's shadow now deflecting on the lower half of his face gave him the sinister look of one who is utterly ruthless and determined. He was supremely confident as he looked down on Zoranda.

Zoranda, not quite so tall but sturdier, wore a tunic of pure white cloth. Round his neck he carried a heavy gold chain and an ankh. His shaved head glowed in the moonlight. As he faced his adversary he kept total faith that light is stronger than dark. His mind held this single truth.

They stared eye to eye.

Sturov knew there were thirty-three black magicians and that the enemy's circle was broken and depleted.

He sneered loudly, his voice full of contempt. 'The control of the portal is mine.' His lips were thin and tight, a fleck of spittle in one corner. 'How stupid of you to imagine you could triumph over me.'

Zoranda ignored him. 'Let light prevail on earth.' His voice rang firm and true. He gazed unwavering into those pale eyes.

Sturov continued, deliberately insulting, 'I penetrated your circle before you even started. What a fundamental error to use someone wounded. A pitiful mistake. Her aura was broken and penetrable.' He laughed. 'Call her a priestess! Did you think she could stand up to Sturov?'

Zoranda was so absorbed by his task that he did not even hear him.

Joanna heard. She opened her eyes and immediately steadied herself in the light. She knew this was her supreme test. With no thought of anger or revenge she called out, 'Let the angels of love touch the hearts of these men.'

It is hard for even the blackest heart to stay closed against the power of love. A chink entered every heart present, including that of Sturov.

Then Zoranda spread out his arms and called again in a clear deep voice, 'I call on the power of the light.'

In response, a bolt of lightning lit up the sky. It flashed around them and illuminated their circle.

Sturov let out a howl. His shoulders slumped and his face contorted as if shrivelled by the light. Slowly his knees buckled and he slumped to the ground. Blue flames spurted from the earth all round him.

No one moved.

Then his thirty-two black henchmen turned and ran from the circle as if all the demons in hell were after them.

After a long time, Sturov lurched slowly to his feet. He cowered under his cloak. With eyes averted, he half-crawled, half-staggered, like a rat into the night.

Wordlessly they reconstituted the circle of light. As they did so, the wind stopped. The clouds vanished. The moon continued to sail innocently across the sky.

Zoranda completed the symbols. Then they chanted the sacred notes while the specially blessed stones and crystals were strategically placed around the city, as directed by the shaman.

As dawn broke, they intensified the sounds and when the first rays of the sun fell on the Intihuatana rock, they stood in a circle round it, while the city was illuminated in the most beautiful light they had ever seen.

Later Marcus said anxiously to the shaman, 'I hope it works.'

'Bless you, son,' the old man replied gently, placing a hand on his shoulder. 'We do not know how much good we have done. We have simply done our best. But you must not give up. You must open the other portals on the planet. It is your task.'

Marcus nodded. 'I know.'

He walked over to the wall where Joanna sat. She was exhausted. Even so, as he took her hand, he thought how beautiful she looked in the early-morning light.

'Whatever happens now, the world will be a different place,' he told her.

She looked around the silent city and agreed.

Also available:

The Silent Stones colour oracle, revealing your past, present and future lives. Put together by Diana Cooper and Yvonne Gray, and published by Findhorn Press, this is available in all good bookshops or directly from www.findhorn.com